"American parachutists—devils in baggy pants—
are less than 100 meters from my outpost line. I
can't sleep at night; they pop up from nowhere and
we never know when or how they strike next. Seems
like the bl_ck-hearted devils are everywhere. . . ."

Found in the diary of a German officer.

Suicide Squad

Ross Carter was one of three men who survived the
suicide stands of his platoon of paratroopers. They
had a three-way destiny—to be wounded, killed, or
captured. But bound together by deep comradeship
and extraordinary daring, the twelve men in his unit
set incredible records of heroism.

Here are the unvarnished stories of ordinary men
faced with the reality of death at any moment. They
beef, get drunk, quarrel violently, take their women
where they find them, and yet achieve an epic gran-
deur in their deeds.

*"Every level of society had its representation
among us. Senators' sons rubbed sho_____
cowboys. Steel workers chummed up ___
from city slums. Farm boys, milli___
brats, white-collar men, factory work__
jailbirds, and hoboes joined for the ___
ture of parachute jumping. And so t__
collection of adventurous men co___
parachute troops."*

From their first jumps in Africa t___
of the Bulge, this is their story—a___
breathtaking suspense and inspiring___

Other SIGNET Titles
You Will Enjoy

Those Devils In Baggy Pants

by

Ross S. Carter

A SIGNET BOOK from
NEW AMERICAN LIBRARY
TIMES MIRROR

SIGNET TRADEMARK REG. U.S. PAT. OFF. AND FOREIGN COUNTRIES
REGISTERED TRADEMARK—MARCA REGISTRADA
HECHO EN CHICAGO, U.S.A.

SIGNET, SIGNET CLASSICS, SIGNETTE, MENTOR AND PLUME BOOKS
are published by The New American Library, Inc.,
1301 Avenue of the Americas, New York, New York 10019

PRINTED IN THE UNITED STATES OF AMERICA

To the Boys in the 82nd Airborne Division

"American parachutists—devils in baggy pants—
are less than 100 meters from my outpost line. I
can't sleep at night; they pop up from nowhere
and we never know when or how they strike next.
Seems like the black-hearted devils are everywhere. . . ."

*Found in the diary of a German
officer who opposed the 504th
on the Anzio beachhead.*

Preface

Through luck, fate or whatever you choose to call it, I find myself again a civilian after three years of comradeship in blood and death in the 504th Parachute Infantry of the 82nd Airborne Division. My friends call me a refugee from the law of averages. My regiment still exists as a name, but the regiment in which I trained, fought and almost died, now lies buried in obscure army cemeteries in ten countries.

Like the Ancient Mariner, I feel compelled to tell a tale of brave and loyal men who are not alive to tell their own tale. I do not propose to tell you a sentimentalized or humorous yarn, although there will be sentiment and humor and many tearful moments in it. The dead men who will come to life in this book were, for the most part, tough-fibered, hard-living and reckless; but no braver, more loyal or better fighting men ever lived.

I well remember a Saturday afternoon in North Africa when I was drinking cognac and wine with two scarred veterans of the French Foreign Legion; the one a murderer from Holland, the other an embezzler from France. Their lives were behind them; their future was to die for causes and for a country which meant nothing to them. I too belonged to a Legion of doomed men, but death is less bitter when the alternative is slavery. Most of us knew what we were fighting for and we knew how to fight.

One thing that people noticed about men of the Legion (the name I will sometimes use to designate our outfit) and that had been impressed upon them many times, often with violence, was the flaming wildness of their spirit. People used to wonder why we were wilder than other soldiers, and I can tell you.

The thing that distinguished us most from other soldiers was our willingness to take chances and risks in a branch of the army that provided a great, new, almost unexplored frontier. In other days paratroopers would have been the type of men to sail with Columbus, or the first to seek out the West and fight the Indians.

Men joined the paratroopers because they couldn't resist the awful thrill of risking their life in a parachute. They were drawn into the outfit as by a magnet and, once in, wouldn't have left if they got the chance. Each man had supreme faith in his ability to take care of himself whatever the odds. For this reason paratroopers were at times a quarrelsome lot because they could never believe that anybody could beat hell out of them.

Every level of society had its representation among us. Senators' sons rubbed shoulders with ex-cowboys. Steel workers chummed up with tough guys from city slums. Farm boys, millionaires' spoiled brats, white-collar men, factory workers, ex-convicts, jailbirds, and hoboes joined for the thrill and adventure of parachute jumping. And so the army's largest collection of adventurous men congregated in the parachute troops.

The 82nd, which landed by boat at Casablanca on May 11, 1943, was the first airborne division activated and sent overseas to join the Allied Expeditionary Forces. Two parachute regiments, the 504th and the 505th, and one regiment of glider troops, the 325th, were the principal units of the division, although there were several battalions of parachute and glider engineers, a quartermaster unit, a parachute maintenance unit, a division headquarters unit, etc. When the 82nd went into Normandy, the 508th Parachute Regiment was attached to the division, and still is. The 504th, in Italy all winter on special duty with the Fifth Army, did not reach England until shortly before D-Day. At the time we were too crippled and too poorly equipped for the Normandy invasion. The 507th regiment, which substituted in Normandy for the 504th, was separated from the 82nd after that mission and the 504th returned to the division fold.

Major General Matthew Ridgway was division commander in training and overseas until the 18th Airborne Corps was formed, which included the 82nd, 101st, 17th, and 13th Airborne Divisions. The 18th Airborne Corps was part of the First Allied Airborne Army, under the command of Lt. General Brereton. The British had two airborne divisions in their part of this army, the 1st and 6th, plus the Polish Parachute Brigade. General Gavin became division commander of the 82nd after the formation of the 18th Airborne Corps.

A history of the 504th Parachute Regiment has been written and a military history will be about the 82nd Airborne Division. What I am writing is not a military history but an eyewitness, participated-in account and the human story of men who fought the enemy to a standstill in many bloody battles all over Europe. I missed only forty-some days of duty with the regiment in three years; and so "was there" when all of these incidents happened.

RSC
Duffield, Virginia
October, 1945

Contents

1. A Beer for Duquesne

At retreat one afternoon, the captain bellowed, "Men, tomorrow we are going to jump out in Andy's field, and after we assemble and get our chutes rolled up, we are going on a maneuver and storm Old Cooly Conch Hill again. The problem is strictly tactical, and there will be no goofing off on the job." Then the top kick beat his gums and told us that reveille would be at eight o'clock and that he didn't give a damn where we went or what we did just so we were at reveille.

We got passes for town, which for us was the Town Pump in Fayetteville, where we drank quite a few beers in honor of the jump to be made next day. Each of us had butterflies in his stomach. We always did before a jump. We toasted each other for luck, hoping that the chutes would open and that nobody's hurt would be more than strawberries, that is, skinned places on the neck, which we often get as the chute opens. We drank the Town Pump dry, and most of us went home early, not wanting to have a bad hang-over which makes it much harder to go out the door.

Just the same next morning many had fuzzy beer heads and furry beer mouths. Duquesne, "Duke," as we called the gray-haired old lumberjack, army age twenty-seven, real age forty-three, was not at reveille. We concluded that he must have had one drink too many. He was about to be turned in missing, when all of a sudden we saw him lone-rangering toward us on an old bicycle.

He streamed up bareheaded, his gray hair sticking to his rugged brown face. When he turned his head to look at us, his bike charged a telephone pole and ricocheted him on his chin, belly and knees to his place in the ranks. We rolled in the dirt laughing, tickled to death at him, because he was a lovable guy, always in his cups, and full of fun. He had an awful hang-over.

Those of us in my plane got together and decided that

we would all yell after our chute opened "A beer for Duquesne" in honor of his Lone Ranger stunt.

We went to our planes, our bellies tickling with the old familiar butterfly feeling. On the way Losyk, a lean, happy-go-lucky Polack, kept ribbing Duquesne, who for once was in no mood for horseplay. The Polack was a good guy. Other than overeating, oversleeping or counting his money—he never spent a nickel spontaneously—he had no observable weaknesses.

The tension mounted as the moment to jump approached. Our nerves were as vibrating as wind-strummed telephone wires. Suddenly we began leaving the plane. As the line moved fast toward the door I sealed my mind with blankness. My chute opened fast. Happy, contented, thrilled, knowing that I was in the best outfit in the army, I yelled "A beer for Duquesne," and floated down like a giant snowflake. I landed unhurt, rolled up my chute, and walked over to join Carlton, a tall, gray-eyed Texan. His face was ashen and drawn.

"What is wrong?"

His mouth worked out a whisper.

"I was second man out. My chute opened, and I was starting to yell 'A beer for Duquesne,' when something bulleted past me uttering horrible screams. It was Losyk falling like a rock with his chute stringing out above him. I saw him hit, bounce several feet and lay quiet."

Officers soon broke up the group of enlisted men clustered around Losyk and screened him from us until the ambulance carried him away. I will not tell you here what an 800-foot fall will do to a man. Let your imagination figure it out. We felt very bad in our hearts and in our stomachs as we worked out the tactical problem of storming Old Cooly Conch. Our minds and feeling of comradeship were back there on the jump field with Losyk. It could have been one of us—but wasn't.

We learned that he was the only man in the battalion who did not have insurance. Nobody would sleep in his empty bunk, so we moved it out and brought in a new one. The new man never knew who had slept in that spot.

My platoon furnished him a guard of honor at the morgue. The army put him in a fine casket, but we never got to look at him again, nor did we want to, preferring to remember him alive. Next day we had a military funeral. Our company, serving as Official Mourners, followed him about a half mile to the church where he was given the Catholic burial service. The army band played sad, wailing music that cut our hearts.

After the Catholic service was over, three Polacks from his town formed the guard of honor on the train to his home. Thus passed the first member of the Legion.

After the funeral we all sat around glumly, each juggling his own bleak thoughts, concreted in his own private little Hell. Finally a poker game and a crap game got going, but nobody gave a damn whether he won or lost.

That night we formed a group in a corner of the Post Exchange to drink beer and ended up singing the Paratrooper's Song of Death, "Cause He Ain't Gonna Jump No More," sung to the tune of "The Battle Hymn of the Republic." It is a very moving song, lugubrious like an Indian death chant. But no man thought of getting out of the outfit because Losyk got his. We were bound to it by forces bigger than ourselves.

2. The Kangaroo Rat Went to Spanish Morocco

We were bivouacked in the desert about two miles from Oujda, in French Morocco, a hellhole if there ever was one. Five hundred of us were living in pup tents out on the level desert. The sun rose in the morning, hung in the sky like a glaring copper ball, and set looking the same. The desert was hard as a rock, our water supply scanty—about a quart of drinking water per day if you got there in time to get your ration. Although we tried at first we couldn't keep clean, so finally gave up, said to hell with it, and stayed dirty most of the time. The wind blew sand into our mess kits and into our food. Millions of flies densely specked the air. We all got dysentery, known in the army as the GI's—and other plainer terms.

We would scoot about the desert all night, and then go to bed before daylight. As soon as the sun came up we roasted inside our tents; so we rarely got any sleep. About eight o'clock some chicken supply sergeant would fall us out to draw some trifling piece of equipment, and again before lunch, and once more before supper. Between times some officer would lecture us on military courtesy and discipline. We sat in a daze hoping he would fall dead or have his guts eaten out by dysentery or some other minor ailment. Then about sunset we would go out into the desert again and play war games all night, get stuck full of cactus thorns, lose our tempers, and fill our guns up with dirt so we would have something to do next day.

One morning we were sitting about doing nothing just as we always did. Some guys had on only their boots, others no more than their boots and a cap, or boots and a shirt, or boots and shorts, or boots and helmet. I just couldn't spot a pair of pants on anybody. So five hundred boys stood around in nearly nothing panting like lizards, all bored with no place to go and nothing to do or read. We had even gotten tired of talking about women, and that is a bad sign in the army.

Well, that was the picture up to the moment when some joker, wearing only boots and a helmet, while strolling about the desert a short distance from the tents, stirred up a peculiar little creature known to zoology as a kangaroo rat. The rat was about the size of a gray squirrel, with hind legs as big as the rest of him. His forefeet were small and weak. His long, mousy nose, inset with beady eyes resembling a pair of pushed-black spectacles, gave him one hell of a funny look. The tail was long and bushy and waved like a red fox's as he bounced in volleys of ten-foot leaps.

So the rat took off with the lunkhead who stirred him up yelping after him like a foxhound. Five hundred men jumped up, five hundred men yelped joyously, five hundred nude men tore off into the desert. The little rat peered over his shoulder, saw with horror the mighty stampede, and really began to get the hell out of there. He would take four or five big jumps, then hit and run a few steps. I don't know what he thought, but I know he didn't like it. When he looked back, which was often, he could see five hundred men coming like a herd of stampeding buffaloes, tearing the sandy air with wild yells and kicking up a vast cloud of choking dust. With good sense, therefore, the little rat headed straight for Spanish Morocco; maybe he knew that Spain was "neutral."

The battalion commander, a little sawed-off guy about twenty-nine, was sitting in his tent catching up on his paper work when he heard the bedlam break out. He ran out of his tent, and there a quarter of a mile away saw his command, apparently gone crazy, heading for a "neutral" country, maybe to be interned for the duration. He didn't waste any time peeling off after his men, all still running hard and some of them even gaining on the rat, which apparently hadn't gotten his second wind yet. There leaped the rat out in front, and then came the battalion breathing hard and beginning to string out like race horses in the last lap, and after the battalion came the little colonel, who didn't know the score but, afraid that he was losing his command, was running hell-bent to get it back. The rat at last got his second wind, or maybe his third, for, suddenly convinced that he was in real jeopardy, he put on a burst of speed that left the stampede behind as if marking time. Finally he disappeared in the distance, still headed for Spanish Morocco, and there he probably is today, unless the chase shortened his life or unless, homesick, he went back to rejoin his family, if he had one.

The men, wind-blown and tired, feeling foolish for raising so much hell over a rat, turned around and started back with the colonel ahead of them, shaking his head from side to side and mumbling to himself.

Up to that time Berlin Betty, who broadcast to us in English and seemed to know all about us, had called us "Colonel ——'s Glamour Boys" because we were paratroopers. When she got wind of the rat episode she began calling us "Colonel ——'s Desert Rats." We "Desert Rats" would listen to her and think what dam' fools we were.

3. The Cacti Grow Tall Round Kairouan

The big shots must have decided that we were tough enough and mad enough for any assignment after living on the desert like sidewinders for two long months. At any rate, one day the first sergeant stepped into the street, blew a big brass whistle, hollered to get us up to him, and then told us to get ready to ride a train for about five days. We tore down our pup tents, threw away the junk we'd stolen and bought from the Arabs, made our bedrolls and got our packs in order. When I picked up my mattress cover to empty the straw, a big rat ran out on a gang of little rats. I felt like a heel for breaking up their home.

We finally loaded onto the famous Forty and Eights, *40 Hommes et 8 Chevaux*, stowed away our gear and tried to find room to sit down, but we had too much baggage to all sit down at once. There were thirty-four men to a car plus water, C rations, our baggage and guns. After only a day's delay we pulled out, making maybe ten miles per hour when going downhill. The sun beat down on the steel cars and fried our

brains; the metal was red-hot, but we had to stay with it, or
desert into the desert; so we stayed with it, ate C rations
which the sun heated for us, drank the hot water from the
cans, and hoped that we would get to sleep one hour out of
twenty-four, which we never did.

So we rolled along, cheating the Arabs and getting cheated,
playing poker, telling lies, eating C rations, drinking hot water,
and cussing the brass hats that had got us in such a dam'
mess.

About an hour before dark on the third day we rolled into
a siding in some little Arab town in Algeria. Pretty soon a train
thirty cars long filled with rations for the British backed in
from somewhere. We looked at and understood one another
without having to talk about it; our officers looked at the train,
at us, and then all disappeared, knowing that we knew they
didn't like C rations either and that we wouldn't forget them.

A Tommy with an Enfield rifle guarding the train was
enough for the Arabs, but not enough for us and he knew it.
He looked at us uneasily, then stood up so that he could see
all of the train.

A paratrooper started for the train, which was on the track
next to us. The Tommy waved him back with his rifle. The
frontal tactics of Ajax having failed, one of the Ulysses' of the
outfit, Sergeant Winters, resorted to guile and craftiness to
achieve our gastronomic ends. Winters gave me the wink, went
up to the Tommy, who looked at us suspiciously, and began
to speak honeyed words, praising the British Eighth Army,
asking about Tobruk, El Alamain, General Montgomery, and
Tommy's family. Tommy, proud of his army, unsurpassed in
his opinion by any, thawed out, praised its mighty deeds and
triumphs over the Germans. We agreed. Winters gave him a
Lucky Strike. Then we climbed up on the car, Winters on one
side of him, I on the other, and a swarm of troopers engulfing
us. The Tommy glowed with good fellowship, we glowed with
good fellowship; and I know that Anglo-American ties were
never more binding than at that moment.

The Tommy, his vision obstructed by the eager listeners, unable to see the other cars, forgot about them. In the meantime
our boys were not idle. Understanding the urgency for speed,
in perfect harmony they worked like a gang of beavers to
transfer the British rations to our cars. Lined up, passing the
stuff from one to another, they soon had our quarters stacked
to the roof with crates of Lend-Lease grapefruit, orange and
grapefruit juice, tomatoes, bacon, corned beef, condensed
milk, roast beef, flour, sugar, pickled cabbage, English plums,
beans, crackers and tins of tea.

Tommy finally remembering that he was on guard stood up and looked. His face paled. He grabbed his rifle, cursed and hollered. The boys looked at the helpless Tommy in innocent wonder. He beamed concentrated hate and gruesome murder at Winters and me, but he could not do a thing about it. Anglo-American ties were never less taut than at that moment.

Darkness came. We wanted to get moving with our loot, but the train stayed welded to the rails. Finally the officers in charge of our car came up, said that somebody had stolen some stuff from the British, and that he had orders to look for it. Had we seen any of it? We told him that we were not the kind of people who would do that to our ally. The officer struck a match and peered inside, pushing his nose within four inches of a crate of beans. We gave him a can and he went away.

The car was so full of rations that we had to ride on top and on the sides but we didn't mind. We ate like kings the remainder of the trip, and then carried the rations with us into the desert at Kairouan.

The cacti grew in hedges so thick and tall around Kairouan that a Sherman tank would have had difficulty crashing through. We used them to shade our tents, but it was a cruel shade because of the dead needles which covered the ground. They penetrated the sides of our boots and worked through our clothes. We spent our spare time picking them out or worrying about getting stuck by them. The tips seemed to be poisonous. An infection often started where they pierced the skin. We kept sulfa powders on hand to combat it.

Bob Hope came to us there and gave a show. Everybody liked him. But we never would have forgotten that night in any case, because two of the new boys making parachute jumps landed in giant cacti trees which held them suspended and screaming from the terrible agony of being made into human pincushions. They died an awful death before we could get to them. The spines being too numerous to pull out, they were buried with them sticking in their bodies.

No one wanted to jump in Africa because of the cacti and the hard and rocky desert. One morning 180 men out of a battalion were carried to the hospital seriously or slightly crippled. After that, all further practice jumps in Africa were canceled.

Meanwhile the Legion learned how to dig a hole in the ground, put a clay pot in the hole, stuff rags around the clay pot, pour waste water on the rags, and pour the drinking water in the pot so that evaporation would keep the water cool, even in 140 degrees Fahrenheit; how to make a good tent with extra blankets on the floor, and drape mosquito nets over the hole to keep out the malaria-bearing skeeters; how to prevent heat exhaustion; how to keep dysentery-carrying flies out of their mess kits; how to keep the blowing sand and dust from filling the guns; and a hundred other ways to make life in the desert livable.

The men sometimes went crazy from the heat and did strange or dangerous things. Benson came in drunk, saw his buddy lying in his tent and said, "Hopkins, I gotta notion to shoot your goddamned big toe off, and if you dare me I will."

Hopkins thought he was joking and said, "Go ahead and shoot it off! It's in my way anyhow, and maybe I'll get a rest in the hospital." Benson picked up a carbine and shot the toe off.

We drew equipment and got prepared for any mission that we might be sent on. We painted green and brown spots on our jump suits, web equipment, and helmets. Some of the boys even painted spots on their tommy guns. Two little death's heads were put on our company's helmets for identification. Later on we discovered that German SS troops wore the same emblem but did not give a damn about that. We were issued water-purifying pills, Atabrine pills to prevent malaria, anti-fatigue pills, emergency rations consisting of K rations and D bars, the latter being concentrated chocolate, one of which sufficed to keep a man fed for a day.

Each man carried an entrenching shovel, a big knife with brass knucks on the handle, a jump knife with a clip blade which was carried in a secret pocket of the jump jacket, to be used when we stuck in a tree, or on the enemy when captured. We jumped with enough grenades and ammunition on our persons to last until we won the fight or reached the equipment chutes. The latter carried Browning light machine guns, boxes of machine gun ammo, 60 millimeter mortars and ammunition for them, extra grenades, rifle cartridges, tommy gun shells, etc.

Extra water was to be dropped in plastic water bags in case we couldn't find any. We also had gas masks and first aid packets containing bandages, sulfanilamide powder, and eight pills of sulfadiazine to swallow with water to keep down infection. In addition, we each had a little kit with morphine and Syrette to give it with. Each platoon had a first aid man who jumped with it. He carried blood plasma and knew how to give it.

We were walking arsenals. Bandoleers of rifle ammunition crisscrossed our chests, tommy gun ammo hung on our sides, and grenades bulged our pockets and canvas bags. The automatic riflemen at first had their guns and ammo brought down in equipment chutes. Later on they jumped with their weapons, although heavy, because often they could not find their guns in the jump area.

Our equipment was checked and rechecked, until finally we had every item we were supposed to have, or might need. We wondered where we were going, how many of us would live through it, whether we would be shot down in our planes, or maybe shot in our chutes as we came down. Only one parachute outfit that we knew of had made a combat jump up to that time. It had made out pretty good, but we considered that jump not a good test of the welcome the dam' Axis might find for us; therefore we were often an uneasy lot, reflecting much on our future, which was bound to be black because the German strength could hardly be considered as scratched in June and July of 1943. I pictured the coming struggle as a mighty black mountain to be climbed at much risk. We had only reached the plain before the foothills and we hadn't yet begun to climb. In joining the parachute troops I had picked a Tartar, but was too stubborn to try to get out, even if the opportunity had presented itself.

4. How Tranquil the Desert

At last the day we had trained for all those hard months had come. The 505th Parachute Regiment had gone into Sicily the night before. Rumor first had it that they had done well. A second rumor said that annihilation had overtaken them, and a third that half were killed in the planes in the air or in their parachutes. Now my legion, the 504th Parachute Regiment of the 82nd Airborne Division, was going to jump to reinforce the 505th.

Loaded down with fighting equipment, we climbed into trucks early in the afternoon and drove across the hateful cacti-studded desert to the airport. How sweet and tranquil that desert appeared to us now! The blossoms on the cacti were in bloom. The dusty, barren desert, now that most of us would never see it again, looked as beautiful as rhododendron blossoms in Virginia. At the airport the hundreds of squat, broadwinged C-47 transports brought a chill to our

blood and a toss to our stomachs. We stacked arms beneath
their wings and spread our equipment on the desert. The
crews joked with us but laughed only with their lips. Their
hearts were as heavy as ours; they were going too.

Our chutes were waiting for us in convenient stacks. Each
man chose two, called the T-7 pack assembly, from the pile,
carried them to his plane and inspected them carefully. We
wanted them to open right on a night such as this one promised to be. Then we were briefed on the jump and turned
loose so we could give our guns a final going over. After that
we went to chow, which included turkey, dressing, and ice
cream. With irony, I thought of the phrase, "The condemned
men ate hearty."

Again we inspected our guns and ammunition. Lone wolf
Casey sharpened his eleven-inch dagger. Conscientious Berke-
ly, the giant, dusted his tommy gun with domestic care. The
Arab brushed imaginary flecks of sand from his gleaming rifle.
The Master Termite slept in the shade of the wing, oblivious
to everything. The Big Polack painstakingly checked his ma-
chine gun before he packed it in the equipment bundle.
Larkin for once didn't seem to be in the mood for a fight.

We had "abandon ship" training with the pneumatic life
rafts on the C-47. That was in case we were forced down in
the water. All had a Mae West (life jacket) that could quickly be inflated with compressed oxygen.

Each of us as he finished checking his equipment sat down
on the desert and thought it over. I could see eyes go narrow,
faces grow grim, jaws jut out. Every man realized that all his
bridges were now burned behind him. Each was accepting his
destiny and reacting to its acceptance in his own fashion.
Casey said nothing, but his pale eyes glistened. Olson's broad
face thinned out into lean, dark angles. Finkelstein alone was
undaunted. He grinned and asked if there were a funeral
thereabouts because of the abundance of mourners. Irishman
O'Connell prepared himself by tying a silk scarf about his
neck. He always wore it when he jumped. Duquesne kidded
his pal Gruening, and inquired if they made good beer in
Sicily. Big Rodgers read a chapter in his pocket Bible.

Cigarette and pipe smoke filtered through dry nostrils into
the desert air. Larkin threw away a butt, smiled sardonically,
and said, "Well, you guys always said you're tough. By God,
let's see you prove it." Benson glared at him, stroked his
straggly mustache and relapsed into gloom.

A rattling of equipment rippled down the line of planes as
we began to get into our harness. A sigh—half relief, half
desperation—ran through the men. Main pack on, leg straps

buckled, chest straps fast, static line loose from back, anchor line snap fastener handy, now reserve chute, both hooks snapped. "Fasten bellyband, buddy!" "Okay, Joe! you fasten mine!" Rifle in case, grenades in pockets, bandoleers already around chest beneath chute, Mae West over neck, gas mask hung on, dispatch case hung on other side. Rations, maps, bail-out kit in it. "Okay, all set. Good luck, pal. See ya in Sicily." "Okay, climb in the plane in order of jumping. Men, you know what to do. Go out fast when I give the word. Jump at ten forty-three on green light. Got that? Okay, sit down. Smoke after the take-off."

One engine starts, now the other. The motors warm up. The roar deadens and numbs our thoughts. Propellers whip up clouds of dust. Hot breezes pour through the plane which taxies onto the runway as the motors step up to stupendous, ear-shattering roars. It's moving, picking up speed, pouring the desert by the little windows . . . air-borne! We are in the air, we are going! *We're off to Sicily!*

We gain altitude and circle. Beneath us on the airport a C-47 takes off every few seconds. Others keep taxiing up to the take-off point. Our sky train grows like assembling flocks of migrating geese as more and more planes join our vast circular sweeps. We begin to fly over larger areas of desert. The planes jockey into V echelons. A plane noses into place about one hundred yards to our left rear; another noses into our right rear. Our platoon in the V echelon is complete.

Looking out the leering door, I could see the sky train quit circling, whip into line, and become one long air fleet with one directing head. We were headed for the turquoise Mediterranean. The time was an hour before sundown. The desert, spotted with Arab villages whose dwellers peered up bug-eyed at the spectacle, flowed smoothly under the air fleet. Camels, goats, horses, cacti, and wheat fields alternated with airports whose Spitfires, Wellingtons, trucks, jeeps, and gasoline drums perched insect-shaped on the desert floor. I sat opposite the door and saw the white beaches of the seashore and then Africa recede into the sunset. At last only water was visible.

Melancholy stole into my thoughts as I looked through the door into the sunset. The orange and yellow horizon contrasted strangely with the fiery red of the sun cutting vertically like a great saw into the blue water. A vagrant thought brought the line of a song, "How I hate to see that evening sun go down." The sun vanished, leaving behind a red glow. The red glow vanished and the water was dark. The men rustled in their chutes as they broke open packs of cigarettes.

Smoke swirled and eddied and then whipped out the door. It got dark. The monotonously thrumming motors shot little flames into the night through the engine exhausts. We sat brooding, prickly as porcupines in our gear, awaiting the word for exit although we were not yet halfway on the long ride for which we had no round-trip ticket.

Suddenly a vague land mass appeared in the distance, Malta! Twenty-two hundred air raids and still fighting! Recognition lights blinked. A plane shot a signal flare in acknowledgment. The lights blinked off and then darkness again and the sea, whose waves porpoised indifferently only a few hundred feet beneath the plane.

In one hour and fifteen minutes we were to jump. The cigarettes went up the side again, crossed the aisle and then back. Spots of fire specked the dark as tight lips sucked the fags to shreds. I ground mine sadistically into the metal floor. Dense clouds of whitish smoke from the battle-torn seaports of Gela, Licata and Vittoria now obscured the sea and shut out even the darkness. The propeller blast, screaming by the jeering open door, fanned it into tenuous, shifting streamers of white in which I fancied that the spent souls of wrecked men twisted and turned.

Across the aisle by the door a tiny red light glowed; simultaneously the strident voice of Lt. Toland, the jump master and platoon leader, cracked out, "Stand up and hook up!" Reeling under the weight of two parachutes and heavy battle equipment, we hooked our anchor-line snap fastener to the cable and waited. Again cracked that strident voice, "Check your equipment!" Each man checked his own chute and his buddy's chute in front of him. The last man turned his back so that the man in front of him could check his back chute. A third time the voice cracked out, "Sound off for equipment check!" The last man, who was to the front of the plane and farthest from the exit, yelled out, "Fourteen okay." The next man yelled, "Thirteen okay," and so on toward the door. Toland was to jump first and I after him. When I yelled, "Two okay," he nodded and yelled in that unforgettable gritty voice, "Okay, we jump when the green light comes on. Make it good!"

Toland stood gripping both sides of the door, head and shoulders out, looking down to see when land was reached. I watched for the red light to turn green, for being second man to jump, I was to prod the officer when the signal came. We stood waiting, our knees buckling beneath our tremendous loads, hearts thudding against our ribs, nerves steeled for the dive into darkness, minds sealed against vagrant, infiltrating, treacherous, nerve-wracking thoughts.

Below, the sea still rolled its dark masses. Suddenly we flew over a ship. I felt a warm glow of brotherhood for our men beneath who were there to help us against the enemy. And then, suddenly, long red streaks of flame began to stab and slice the sky into weird patterns of flashes and bursts, above, below and around us. Whether by friend or by foe, we were being shot at! I felt the urge to kick Toland through the door and to get into space before our plane became a burning coffin, I was mentally churning the matter when number three man punched me in the ribs. The green light! I gouged the officer, and in a single, swift movement, the door was empty; and then I too soared out and, falling tense and breathless, sweated it through the few seconds, which seemed an eternity, until the opening chute as if gripped in a giant fist first stopped and then swung me back into the sky. Above me like a great bat floated the big transport plane spurting fire from the exhausts. Between me and it other chutes were opening. To the left the full moon, seemingly on a level with me, smiled its contentment at being 240,000 miles from the hell into which I was dropping. A double stream of red tracers seemed to be going between my legs. Ack-ack shells exploding around me splattered little puffs of smoke against the moonlight. Some of our planes tumbled out of the air like burning crosses; others stopped like a bird shot in flight, crumpled and plummeted. Still others exploded and disintegrated.

The double stream of red tracers was still climbing into the night but farther away from me now. I spread my feet and relaxed. Below, the earth, though still vague and hazy, was arising to meet me. Peering over the reserve chute that had now slid up to my chin, I saw vegetation and then a few seconds later tumbled to the ground in a heap.

5. Big Rodgers Came Strolling Through the Vineyard

I had landed in a vineyard. Stunned and breathless, I lay on the ground tangled in my chute and fighting equipment, expecting German infantry to pounce upon me any second. I put my rifle together and got on my feet. Fifteen yards distant a double stream of red tracers bubbled skyward over a stone wall about eight feet high.

New at the fighting game, I never considered that I was watching *red* tracers, whereas Germans use silver tracers. With a grenade in hand, I sneaked up to the wall. At that moment the gun quit shooting and I heard, "Man we gave it to them Nazi bastards."

I realized then that our own men had been shooting at us. I had been on the point of killing some of our soldiers, who must have killed some of us.

At that moment Big Rodgers came strolling through the vineyard, plucking grapes, eating them and spitting out the seeds as calmly as if he were back home eating a watermelon on Sunday afternoon in Andalusia, Alabama.

"You know, Ross," he said in his self-effacing, soft southern way, "there could of been a little memorial service on the hill for us back home and we wouldn't have knowed nothing about it. It sure would hurt my feelings to get it up in the air where I didn't have a chance to fight back. Course this is just between us, Ross. I believe our own boys got mixed up and got to shootin' at us! What do you think? I said a little prayer up there in the vines just a minute ago. I know you and the other boys don't think it helps much, but I just naturally feel more like fightin' when I pray!"

Quiet, unobtrusive and retiring, Big Rodgers smoked little and never drank or cursed. He would volunteer for any work detail however disagreeable and for the most hazardous patrols. When asked to accept a dangerous assignment, he would reflect a moment and then answer quietly, "I'll go." He never passed snap judgments on any matter or spoke until he had thought over what he had to say.

Big Rodgers, former Golden Gloves champion, never picked a quarrel or acted the bully but if challenged he gave his fist mate a beating to remember. In training he gave the impression of being awkward but in battle action his soldiering came to be the talk of the Legion. I could write a book about this sincerely religious man to whose heroism some of us owe our lives and who earned among us a respect that we accorded to no other man.

We hid behind a stone wall, listened and looked for a few minutes, then worked along it until we heard a jumble of voices coming from behind a large shed. T. L. readied a grenade and edged toward it while I covered him with my tommy gun. Suddenly I heard a sentence which sounded like *Pausiren sie?* T. L. loked at me. I nodded the okay-let-her-fly signal. He flexed his arm for the throw when suddenly we heard, "Poughkeepsie? Hell yes, it's on the New York Central!"

"That's Gruening!" T. L. put on his serious face. "I might o' killed him, Ross, and whoever's with him."

"Where Gruening is Duquesne's close by," I said.

"Now in the old army, Gruening . . ." we heard the old lumberjack start to chide.

"A pair of jokers," I cut in, "who got to arguing about the New York Central and let scouts slip up close enough to hand-grenade 'em would have been court-martialed! Poughkeepsie back of this shed sounded like *Pausiren sie?* We thought you were Germans! Another second and T. L. would have really mixed you up!"

"Now, Gruening, I've been telling you all along that the New York Central ain't worth a damn! You see! It almost killed both of us!"

"Boys, I would have and I would have sure hated it too. Things wouldn't be right if we couldn't hear about that railroad, would they, Ross?"

"T. L. you go to hell!" grinned Gruening, who, like the rest of us, never got sore at Big Rodgers.

"I reckon I won't do that," he drawled, "but I believe we'd better be going to look for the other boys."

Before long we came across Berkely, Casey, the Arab, Finkelstein, Carlton, the Master Termite, Larkin and Olson, who had already found the equipment chutes. Accompanied by one officer we tried to find our way to the jump field, not knowing it was twenty miles away. Before dawn we gave it up as hopeless, set up a defense along a rock wall, put out guards, draped ourelves with the parachutes to keep off the dew and settled down beneath a big tree to await developments. We didn't know whether we were among Germans or Americans.

When dawn came our spirits rose. We filled our canteens from the water bags, ate a K ration and looked about us. A Messerschmidt flew by skimming the ground, reconnoitering the chutes scattered over the vineyards. It was the first Nazi plane we had ever had a close view of in the air and we gave it a good looking over.

It turned out that members of my battalion were for the most part close together. Other outfits were not so lucky. Some of our men landed behind German lines. Almost one entire platoon disappeared that night without trace. A trooper named Sawyer attached himself to a 45th Division reconnaissance outfit and went through the campaign as a machine gunner on a fifty caliber.

Two paratroopers disarmed the friendly Italian garrison

of a town deep in Sicily, found plenty to drink and celebrated for three days. Finally some of Patton's tanks roared into town and the paratroopers were arrested as Germans. They explained that they had taken the town three days before.

"Taken hell," a weary tankman yelped, "we fought through a Panzer division to get here."

The drunk paratrooper opined patronizingly that the Germans must have known all along that the town was in American hands and for that reason had avoided coming into it!

Another paratrooper took over a town and was riding a jackass up and down the square in drunken revelry when two Messerschmidts flew over and strafed it. The drunk waved gleefully and hollered, "Try again, you Nazi bastards," and then gigged his jackass into a gallop.

All the paratroopers were not so lucky. One company jumped on a German tank outfit in the dark and got badly shot up.

We spent the day watching our first dogfights, listening to rumors and wondering what next. My platoon was together again, but no one knew anything about the remainder of the company. A rumor scuttlebutted that they were all dead; in the afternoon, however, most of the boys showed up. The battalion re-formed under the command of the ranking captain, who made a short speech of encouragement, and then, just before dark, we moved off toward Vittoria in battle formation.

We learned later that the colonel and some of his men had landed in the front lines among the 45th Division. The colonel had with him parts of his 81 millimeter mortar platoon. He arranged to have a major of the 45th Division furnish riflemen to protect his crew while they were fighting with their mortar. Some German tanks attacked. The mortar men fired on the tanks with the 81, knocking out one light tank, and then withdrew. A paratrooper named Gordon, dug in with his machine gun near the mortar, was so busy fighting that he didn't bother to run from the tanks. He crouched behind his gun and fired until the tank machine guns riddled him from pointblank range. He was found a day later, stiffened behind his gun in firing position, finger on the trigger. Drops of blood had soaked down into his big mustache from a wound on his forehead. He was a brave picture of a fighting man. He was buried in his firing position since his body was too stiff to bend into natural shape.

The enemy captured two paratroopers in their chutes, tied them to trees, doused them in gasoline, threw a match at them and left them there as flaming torches. Those two burnt, charred bodies symbolized the raw, naked brutal force we would have to overcome to win the war. We never forgot them.

6. The Arab Captures a City

The second night after the jump we marched until four in the morning. We didn't have the vehicles to carry our rations and heavy equipment—machine guns, mortars and ammunition—that regular infantry divisions have; consequently we carried all this stuff on our backs. We reeled along on guts and some on bloody feet. Olson carried his 60 millimeter mortar about twenty miles that night. He staggered along, wheezing, oozing sweat, his feet dead, his short, powerful legs buckling at every step, but indomitable. Benson, sagging from the weight of his mortar ammo and other equipment, cried because he was unable to carry his load as easily as the other ammo men carried theirs. T. L. Rodgers, though bowed beneath the weight of two boxes of machine gun ammunition, his rifle and grenades, was tough enough to add the machine gun to his burden and carry it for miles.

We stopped in the edge of a town, put our heavy stuff in a pile, put out guards, and passed out in the vineyards along the road. At daylight we got up. Casey felt of his chin, wiped away blood, swore snarlingly and looked up at the rock wall by which he had been sleeping. He noticed and picked up a bloody rock the size of his head. A grinning sentry told him that a Nazi plane had dropped a bomb on the other side of the wall at five o'clock. It had dislodged a rock which had fallen on Casey and put him into still deeper sleep. No one except the sentries had heard the bomb or plane.

K rations were brought up in an old Italian truck. Carlton and the Arab, craving vegetables for their meal, went into an Italian garden, helped themselves to tomatoes and returned with the garden gate, being in need of fuel. The owner, a fat signor, ran out spouting words like rain, but the twosome, their heads bowed in shame, brought it along. Berkely got a mule from a peasant and we tied our equipment on the poor critter. As we marched, Carlton spied a fine riding cart, re-

cruited Berkely and the Arab, went into the peasant's yard
and requisitioned it. Thus the Legion procured transportation
as it marched along the road by the Mediterranean! A donkey
here, a mule there, a buggy from a shed, a little car in some
town, an old Italian truck which ingenious mechanics sal-
vaged, bicycles, motorcycles, horses from roadside pastures,
and finally some army trucks begged from the 7th Army to
haul rations and ammunition.

It never rained, so the campaign progressed rapidly. There
was plenty of wine. Cantaloupes, tomatoes, and grapes
abounded. At night we slept where we stopped. Occasionally
an enemy plane flew overhead or dived down and strafed
but did little damage. Life was wonderful. We were convinced
that war had never been like this in the history of the world.
Cheering crowds greeted us in the towns. Peasants brought
food and drink when we stopped. Barbers shaved us for a
cigarette. Many girls could fall in love for a chocolate bar or
a few cigarettes. We took more Italian prisoners than we
could feed. On seeing us coming they cheered and hastened to
surrender. *"Buono soldato americano!" "Avete una cigaretta."*
When we would tell them to go home, that we didn't want
them, they would protest, their faces expressing woe, shoulders drooping, *"Nienta, mio prisionero."* So we would ac-
commodate them. Every third Sicilian or Italian had been in
Brooklyn. "I worka on da dock eighteena year. I bootleg da
wheesky, maka moneta grande, return to Sicilia." *"Buonos
americanos."*

But all the Italians were not friendly. An American paratrooper who spoke Italian fluently, while on advance scout
for a twenty-man patrol, was captured by an Italian outpost
of seven Italian officers, one German officer, and several
enlisted Italian soldiers. An Italian officer questioned him
in English and he replied in Italian. "Traitor!" the officer exclaimed, pulled his Beretta automatic, and emptied it into the
soldier, who fell to the ground, wounded but not killed. The
officer then threw an Italian concussion grenade between his
ankles. It exploded shredding most of the meat from the
trooper's leg bones. Still conscious, he continued to curse the
officer in Italian. Enraged, the Fascist officer took an American grenade from the paratrooper's belt and dropped it between the prostrate man's thighs. It spread his stomach over
the ground. The twenty paratroopers came up, handed the
officers shovels, made them dig eight graves in a row, lined
them up by their graves and shot them.

We continued to march up the coast, covering twenty or

twenty-five miles daily. One day, when our feet were blistered and our backs breaking, we came up to some light tanks.

"Pile on, men, you're riding tanks into battle today," an officer said. We climbed gaily on the iron steeds, preferring to ride the tanks to hell and back rather than walk another mile.

Berkely, Homer Carey, Olson, Finkelstein, the Arab, Sgt. Winters, and I were on the lead tank. The other men mounted the four tanks in the rear, and with a jeep in the lead to look for mines we took off with an abundance of noise, happy as a cat in cream to ride after walking a hundred miles! Perched like Caesars on those tanks we roared on into enemy country.

We pulled up at a stone bridge which was mined. A transportation colonel came up and commanded that some paratroopers be sent over the hill to see if there might be an ambush awaiting the tanks after they crossed the bridge. Duquesne, Winters, the Arab, and I were picked to go.

We never did return to report. When our outfit pushed over the bridge and beyond the hill, they saw ahead a city bedecked with white flags. Our patrol, grinning happily, climbed on the lead tank and in majestic triumph handed the city over to our commander. A bottle stuck out of the Arab's pocket and a small ebony, curiously wrought pipe jutted from his mouth. I could tell you how he came by these items and what happened to us, but I think the Arab's version will make better reading. Here's how he'd recount *our* feat after he'd belted a few drinks.

"I'm just a dam' two-bit corporal," the Arab would grin, "but, igod, I and three other jokers, mostly I, took a city of forty thousand. What a story! Winters led the patrol. When we saw that damned city ahead of us, Winters set off towards it at a jazzy rickshaw trot and we after him. On the edge of town the road split. Winters said for me and Duquesne to take the left-hand road and meet him and Carter somewhere in town. Now, igod, imagine four men assaulting a town that big! Duquesne's rifle was screwed up, so he carried his pistol in his hand. When we first got into the city, the Ginnies on seeing us would shrink back. But they responded with cheers to our grins and *'Soldato americano'* and offered us wine and spaghetti. Nine grinning Ginnie soldiers came up. I bummed a cigarette from them. They walked along with us through the big cheering crowds. Many people cried for joy, especially the women. An old Ginnie who spoke English guided us through the gleeful throng into a big building which turned out to be the Fascist party headquarters. Inside an impeccable old gent looking up, snapped to attention, gave me a tailormade salute and spouted a bunch of formalities in the Ginnie language. I gravely returned the salute, then asked my interpreter what the hell he'd said. He replied that the fancy dude was the commandant of the city, was turning it over to me and wanted to know what I was going to do. Hell, I didn't want the damned city! What could a dirty dogface like me do with a city? I told him I just wanted credit for conquering it, not for running it, but that I would like a pistol as a souvenir. He had no pistol, but he did give me this little pipe and the fine bottle of cognac whose smiling neck you see protruding from my pocket. You are now looking at the conqueror of the sovereign city of Menfi. It is on the map, and wait until I write home about it!"

In the States the Arab, a nickname we gave him in Africa, was a fair soldier but not outstanding. He carried out orders conscientiously, but never seemed really to give a damn nor to be ambitious for promotion. He had had a good education, but aside from helping the boys with their spelling when they wrote home made no show of it. Off duty he spent a lot of time reading and on duty if he got a chance. While the rest of us played poker, shot craps or bulled, the Arab read Homer's *Iliad* and *Odyssey*. Sometimes he told us about the adventurous Odyssey of Odysseus, also called Ulysses, who spent ten years at Troy and ten in wanderings before he finally returned to his home, and he said he felt like a modern Ulysses, the difference being that he would crowd his adventures into two or three years and then go home . . . maybe. The Arab read his Homer and carried it with him as some troopers did the Bible. The boys learned to leave Homer alone after the Arab beat the hell out of Gruening and broke a rib for Larkin because they hid it. When he got tired of reading Homer, which was seldom, he sent away for other books, epic poems if he could get them.

The Arab was from hillbilly country and proud of it. He said that his ancestors hunted with Daniel Boone on the Wilderness Trail and that his father had found a letter a few years ago written by Boone to one of them. Although he tried hard to do close order drill and calisthenics, he could never do the complicated exercises thought up by jokers who should have been circus clowns. He said that he was a squirrel hunter and fisherman, not an acrobat.

The Arab's easy good humor and imperturbable air endeared him to most of his buddies. Except over Homer he never had fights and seldom got on any of the mean drunks or crying jags that some of us did. He was merely waiting for the war to end, he said, so that he could go back to the hills to read, philosophize, squirrel hunt and fish. I once asked him why he volunteered for the Paratroops. He shrugged and said, "I had to," and that was all I could get out of him.

In Africa we began to notice that the Arab always had the shadiest spot for his tent and the best and most drinking water, which he kept cool in a pot buried underground. He could always dig up eatable rations, extra blankets, shelter halves, mosquito netting, oranges, and other desert luxuries. No one except Berkely, Carey, and I knew where he got this stuff and we were too wise to tell. He was a clever thief; so in admiration we called him the Arab, after the regular Arabs, who have more taking tricks, in my experience, than any people in the world.

The Arab never played games or exerted himself if he could avoid it. If newcomers, viewing his listlessness, concluded, as they usually did, that the Arab was feeble, in bad health, perhaps a hospital case, they had a different opinion of him at the end of a ten-mile hike. The sluggish slob, looking fresh as a Swiss milkmaid, sometimes chanting lines in Latin from the *Aeneid,* bellwethered the boys home.

The Arab tented in Africa with a kid named Carey, who was as lazy as he was. They would argue for hours about whose turn it was to do the tent chores. When their patience was exhausted they decided the issue by force. Carey, the son of a Texas oil man, had never worked in his life, but he took to the desert like a duck to water. Soon he was as scurvy in appearance as the Arab. It was never clear why the Arab nicknamed him Homer, but the name stuck. One thing is certain: the Arab would not have conferred the title on a joker he disliked. Homer was an engaging character, full of joy and zest, whose one peculiarity was wheezing in such a way when he got drunk that it made us all laugh.

The love life of Homer was an open book. With a little priming he would report on his amorous exploits and adventures in detail, with the exception of an affair he once had with a one-legged woman. We were curious to learn the details, but for some reason he would clam up on this subject and tell us to blow it out our barracks bags.

The calm, quiet, good-natured, Homer-reading Arab turned out to be one of the fiercest, craftiest fighters in the Legion. It surprised us but shouldn't have. It is hard to predict the fighting cock in the chick and the true soldier before he has been in battle. A man who is a man doesn't say so. A man who isn't often does.

I wish I could tell you more about the enigmatic con-

queror" of Menfi. I never figured him out as long as we simply
lived and fought side by side. Now that the war is over,
though, I sometimes think I've discovered his meaning but
I'm not sure.

7.   Casey Needed Wood to Cook His Rations

Castellammare di Golfo, population 20,000, was a fine town
with sea breezes fanning it continually. My platoon got the
plum of administering it until the real Military Government
jokers arrived. The people seemed to be friendly. We took
over the former Fascist party headquarters, which were in
the best building in town, containing a good radio and much
Fascist literature which we used to cook our rations.

For some reason or other Fascist literature wouldn't cook
Casey's rations. He needed wood. The Fascist party emblem
above the door, a bundle of sticks with the blade of an ax
sticking out, caught his eye. Casey hunted up janitor Maggio,
pointed out the emblem, asked him to tear it down and split
it into kindling. A crowd of Ginnies gathered, thinking that
we were destroying the symbol of Fascism, whereas Casey,
ignorant of Fascism, only wanted some stovewood. With each
lick Maggio grunted, yelled, and laughed, *"Fini* Mussolini."
Spectators applauded.

Casey gathered up the wood, retired to the park amid
deafening applause, cooked his corn pork loaf, and wondered
what had caused all the hullabaloo.

There were men in our Legion and there was Casey. He
said to call him "Al" when he first joined us in Africa. In
many ways he was the strangest creature I met in the army.
He was six feet one and weighed 190 pounds. His arm muscle
was as big as my leg and I am no runt. The jugular veins in
his columnar neck seemed to serve as guy cords for his long
head on which the tawny hair grew in little knots and bunches
like small patches of grama grasses on our Western ranges.
He had a wide, thin-lipped mouth set with long, wide-spaced
sharp teeth, a slim high-bridged nose, long pointed ears, and
narrow, pale, ice-cold mica-tinted eyes which had a phos-
phorescent greenish glow in the dark. His hands with thumbs
almost as long as the fingers were as slender and fine as a
musician's. No one knew his age, which could have ranged
anywhere from twenty-five to forty. One thing was certain:

he had been around. Aside from admitting that he had been a cowboy, a rodeo bronc rider and bulldogger, and a citizen of Wyoming when he enlisted, he had no past that he ever told us about.

Casey spent hours cleaning his rifle and polishing his jump boots which he kept as soft as glove leather. In Africa he spent hours in the desert shooting the flowers off the giant cacti. Sometimes he came in with a bottle of cognac which he had gotten from an Arab and sat and drank until the bottle was empty. He never got drunk, but with his pale eyes gleaming tigerishly he would stalk around catlike for a few minutes and then go to bed.

When Casey jumped, his face remained expressionless and he usually landed standing up. He never said anything much about anything so we couldn't tell what he thought about jumping. One day they showed us some German prisoners from the Afrika Korps. He didn't say a word. He walked up and stared and then tiger-footed round and round them until those tough boys got nervous. Finally he nodded his head as though satisfied and turned away.

He was a very efficient soldier and hell on patrol assignments. The lieutenant figured that men would obey a man like Casey, so he offered him a job as corporal while we were still in Africa. He just looked at the lieutenant and shook his head but never said a word, and that was the end of it. We figured that he would be a lone wolf in battle and that's what he turned out to be.

I used to look at Casey and imagine him in a skin suit, spear or club in hand, stalking saber-toothed tigers or dinosaurs or other beasts now dead and gone. I would watch him sit cross-legged with his eyes fixed on the desert, his head wagging slowly from side to side and his slim nose aquiver like a dog's scenting game. I don't know that he could smell as well as a dog, but I had the feeling that he could smell about as well.

One night Casey disappeared for about an hour into the desert and came back with a big hunk of camel meat. We think he killed the camel with the eleven-inch blade dagger he carried, but we never could verify it. He built a little fire in his pup tent, broil-seared the meat just enough so the blood wouldn't drip, then cut big chunks up into little chunks which he ate from the point of his knife without salt. He tore into the tough meat like a wolf. We watched him eat and never said a word to him and he never said a word. After he finished he wiped his dagger, looked up and said:

"Carter, antelope tastes better than camel. I like the sedge taste."

In spite of his strangeness we all respected Casey and liked
him and knew that he was a man we could depend on. He
always was.

There was a bakery in Castellammare di Golfo, but with
the transportation system broken down there was neither
wheat nor flour for bread. The people being hungry and dis-
contented, a lieutenant set out to look for wheat. In an old
Italian truck, repaired by Berkely, and accompanied by two
or three of the boys and some Italian guides, he drove to the
estates of some rich Fascist landowners and offered to buy
wheat at the market prices. They blew their stacks, but we
shut them up. The lieutenant had the wheat made into bread
and distributed in equal shares to the hungry by ration tickets.

In the bread queues there were some favorites of the Ginnie
policemen who did their job subject to our orders. Ex-lumberjack Duquesne, seeing a policeman escort a friend from
the back to the front of the line, skull-bashed the copper to
sleep and, when he came to, booted him, midst thunderous
applause, twice around the square. Then Casey took over
and toe-bounced the favorite's rear back to the end of the
line. Our military government was hitting on heads and tails!

It was a very happy time that we had in that town. Casey
and some of the boys, while scouting the country, had found
three sweet girls and installed them, with a housemother, in a
mansion overlooking the sea. The boys purred day and night
with joy. A few men attached to an armored outfit came
through town, found out about the love nest, and with haste
approached its portals. There the Master Termite and Casey
with "MP" on the front of their helmets politely barred the
door.

"Boys, it shore beats hell," the Master sympathized, "but
this place has just been put off limits. The damned army won't
let a man have any fun."

When the antsy armored boys had departed, the Master
and Casey rubbed off the MP markings, grinned and disappeared into the love sanctum.

8.   Hill 424

On the afternoon of September 13, 1943, the Legion was
called together, told to put on its equipment and march down

to the airport. In my platoon all were present except Hastings and Stanly, who had gone out to try to steal some white turkeys. We had to leave camp without them.

There was an air of urgency in the demeanor of the brass hats that had been absent in the hours before the Sicilian jump. It was clear that something was wrong somewhere. We were not briefed, nor given a chance to study aerial photographs as we had before for two other jumps that had failed to come off.

We picked up our chutes from a shed and marched out to the planes. Hastings and Stanly joined us there. They were almost too drunk to walk. A friend of mine came up to me with a rumor: "They say that Mark Clark's men have only got six hundred yards of beach left to fight on. The Krautheads are pushing them into the sea. We're going to jump in the middle of the Krautheads and hold them off so that Clark can evacuate the wounded and save some of his men. A suicide mission, that's what we're going on."

Goddam! What a story to spread just before a jump! We hadn't been told yet where we were going. But soon Lt. Toland gathered us together and announced that we were going to jump at Salerno within the Allied beachhead to help out Mark Clark's men who were having rough going. When our planes approached the beach, a beacon was to be lit to guide us in. It was still a rough deal, we thought, but at least it sounded better than the rumor. The 1st and 2nd Battalions of the 504th (the Legion in this story) were to jump that night. The 3rd Battalion was to come in by boat. The 505th Parachute Regiment, our sister regiment, was to stand by to jump if needed.

Once more an awful feeling of strain and fear bore down upon us. We thought of the Sicily jump when the army and navy shot us all to hell, and wondered if it would happen again. We had had a good singeing already. This time we figured that we'd really get it.

The men were reacting characteristically. The Master Termite philosophically puffed on a cigarette. Berkely, now a squad leader, was meticulously checking all of his men's equipment. Finkelstein was grinning. Casey sat gazing into the olive grove on the hill. Big Rodgers was silent as usual. Hastings was scrutinizing his parachute with distaste. Duquesne was wondering where he'd get his next beer. Gruening, his boon companion, was speculating on his chances of going back to work again for the New York Central. The Arab was deciding how he was going to hold his rifle when he jumped. Carey for once wasn't thinking of women: his round cheeks were set firmly with the pressure of his thoughts.

All were priming themselves for desperate action. The air was blue with cigarette smoke and just blue.

A jeep drove up. Colonel Reuben Tucker, the regimental commander, was standing up in it, his flushed, bemustached intense face set in deep lines. He halted at every plane and yelled, "Men, it's open season on Krautheads. You know what to do!"

We climbed into the planes. It was already dark. We taxied onto and roared down the runway. The second great adventure of the Legion had started.

I was again to be second man to jump. From my seat opposite the door I watched other planes sway up and down as they hit air pockets. The long minutes wore on. Our minds were full of speculations about the battle conditions we would find at Salerno as we sat with our bodies cramped by the heavy chutes and equipment. Finally the crew chief came back and told Lt. Toland that we would jump in twenty minutes. We woke up the sleeping men. At seven minutes to jump time we checked our chutes. The red light was on. Toland stood in the door. I looked at the signal light. When it turned from red to green, I nudged the lieutenant. He dropped into space. For a second the jump door yawned wide and dreadful, then swallowed me. The chute opened and I looked around. It was peaceful. No one was shooting at us. I landed, stunned by the shock. Carey came to me and helped me out of the chute. The platoon began to assemble. Berkely looked in vain for the equipment chute containing the squad's automatic rifles and ammunition. Apparently the crew chief hadn't pulled the release switch.

It was three o'clock in the morning of September 14, 1943. We didn't know where we were on the beachhead and few of us ever learned much about it except that we had jumped at a place called Paestum, just south of Salerno. All next day, hidden in a small valley, we listened to a terrific battle taking place a couple of miles away. We were in position to repel the attack if it reached us, but it never did. That night we put out guards and finished digging foxholes. Sometime in the night a brilliant light illuminated the country for miles around. Later I learned that a Krauthead shell had passed into the open hatch of a Liberty ship loaded with 80,000 gallons of gasoline.

On the morning of the second day we prepared for an approach march to somewhere. At twelve o'clock the battalion pushed off. At a fast pace we went through a valley and up a mountain. The sun bore down on us. Our chests were bursting. Soon our water was gone, our throats parched. Shells

screamed over and hit on the opposite mountain. The descent
led through tranquil vineyards and orchards to the bed of a
rocky stream that had its source in adjoining mountains, un-
poetically designated by military strategists as Hill 424 and
Hill 415. The town of Alta Villa was on Hill 424. It developed
that my battalion's mission was to take and hold Hill 424.

The 36th Division, whose primary objective on landing
was to seize and hold this hill, had unexpectedly found Krautheads dug in and waiting for them. The troops landed in spite
of fierce opposition and pushed on to Hill 424, the key Krauthead observation post which it had already taken and lost
three times by the time we arrived. The 36th being too weak
because of heavy casualties to seize the hill, it was up to us
to try our hand, backed up by the 2nd Battalion of the 504th.
At the time, of course, most of us just obeyed orders, not
knowing what we were supposed to do.

When we were about a mile from those two hills, a Piper
Cub, on an observation mission, flew over and dropped a
wrench with an attached note stating that the hills were occupied in strength by the enemy. The information made it
seem wise for us to march farther apart, but did not deter our
approach to the two hills, which were rather close together
with a saddlelike little draw connecting them. The sun had
gone down and darkness was falling as we approached the
foothills and began to climb.

Carey, Lt. Toland, the Arab, and I were lying in a little
ditch in a vineyard waiting for the column to move out ahead
of us when a shell followed by three others screamed over
the hill, hit mere yards from us and exploded, each explosion
covering us with dirt and rocks. I'd never known real terror
until that moment.

The column moved on up the hill under shells moaning
high overhead, heading for the beaches. In the darkness a
machine gun opened up on us. I dived headlong into a pile
of rocks and skinned my nose from tip to eyebrows.

Pushing on, we gained the top of one hill. Krauts on the
reverse slope saw Berkely outlined in the dim light against
the skyline and shortened the grass around him. At one
o'clock a major from the 2nd Battalion informed us that we
were on Hill 415, which the 2nd Battalion was supposed to
occupy. We moved down the saddle and up the slopes of
Hill 424. Just before daylight our scouts approaching the top
of the hill made contact with the enemy. Acting with speed
and daring, men of the battalion stormed the hilltop and
kicked the Krautheads off before they fully knew what had

happened. We had done something the army field manuals often talked about: infiltrated into enemy territory, chased out the enemy, and taken over his positions.

Filled with apprehensive trepidation, we watched the shadows disappear and dawn came. Dug in between two spurs of the hill, we gazed around uneasily and on noting the gaps in our lines quickly made positional readjustments. A narrow gully was the only avenue of communication between us, the 2nd Battalion and the remainder of the beachhead. A strong point of Krautheads in the valley covered all approaches except the gully.

Cadavers lay everywhere. Having seen only a few corpses in Sicily, it was a horrible experience for us to see dead men, purpled and blackened by the intense heat, lying scattered all over the hill. The body of a huge man, eyes bloated out of their sockets, who lay dead about twenty yards from me, had swollen and burst. First lieutenant's bars were on his shoulders. His pistol belt with open compass case and empty binocular case bore witness to the quality of our equipment: the Krauts had looted them. A broken carbine lay by the body.

The Arab, who had lost his pistol belt with his compass and canteen during the night, callously observed the dead lieutenant's empty accessories. He grinned. "Way it looks I'll have a compass by noon to go in my belt. All hell's gonna break loose in a few minutes." He walked over to another body, appropriated the canteen, and carried it over to the Master Termite, busy deepening his foxhole with an enthusiasm never manifested in the States. "Master, I found a canteen for ya. I knew ya didn't have one."

"Thanks," mumbled the Master between shovelfuls of dirt. "Where'd you get it?"

"I got it from a thirty-six guy over there. He don't need it no more. Dead men don't need water." The Master discarded the canteen in haste.

"Arab," he said, "you got no respect for the dead."

Berkely and I, always delighted by the verbal jousts of the Master and the Arab, had just made our way through the rough terrain in time to hear them. The Master kept on digging while the three of us sat and watched and the Arab verbalized:

"The Master whipped by fear has mastered the art of digging a foxhole. Once in Fort Bragg I saw the Master Termite throw down his shovel and cry. In them days the Master's foxholes weren't good enough to please the kid corporal. I have seen the tears roll out of those wide gray eyes and dribble down that quivering chin into four different foxholes in six hours. But that was back in Fort Bragg. Berkely, you and Carter were there and saw it happen. That was a long time ago. Now the Master can dig faster than a badger."

"Ah," said the Master who, moved to tearful reminiscence by the Arab, contrived a smile. "When before had a Master Termite endured such indignities? In those days I was just a make-believe termite digging unnecessary foxholes in a make-believe war and it was too damned much. But now I'm a real termite in a real war and I can dig a real foxhole."

"Master, why do you weep?"

"That's easy, Arab," said Berkely. "The Master misses the chirp of the three sweet chicks and the downy nest in Castellammare di Golfo!"

Tears overflowed the Master's eyes and he went back to his digging.

The Master, a whimsical hobo for fifteen years until the army claimed him, was a gay, droll, sentimental individualist for whom the dictatorship of the officers and noncoms was baffling and inexplicable. Never in his life had he taken an order from anyone other than a harness bull in some hick town. Now his every action was subject to discipline. He submitted to the army and did his best, but after all he was thirty, and the big kid corporal who had made him dig foxholes was only twenty-one.

Perhaps it was because he needed an escape from the hard reality of the army that he thought up his droll game of make-believe; anyhow, he announced one day that he was a Termite, the Master Termite, Boss of all Termites, indisputably the King of Wood-eaters. What corporal's stripes approached his Royal Dignity!

The Master Termite metamorphosed, when he was drunk, from make-believe into the real thing. Once he approached me, smiled whimsically and said, "I'm the Master Termite." Suddenly he hurled himself through the air and sank his strong teeth sharpened on stale bread through my shirt into my arm muscle.

The Master and Duquesne were living a grand life in Birmingham until an MP put the old-timer in the clink. The Master said to the MP: "You put my buddy in the clink?"

MP: "Yep."

Master: "You won't turn him loose?"

MP: "Nope."

Master: "If the clink is good enough for Duquesne, it's

good enough for me." He knocked out the MP, got into the clink and sent the following telegram to the captain:

IF YOU WANT MY SERVICES, YOU'LL FIND ME IN THE BIRMINGHAM JAIL. FAITHFULLY, MASTER TERMITE.

The Master, like most bums, was eminently successful as a lover. His girl, named Angel, lived in Brooklyn. She called him "Wings,"—Angel's "Wings." The Master Termite often read us her letters in which she described the house they would build on Hoboken Bay when the war was over. Angel and Wings . . . and the House by the Side of the Bay. . . .

In Naples the Master found his brother, Private Peter Termite, whom he had not seen in five years. Overjoyed, he suggested that his brother get a pass so that they could tour the city together. Private Peter stepped up to his Old Man, saluted briskly, said, "Sir, Private Peter Termite requests an overnight pass so that he and his brother, Private Master Termite, can get drunk."

The Old Man informed him that a parade was on hand, that he could not go. The brother saluted, turned on his heel, and told the bad news to the Master.

"Whatcha gonna do, brother?"

"Do, hell!" brother Peter retorted. "Nacherally we're gonna get drunk."

Next morning the Master staggered into camp, sat upon a stone, put his head into his hands and moaned and wept, "Oh, that this should ever be! How am I ever gonna tell my mother? Boys, my brother, Private Peter Termite, is a drunkard!"

While riding the train across Africa, the Master, alcoholically overstewed, took offense at Gruening's mustache. Gruening challenged him to a fight. When the train stopped the two staggered into an improvised ring. Gruening, fond of the Master and not wanting to damage him, entreated him with tears in his eyes to withdraw his remarks. The Master refused, reaffirmed his opinion that the mustache *was* scurvy, offensive to the eye and fit only to strain soup through. Gruening dropped him with one blow on the left eye, hopped, straddled the Master and tearfully addressed him in these words, "Master, apologize, I'm begging ya. I don't wanna black your other eye, but I got my honor to think of. Please, Master, apologize." But the Master merely smiled at his conqueror and said, "It is a matter of principle. I don't like the dam' thing, and I won't lie to dodge another black eye." Sorrowing, Gruening blacked his other eye. . . .

A thunderous barrage of random shells, mostly from mortars, broke up our chat and reminiscences. We hugged the bottom of our holes, shrinking as we heard the soft whisper of the shells just before they hit. A staff sergeant in charge of battalion communications, who happened by just before the barrage began, looked scornfully at our holes and said, "Hell! A man just has to lie down under a tree when a shelling starts, and he's as safe as in them gopher holes." And he lay down beneath a gnarled olive. Presently I heard a tremendous explosion. The staff sergeant lay beneath a tree, his foot, neatly severed at the ankle, close beside him. A medic came running, applied a tourniquet, stopped the blood, gave him a shot of morphine, some sulfa tablets, bandaged the stump, and called for more medics to carry him down the hill. The guy lived, made the States, has a cork leg, and sells insurance for a living.

The Krautheads began counterattacking. Since only a few of our machine guns and automatic rifles had reached us, it was up to the riflemen and tommy gunners to hold off the assault. The boys lay in their holes around the top of the hill and calmly squeezed off their shots. A Kraut machine gun would cackle, and then a heavy, deliberate trooper's rifle shot would lay the egg! The machine gun would remain silent. American riflemen were always the best in the world, and our Legion riflemen were among the best in the army. In about thirty minutes the attack was broken up.

Kraut medics moved fearlessly about on the battlefield giving first aid to their wounded. Our medics left our lines and helped save the lives of some of the stricken Germans. They worked side by side in a kind of truce until all the wounded were disposed of, then both parties withdrew.

Jokers who began to fight during and after D-Day may doubt that the medics helped each other out. However, at Salerno the Krautheads were not so desperate as they were later. The Italian campaigns were fought more according to the Geneva Convention than later stages of the war. The killing of prisoners on both sides didn't occur very often until the Normandy campaign began.

Sergeant Corwin came by with orders to take a patrol down into the valley behind us to contact the 2nd Battalion and find out their positions. Since the numerous mortar shells hitting around us made the valley seem more safe and peaceful, the Master Termite and the Arab volunteerd to go on the patrol.

Eight men moved down the gully and came to a big house where they stopped to take counsel. Some Krauthead mortar observer spotted them. A cluster of shells landed a hundred yards to the right of the house and two behind it. In the midst of it, it is surprising that others did not react as did the Master, who said he felt compelled to obey a call of nature. He moved into a little path and took down his trousers. The uneasy Arab urged him to hurry. The comfortable Master was in the act of spinning a philosophical comment about nature's abhorrence of haste in such matters when a pattern of exploding shells circled him and sent him scurrying, hobbled by his pants, to join the others in the deep gully, which the enemy observer began to shell-stitch. At that moment a patrol with a sketch of the 2nd Battalion's position dropped in on them and Corwin's patrol turned back. Going up the hill, they met a bunch of wounded men coming down. The war correspondent Richard Tregaskis and Colonel Freeman were among them. After they passed the wounded, the patrol saw a mortar shell land in their midst. Tregaskis earned his pay that day. Stamey, a member of the patrol, was missing.

A second counterattack was launched and again the boys picked the Krautheads off like squirrels. Kearny, lying by a thicket, saw some bushes quivering. Covering it with his rifle, he waited. A head stuck up into sight and Kearny shot the left eye out. Schneider, a German-American whose twin brother had been killed in the 9th Division in Africa, had the obsession that if he met enough Krautheads in battle he would at last find the man who had killed his brother. He was watching a stretch of ground with another trooper when he saw an enemy machine gun squad advancing to attack. Schneider asked his companion to crawl over to the left. Schneider killed the sergeant and yelled orders in German to the remaining Krautheads. "You dumb bastards, move to the right, or you'll all get it." They obeyed the orders because they thought one of their own men was giving them. Moreover, in the strain of battle men obey anyone who appears to know what he is doing. Their right now being the other trooper's left, he killed three more of them. Schneider then raged out at them again. "You dumb sons of bitches! I said go to the left. You're all going to get it if you don't listen to me." They moved to the left in front of Schneider, who killed two more. The others got the hell out.

The little colonel was up to his ears in battle and seemed to be having a hell of a good time. Alta Villa, where the enemy had heavy infantry and tank forces, lay under the hill and slightly to the rear. The little colonel turned to a Greek-American paratrooper named Perici:

"Perici, take six men and go into Alta Villa and find out how many Krautheads are in it."

Resolutely Perici replied, "No, sir, I can't go to that town."

The little colonel, gasping with rage, pulled out his 45. "Perici, why can't you go into Alta Villa?"

"Sir," rejoined Perici calmly, "I've been in this army for four years. I done learned that I can't go to town without a pass. The MP's would get me as shore as hell is red-hot."

With a tight smile on his lips the little colonel wrote out a pass for Sgt. Perici to enter the town with six men. Perici, satisfied, went into the town where he and his patrol got shot up. They found out the Krauthead strength and although wounded Perici returned to report as follows to the colonel: "Sir, they's MP's in that damn town with tanks and half tracks. A rough bunch, sir!"

The Krautheads didn't know a bad thing when they saw it. They attacked a third time and again got butchered. They could be seen forming for a fourth counterattack at the foot of a mountain. By now our ammunition was running low. Fortunately an artillery observer detected the counterattack preparations and radioed back to his twelve 155 howitzers who dropped 160 rounds on them. That broke up the attack. My platoon and one other scooted around the hill, encircled some die-hard machine gun nests and chased them into a thicket. The hand-to-hand fighting for Hill 424 being over, a slight lull ensued in the battle.

Sergeant Winters out on patrol found a 36th Division casualty in an old house who had a chunk as big as a coconut blown out of his leg. He was stark naked, wearing only his dog tags and barely alive enough to talk. He said he'd been there three days without water as prisoner of the Germans, who had stripped him of his clothes.

Krautheads, some newly killed, others dead in the 36th's battles, lay all about. I'll never forget a slender, blond, blue-eyed young fellow we found lying on his back in a thicket. His clean-cut, intelligent-looking face and eyes bore a surprised expression. Evidently Hitler hadn't told him about things like this when he promised him *Lebensraum*.

We took over the Krauthead positions and where needed dug new ones. We had no rations, so we pulled ripe figs and apples from the trees. For a while we took water from a caved-in well until a Nazi floated to the top. It was good water, close at hand, and easy to draw. Casey wanted to shoot him again, but the Master Termite reminded him that only a coward would shoot a dead man.

"You must always be gallant toward the deceased," said the Master, "and gentle with women!"

Casey said "Hell!" and walked off.

The lull in battle soon ended. From a big valley and from the foot of a hill, a terrible barrage of projectiles from 88 millimeter guns on tanks or on self-propelled mounts, and from a battery of 81 millimeter mortars, began to erupt on us in a never-ending stream. I likened each explosion of mortar shells to the fierce, trailing bark of a giant hound whose bay-ings, snuffings and growlings intensified in terrifying ferocity as he approached the prey. It was during this barrage that I first calculated that a direct-firing 88 shell traveled about three hundred yards ahead of its sound. A man had no time to duck before it arrived.

A shell completely buried Kirby except for his hand. We were pulling on his hand expecting to uncover a corpse, when a muffled voice spoke from beneath the earth. "Dig my other hand out, and pull on it too." Kirby dug the dirt from his eyes and mouth, and walked away, apparently undamaged. An hour later he went into convulsions from shock and was evacuated.

I heard someone calling, "Casey! Casey! Casey!" My guts knotted up at the awful prospect of climbing from my hole to give him first aid in that deadly hail of flying steel. "Casey! Casey! Answer, you bastard," I yelled. No answer . . . It was up to me to go to him as I was the closest. I found him flat on his back in a shallow slit with his mouth open and flies crawling in it—asleep. The area around his foxhole re-sembled lunar craters, yet there he lay snoring in the midst of the damnedest bunch of noises I ever heard. As I dashed back to my hole I cussed the bastard and regretted he hadn't choked to death in Africa on that raw camel meat.

Oldring, Carlton and Hastings were looking over a wall in the early morning when a shell killed Oldring instantly and wounded Hastings in the great blood vessel where the collar-bone is nearest to the neck. He bled to death in ten minutes. Carlton escaped.

When I think of Hastings I always remember the time he stole a mule in a North Carolina town and galloped it precipi-tately up the street with three coppers on his trail. Once Ol-dring and I were outposts in the pine woods at Fort Bragg. It was cold and snowing and we had neither blankets nor extra clothes. A fat mongrel dog came along: Oldring grabbed it and disappeared beneath a shelter half. We took turns cuddling the cur, which radiated heat like a stove. The surprised canine

was happy to have our selfish affection. In gratitude we left
him a peanut-butter-and-jelly sandwich.

Oldring and Hastings . . .

There was a joker in the platoon named Lewis, who always
contracted a fierce dose of religion in battle, but on leave hurried to the red light districts and to the taverns. On Hill 424
he got religion very intensely, for it was, as you already know,
a very rugged battle, with men getting it right and left. On the
second day, during a lull in the shelling, the hungry Arab cautiously crawled out of his hole and journeyed warily over to
some fig trees. Lewis, a shovel in his hand, stood deep in a
hole, tears flowing down his cheeks, deep emotion exteriori-
zed in his care-etched countenance.

"Arab," he said huskily, "I guess you're thanking God for
delivering you from death. He saved my life, and I've been on
my knees to Him all morning. I think we ought to have mass
prayer."

The Arab surveyed the holder of such pious gratitude, then
commented in thoughtful reflection, "Lewis, looks to me like
you've been down on your knees digging. If the Lord loved
me He wouldn't a got me in such a damned mess. He ain't
looking after me. I'm a-looking after the Arab. You don't
trust Him either, or you'd never have started that hole!"

Berkely and I joined the hungry Arab as he continued his
stroll among the fig trees, his short entrenching shovel banging
on his hipbone.

"Arab, why do you carry a shovel when you're no farther
from your hole than a ground hog?"

"Berkely, I considered you a man of more wisdom. Figs,
my good fellow, stimulate the bowels!"

"Arab, if that's the way it is, I wouldn't need your hip-
spoon. I've crammed enough figs to need a steam shovel!"

And so he had. During the hour we had been under the
trees, F. Dietrich Berkely had eaten enough figs to stock a
grocery store. Suddenly he gasped, "It ain't big enough, but
give it to me anyway, Arab! Quick!"

"Give you what?"

"The shovel! that hip-spoon! It'll have to do!"

The Arab and I rolled gleefully in the dirt as the big man
made for cover. F. Dietrich Berkely was the Arab's and my
closest buddy in the war. I know that he was the most conscientious tech sergeant in the army. At night he often lay
awake contriving schemes to promote the comfort, safety and
efficiency of his boys. They knew it and would go through hell
for him. There wasn't an atom of chicken in him.

Berkely was tall, broad-shouldered and bull-necked. It was

curious, but no matter how hard he trained he always wore a
small cantaloupe belly which made him appear to be double-
chested. His black hair, dark tan complexion, X-raying black
eyes, perfectly aligned teeth and boyish expression made him
one of the best-looking men in the Legion. But Berkely, big in
character as well as in physique, a man's man and a woman's
dream, was too modest to be aware of his good looks.

"Arab, there's a real guy."

"Yeh, he's a good 'un. But I wish to hell he'd stop flippin'
his hands when he talks. He makes 'em into a windmill. I
guess he's choked with more to say than he can find words to
say it with."

In argumentative combat his mental dissociation was such
that any object he had in his hand could be taken from him
without his knowing it. I've seen him give away ten-dollar bills
and even his watch. Later, when he missed them and began to
bellow for his property in his queer deep voice, the takers lost
no time in handing the items back. Easygoing, likable Berkely
could freewheel hell when he had good cause and the boys
knew it.

Berkely had one other notable eccentricity. He couldn't
stand to have a listener twirl a chain while he was talking. Unconsciously he would reach out his long brown left hand, of
which the second finger was coffee-colored from chain smoking, and take it. When the conversation was finished, he would
notice the chain in his hand and ask whose it was!

"Carter, my figs are conversing impolitely in my paunch. I
guess I'd better follow my shovel!"

The Arab started out in a brisk walk, broke into a trot, and
finally loped for the cover into which Berkely had vanished.
He had barely pushed into the bushes when I heard him yell:

"Snake! Snake! Jump, Berkely, or you'll get bit!"

The thicket first rustled, then surging convulsively as if
shaken by an earthquake, erupted Berkely kicking off his
pants which, caught in the momentum of a final desperate leg
heave, worked free and sailed high over his head into a bush.
The pantless giant thudded the earth to where I stood grinning.

"The wily Arab really put one over on you!"

Berkely looked at his bare legs, at me, at the bushes. "That
scurvy blank of a blank and damned blank! I'll maul his stink-
ing guts through a granite rock!"

"Don't blame the Arab," I said. "He's pulled it on you before."

Berkely, a teammate with T. L. in dauntless courage and
resolute bravery, feared nothing but snakes. Many a time I've

seen him walk into what looked like certain death in combat
and then run like hell from a black snake.

Suddenly the Arab unfurled a terrorized shriek.

"I wonder what he's up to now? I'll be blanked if I'll go to
find out."

Soon he strolled leisurely out of the thicket and rejoined
us.

"Arab! you . . ." Berkely began, intending to cuss him from
Lombardy to Sicily and then toe-kick him back into the
bushes, ". . . smell bad!"

"Yeh," the Arab said sadly, "there *was* a snake in 'em
bushes!"

Sergeant Winters, who had great faith in the protection of
the earth, dug his foxhole, when the soil permitted, in the likeness of a grave. First he made an excavation six feet long,
three feet wide, and four feet deep. Centered in the bottom
was a hole five feet long, two feet wide, and two feet deep. In
the center of the smaller hole was a third excavation project
about two feet wide and two feet deep. Shelves of varying de-
signs and intricacies made the sides of the main hole resemble a cliff dwelling for midgets.

Little Finkelstein, unperturbed by the torrent of hot steel
flying about, finding a packet of K ration in the debris of his
pockets, stuck his head out of his hole and hollered, "Winters,
I got a K ration coffee!"

Winters lifted his head above the opening to his grave-
house and shouted, "I got some water. Come to my boudoir
and we'll make coffee."

Finkelstein waited for a lull and darted over. They perched
contentedly on the topmost terrace. Winters produced a canteen cup, carefully poured in water while Finkelstein held it,
then tore open the coffee, shook out the coffee powder and
was searching vainly for sugar when an 88 came their way
burning the wind. Winters fell to the bottom of the hole within
the hole. Finkelstein did a barrel roll after him. The shell
only cut the top of a tree. Triumphantly Finkelstein held out
the cup.

"Winters, see, I never spilled a drop."

Winters looked at him and shook his head.

People who express prejudice against Jews in front of troopers who knew Finkelstein had better call an ambulance ahead
of time, for they will certainly need to go to the hospital for
new teeth and a jaw job. Weighing only 115 pounds and being
only an inch or so over five feet tall, he was barely large
enough to get into the army. In fact, he was the smallest man

in the battalion. He could have gotten into some easy racket, but instead stouthearted Finkelstein immediately volunteered for the paratroops, and they let him because he insisted. He was strong, well muscled and asked no favors because he was little. He did his part and more. Finkelstein was a man's man.

He could never find a helmet to fit his coconut-sized head, nor jump pants that wouldn't hang down to his heels, nor a jump jacket that didn't fall below his knees. But he was so happy to be a trooper that he went about grinning and didn't give a damn because he had to take off his helmet to look up. We liked him so well that anybody who tried to abuse him could count on getting hell stomped out of him. With dancing black eyes, smooth dark skin, and a full-lipped mouth displaying a set of even white teeth, he was a man who made women forget what mother had told them. He strutted like a bantam rooster whenever he went to town wearing his tailor-made uniform and his special-order number five boots.

He would challenge Carlton, the big Texas cowboy, to a wrestling match, and a mighty struggle would take place, with Carlton laughing so hard he couldn't wrestle, letting Finkelstein tie him in knots. Finkelstein would then arise, stick out his little chest, rub his hands together, declare that Carlton was a pushover, and ask if there were any *real* men in the outfit.

In Baltimore Finkelstein and his crony, six-foot-three beanpole Donlevy, went to a vaudeville show so crowded that Finkelstein couldn't see. Donlevy climbed on a table and was reaching down for Finkelstein when people started protesting. Finkelstein climbed up beside him, stuck out his chest in challenging belligerence and hollered he could lick any man in the house. The two standing together were so funny that the crowd went into hysterics, forgot the vaudeville show and showered them with coins and bills. They used their sack of money to go on a drunk, got thrown into jail and came back to camp late.

Finkelstein was offered a chance to get out of the outfit because of his size just before we went overseas, but he stuck out his chest and told the colonel, "I am a man, not a damned midget, and I am going with the outfit. This is my war, sir!"

Stamey, the missing member of Sergeant Corwin's patrol returned the third day. He had jumped into a gully on top of some German scouts. They were on the way with him to their local headquarters when the fire of American 155's caused them to scatter. In the confusion he escaped and got back to us two days later.

On the third day it was reported that the general in command of the 82nd having had no specific news from our battalions and thinking that they were annihilated, sent orders to Colonel Tucker to withdraw his regiment from 424. "Hell no!" the colonel is said to have replied. "We've got this hill and we are going to keep it."

That day a regiment of the 36th Division relieved us. We walked down the hill through Alta Villa, where the villagers came out of their wrecked homes to cheer us. But as we went through the town we could not forget the old man who had sat in his house by a bend in the road and posted the enemy by telegraph on our movements. By the time he was detected and apprehended dozens of our vehicles had been destroyed. Our regimental intelligence officer caught the old man sending signals and had him shot on the spot.

At the foot of the hill an American bulldozer scraped two long trenches; one for the American dead, mostly 36th Division boys, the other for the Germans. My battalion had twenty-one men killed and many wounded. The 2nd Battalion, on hill 415, had slight losses because the battle didn't go their way. A Lockheed Lightning dropped a 500-pound bomb on the hill and killed five men, but that was the only big loss they had.

Thus ended the historic battle for Hill 424. The 36th Division got all the credit, for we were never mentioned officially On that hill we inflicted eight times the number of casualties we ourselves suffered. In Germany many months later we took prisoner a Krauthead who fought hell out of some of the best units of three Panzer divisions.

Sam D'Crenzo made a painting in England on the wall of the battalion mess hall which showed two 88's crossed, with the legend Hill 424 at the top, while at the bottom were the words: *Those 88's are breaking up that old gang of mine.* They made a start.

9.   A Night's Labor Lost

After the Salerno battle the Legion loafed for a few days, then one morning piled onto trucks, rode down to the beach at Paestum, boarded LCI's, and headed north. We waded ashore at Maori Beach and rode up into craggy-looking mountains in trucks. It was raining. My platoon took up positions in a vineyard, just under the crest of a hill which was said to be near Chieunzi Pass—Shrapnel Pass or 88 Pass, or any damned thing you want to call it. Krautheads were supposed to be just over the ridge.

Giant F. D. Berkely, who had earned a mighty reputation for bravery and daring at Salerno on Hill 424, and I were dug in side by side. The army knew that the dogfaces would smoke, orders or not, so they sent down a diplomatically worded order that merely said no lights could be shown.

Presently a cigarette tip glowed along one of the vineyard paths. Berkely sprang on the smoker. A scuffle followed and then a Britisher spoke.

"My word, old man, but you're a bit rough."

Then I heard the deep voice of Berkely. "Sorry, Tommy, we had orders for no lights."

"Quite all right, old man, quite all right. Orders, you know," and he returned to his bivouac, which was nearby.

Next morning a British captain came up to us and said that he had lost a "pip" from his shoulder in the vicinity the night before and asked if we had seen it. Berkely grinned and said no. . . .

One afternoon we started toward the pass with full equipment. The 1st, 3rd, and 4th Ranger Battalions, plus the Legion's 3rd Battalion, were holding the pass. That night the Rangers were to lead the way down the enemy side of the mountain, on the left of the pass, to a bridge which had been blown out but was thought to be still held by the enemy. We were to hannibal it down the precipitous terrain, take the bridge site at night and a town called Angri by daylight. After the objective was taken British engineers were scheduled to build a Bailey bridge.

All night long, with the Rangers in the lead whistling signals to each other, we went up and down the mountain. It was hellish. Men fell over cliffs, tumbled for yards down the rugged slopes, groped for their rolling helmets in the undergrowth. It was so dark in thickets that we formed a human rope by hanging on each other's belts, to keep from getting lost.

Big Rodgers temporarily went off his nut, fell over a bank onto Nixon, his big red--headed buddy, and yelled tensely, "I got him, I got him. There he is."

Nixon drawled, "Who in hell you got besides me? You're sitting on me." Rodgers let him up, continued to march down through the thickets in a daze.

Sometime during the night we got separated from the Rangers. At daylight, our limbs no longer working automatically, we rubber-legged into a clearing above the bridge. We had to pick out the spot where we wanted our feet to be and deliberately set them in it. When we reached the bridge, we found the British engineers already on the job. The labor of that terrible night had been for nothing.

On arriving at Angri my platoon was detached from the company and sent to the left to set up a defense in an orchard. The Krautheads, who had already withdrawn, began to shell the bridge. One shell landed by a jeep, killed two Tommies, and blew three paratroopers, unhurt, into a ditch. One went off his nut later in the day. When shells came over he would try to crawl under his stretcher.

The next night we walked several miles before we reached the trucks which were to take us to Naples. One the way Larkin, who was marching between Duquesne and me, first started to mumble, then really to blow his lungs.

"The blank obscenities! The obscene blanketies! The blank obscenities!"

"Carter, Larkin needs a beer! When a man started to talk like that in the old army we always said he needed a beer!"

"They'll pay for it! Blankety obscenity, obscenity blank on the blankety blank . . . itches!"

"Listen to him, Carter! That boy needs a beer and he needs it bad. Course I ain't caught on yet to how they do things in this new hardware army, but in the old army . . ."

Duquesne spun, crossed the dirt road and came to rest against an embankment. A second later Gruening dropped Larkin into a mudhole with a chin punch and started to stomp him.

"It's okay, Gruening! All he needs is a beer," Duquesne groaned.

"What the hell's going on?" roared Berkely. "Didn't you get enough of it on Hill 424?"

"The blankety itches! The blankety, blankety itches!"

"Larkin, leave your blankety, blankety itches in that mudhole and let's move. It won't be long till we get to the trucks. Let's get going!"

Larkin got back into line. "Duke, I'm sorry!" he said a few minutes later. "I was cussing the Krautheads because of Oldring and Hastings."

"It's okay, Larkin. Just like I was saying, you need a beer . . ."

Larkin hit Duquesne, Gruening hit Larkin and Larkin grinned as he said:

"Duke, I'm still sorry, but I don't need no beer and if you keep on saying I do I'll stomp you into this muddy road and turkey-gobble tread you."

I don't know why Duquesne kept salting Larkin with the beer razz. Maybe he figured we'd been through enough to take the fight out of him. Larkin had his good points and plenty of them, but we'd learned a long time back not to argue with him because it usually ended in a scrap and that got to be pretty monotonous.

In training he had had at least one fight a week and didn't seem to care whether he won or lost. He nearly always had a skinned head, a black eye or a knot on his jaw. If some trooper knocked him down and stomped him, he would get up grinning and start all over. If a trooper said that black was black, Larkin would affirm that black was white and they would fight. You couldn't win with Larkin; you just had to agree with him or fight him and get it over with.

In the States Larkin fought almost every man in the platoon and in Africa he started over again. He had fought several times with Oldring, who had always licked him. He always admired a man who could beat hell out of him. Oldring always could. He got to thinking about Oldring as we marched along, I guess, and unshackled his fists against Duke since there were no Krautheads around.

One time in the States our company executive officer read us the articles of war and informed us that our fighting would have to take place outside the barracks or the fighters would be court-martialed. Oldring asked some ordinary sort of question, but before the officer could answer it, Larkin, who never looked at Oldring without taking him on, yelped out, "Oldring, I gotta notion to kick the hell out of you." Oldring bristled, stepped up to Larkin, grinned, and said, "You dam' four-flusher, start kickin'!" The officer stopped the fight; Larkin and Oldring then grinned at one another to show their mutual respect.

In Africa the company commander ordered everybody who wanted to fight to go at least four hundred yards from camp into the desert. In one week Larkin went four hundred yards into the desert and several rounds with McGinty, Alvarado, Hastings, Christoforo and Payne. He made the mistake of calling Casey one day and Casey, who never said a word that was not necessary to any man, just beckoned to Larkin and pointed to the desert. Casey came back alone. We carried Larkin into camp and got the medics to patch him up and set his dislocated shoulder. After that Larkin would eye Casey in the way stray dogs eye each other, but Casey never seemed to see him.

The corporal of the guard on one occasion had the mess sergeant save some chow for Larkin, who was on guard. Larkin walked up to the mess sergeant, a giant red-headed man, and without bothering to find out if some chow had been saved, said:

"South, you are a chicken son of a one!" South, a man of deeds and few words, took off his apron, stepped out of his tent and planted Larkin with one swing in four inches of dust and then stomped him. Larkin got up grinning. South queried, "Larkin, what in the hell was this all about? I saved chow for you."

Larkin kept grinning as he wiped the blood and dust from his face and then remarked, "I was in the wrong, South, but I still think you're chicken."

South started for him, but Larkin held up his hand to indicate that he had had enough for that day.

Such was Larkin.

We made the rest of the hike to the trucks without incident and after riding most of the night in the train wound up in Naples at daylight.

10. Naples Went Wild Western!

Naples. Napoli, a city of eight or nine hundred thousand people, was once known to the virtuous as the "City of Sin." At the time we entered it anything went. The narrow alleys leading off from Piazza Garibaldi swarmed with little boys pimping for prostitutes wearing fur coats and silk stockings. Little hole-in-the-wall bars did a rushing business. Red and white wines, kümmel, Marsala from Sicily, cherry brandy, cognac, champagne for seventy cents a quart, and vermouth were available by the bottle or the drink all over the city. Thousands of Italians lived by selling trinkets and postcards to unwary soldiers.

Men were killed regularly in the bars and brothels. Robberies were frequent. It wasn't safe to go to town without a gun. Italian gangsters and Allied deserters joined forces to run brothels and black markets and to hijack Allied supply trucks. One prosperous Italian whom I knew kept servicemen

drunk until their absence was classified as desertion. Then
he persuaded them to join one of the hijacking outfits.

Among the various night spots that soon made their debut
the Arizona Bar was one of the most famous. The proprietor,
an English-speaking Italian, encouraged Italian prostitutes to
make his place a center for picking up Allied servicemen. An
MP was never safe in his joint. Once or twice a night it was
routine for soldiers to shoot up the place. Next day Tony
would take up a collection to pay for the damage.

From the balconies of our eight-story apartment house on
a hill overlooking the harbor we could see Pompeii and
watch Vesuvius smoke and eject spurts of flame. At night
we had a grandstand seat for the air raids which continued
regularly for a long time.

My company had a most pestiferous patrol task assigned to
it. The Krautheads, in exchange for stuff they needed from
the Italians, had supplied Naples with large quantities of low-
grade coal which was piled in a big field in six large heaps. It
was the only winter fuel on hand for 800,000 people. The
Germans, with typical thoroughness, not only had blown up
the gas system but had also poured gasoline on the coal piles
and fired them before withdrawing from the city. One pile
was put out by the Italians before it caught, but the other
five piles burned fiercely. We never succeeded in extinguish-
ing them.

We had orders to distribute coal only to authorized agents
of bakeries and hospitals. Thousands of people carrying buck-
ets or tow sacks, having neither gas nor coal for cooking,
formed mobs at the entrances to the coal piles. At night the
problem was particularly bothersome. The daring and the
hardy would scale the walls, sneak up to the burning coal,
pour water on it, put the red-hot cinders in their sacks and
try to escape. It broke our hearts to turn away weeping old
ladies, rickety children and good-looking girls. Desperate
fathers would sometimes try to bribe us with wine, money
and occasionally with their daughters.

One morning an organized mob of 400 men, muttering
sullenly, attempted to storm the field policed by only four
guards armed with rifles and pistols. Bighearted Berkely, who
was in charge, felt extremely reluctant to fire on the poor
people, but orders being orders, he was determined that not
a mother's son would get any coal. The mob was storming
through the gates when camel-eating Casey imperturbably
drew his 45, looked over the mob, spied a light-post with the
small bulb still in place, took calm aim and broke it at
twenty-five yards. The mob dispersed.

Our apartment house had a flat roof from which we used to watch the air raids. One night Dolan, a mortar sergeant, sat on the roof listening to the *crump, crump* of dropping bombs down in the harbor and watching exploding ack-ack. A terrible rage welled and began to lash his drunken Irish heart.

He exploded, "Why, those chicken sons of bitches are killing our boys down there! I'll stop their goddamned clock."

He dashed downstairs, brought up his 60 millimeter mortar, got some of his three-pound mortar shells, hollered, "Range fifteen hundred, ten rounds," and dropped the shells, as he yelled, one by one into the tube. Far below in the silent streets we saw the wicked little barrage explode. Dolan claiming he had knocked down two planes, went to sleep with a smile on his Irish lips.

At midday, shortly after we got to Naples, I was sitting on the balcony looking down toward the harbor about a quarter of a mile away when suddenly half of a big stone building housing some parachute and 36th Division engineers soared five or six hundred feet into the air. We went down to help British Tommies and American soldiers clear away the debris in which an unknown number of men was trapped and buried. I helped Berkely pull out a man whose right leg was ground off at the hip and whose stomach was hanging out. His mouth was open and his eyes bulged. We dug out one man who was still alive though dusty, tattered and dazed; falling debris had formed an arch over his body and protected him. We helped him to his feet. He said, "Nice work, boys, thanks," walked ten feet and fell dead. Fifty-eight men were crushed in the building. The Krautheads had left a time bomb set to explode at twelve noon, the hour when most soldiers would be in the building.

My company concluded that the time was ripe for a party. We arranged to lease for a night the swank Five O'Clock Club, which had a smooth dance band. The Arab and the Master Termite were commissioned to supply plenty of strong drinks. A sister company in the battalion agreed to provide six bouncers under oath to keep sober and to throw out all intruders. A Moorhead, Kentucky, ex-moonshiner discovered a little copper still and enthusiastically distilled sixty gallons of red wine into six gallons of a clear, colorless liquid that would blow a man's head off. The captain who wandered in one day to inspect the distillery took a swig and staggered out in a daze.

One morning the first sergeant stepped out of his room, hollered and blew a blast on his big brass whistle. "Men," he orated, "what kind of women do you want for the party? We can get a detachment of Wacs who will come at seven thirty and leave at eleven thirty. Although we're all gentlemen and aristocrats, they distrust us to the point that they refuse to come without chaperones. Or on the other hand, we can get the ladies in fur coats to come. They'll stay till hell freezes over and the sky's the limit. Who do you want?" With one voice the troopers yelled, "Bring on the *signorinas*."

We piled into trucks and went to the party. Two dance bands noised things up, their rhythms invigorated by plenty of champagne, cognac, brandy, and our own liquid dynamite. The six tough troopers threw out the gatecrashers while the hundred beautiful ladies in fur coats danced with the boys.

It was a hell of a party. Honky-tonk jitterbuggers kicked the shanks of sentimental waltzers. Sheraton did the Mexican hat dance around a bottle of brandy borrowed from the Master Termite, who sat drinking all evening, his bent elbow seesawing meaningless, monotonous rhythms. Ex-lumberjack Duquesne treaded the floor as if it were a rotating log in a millpond while his pal Gruening told an uncomprehending artificial Neapolitan blonde about the wonders of the New York Central. Carlton, stirred by some fancied wrong, sent a former company commander, too drunk to know who hit him, through the door with one punch. Larkin feuded until fat-cheeked Miland knocked him out and had him taken back to camp in a truck. A hot-looking squat brunette melted the ice in Casey's pale eyes and he left the dance, a bottle of brandy in his pocket, while he was still sober. Casey chased one of the band leaders down the stairs, then took his place on the podium. Barnette, tears running down his face, played the piano with about the same skill as an ape in the St. Louis zoo. Dolan grabbed a bass fiddle, did an initial flourish with the bow, then plucked the strings till they broke.

Early in the evening the boys who preferred women to bottles began to drift away with their dates. By midnight a few were still dancing in and out among the sprawling drunks, but for the most part the dance floor belonged to the couldn't-hold-it disciples of Bacchus.

Berkely, the Arab, T. L. Rodgers and I began to carry them to the trucks. T. L. and I carried them out and they threw them in. Berkely held the drunk's feet, the Arab his head. Before tossing them in, they chanted in unison, "One for the money, two for the show, three for the money, and there he goes." The drunk would soar into the truck like a sack and on landing crack his head on the steel floor or on some trooper's head. Next day, several drunks, feeling knots on their heads and all banged up, inquired as to who had beat hell out of them. The origin of their injuries continued to remain a mystery. Four men, including Wild Bill McMurty and Nixon, were missing for reveille next morning.

11. "Tell the Boys I Wish Them Luck"

The Fifth Army had run into a very rough deal north of Naples. Mark Clark, much impressed by the deeds of the 82nd Airborne, requested that he be given one regimental combat team for a special mission in that area. General Ridgway lent him my regiment, plus the 376th Parachute Field Artillery Battalion and Company C of the 307th Parachute Engineers. That made up the 504th Parachute Infantry combat team. The remainder of the division sailed for England. The Krautheads had set up a temporary line on the Volturno river, which for miles angles through rugged mountains. A few bridgeheads had been thrown across, but the men holding them were being chewed up. The general wanted us to be the liaison unit in the rough terrain that lay between the 5th and 8th armies. We were to climb through the mountains constituting the rough, precipitous center of the Italian peninsula.

We got orders to roll it up and get ready to move. Berkely had been forced to go to the hospital with jaundice and the Arab had taken over his squad. All the other jokers were still healthy enough to be killed. The Arab, discovering that he was minus a rifle grenadier, decided to ask Gruening to take over. The job involved carrying a model 1903 rifle with a grenade launcher, used to knock out tanks and pillboxes. The regular grenadier had been transferred and only Gruening had had enough experience to use this equipment. The Arab hesitated to impose the task on the independent old joker, one of the favorite soldiers of the squad. The following dialogue was repeated a dozen times.

"Gruening, you'll have to be grenadier."

"No, by God, I won't."

"Yeah, you will, you're the only man who knows how."

"I'll see you in hell first." And there the classic feud stood for some time.

Finally Gruening said that he wouldn't do it unless the Arab gave him a "direct order." Now a noncom hated to give a "direct order" for if it was disobeyed, the only recourse left to maintain discipline was court-martial. There were frequent and long arguments over the difference between a "direct" and a "lawful" order. The Arab placidly puffed on a long clay pipe and grunted, "Okay, it's a direct order that you carry the damned thing." Having no ammunition pouch, Gruening had to carry the heavy grenades in his hand in a little bag much like a shopping bag. These rifle grenades turned out to be the humorous side of the whole mission.

We spent two days in a muddy willow thicket near the pontoon bridge across the Volturno, then crossed it, camped beneath the south side of a mighty mountain, and the following morning at six we began to toil up its rocky slopes. We didn't reach the top, covered by clouds, until three P.M. Below, whenever the clouds cleared, we could see a little emerald-green valley, terraced from a point far up on the mountains down to the valley floor, a spot that merited to be remote from every strife and disease of man.

Descending, we found a pass leading into another valley as remote and exquisitely beautiful as the previous one. A ruined medieval castle stood on the side of the pass where my platoon was ordered to set up a defense. The 36th having seized the pass leading out of the valley on the north, the trapped Germans might try to escape through our pass. As a company of the Legion began marching down a winding road leading into the valley, a unit of the 36th began to shell the little town. Perched like eagles on our mountain precipices, we witnessed the terrible effects of the barrage on one of the most picturesque towns I saw in Europe. People in the States were paying money to see a few pictorial battle scenes; we were viewing a vicious battle, without cost, from a grandstand seat. At the end of two hours what was left of the town was ours.

The battalion wound up the hill and through the pass, marching after the retreating Krautheads. My company, turning left, entered a narrow, precipitous valley. A Krauthead observer saw us. Soon over the northern hill we heard the disheartening *chug* of a mortar and we crouched in the rocky stream bed waiting for the missile to complete its lofty trajectory and hit. It plunked into the bank six hundred yards to the rear. We got up and journeyed on. *Chug*. We ran a few steps forward and fell into the ditch. It hit a hundred yards closer. We moved on at a snail's pace. The company commander, a quarter of a mile ahead of the rear of the column, didn't have the pernicious shells creeping up on him. He was safe. A man in jeopardy has to blame somebody. *Chug, chug.* Two more exploded. A *b-b-r-ng* of steel whined over our backs. We moved again, still cursing the front of the column. *Chug, chug.* The damned things landed a hundred yards behind. One more correction of his mortar and he would have us. *Chug, chug, chug, chug.* This would be it! The death givers plowed into the stream bed just behind us. We were frantic. Gray-headed old warrior Duquesne said as he arose, "Mac, I'm saving two sticks of gum for us; I call it my excitement gum. I only chew in emergencies."

The mortar quit. We climbed the slope to the left, angled off on some tree-covered terraces and stopped. Carlton raged, "Those chicken bastards up front, stopping and leaving us to get the hell shot out of us! I'll shoot that no-good son of a bitch if I ever get a chance." We didn't look at him. Our looks might rub him wrong and get us shot. He moved forward a few yards, puffing fiercely on a cigarette. Old Duquesne and I remained alone on the little terrace over which giant trees indifferently nodded their great age. In the distance we heard the terrible bass of heavy artillery and a second later felt the terrifying rock of a screaming, whistling barrage of shells exploding in the woods just above our terrace. Duquesne and I lay on the ground trembling. We lit cigarettes. We heard the nerve-tightening scream of "Medic, medic, for God's sake send a medic, three men hit!"

Old Duquesne pulled out two sticks of sweat-melted gum which we crammed into our mouths, paper and all. "Mac," he gritted, "now's as good a time as any to chew my 'citement gum." I agreed.

Lanky Donlevy beckoned to us: "Moving out." We wound around the hill through the dense woods, rejoicing over the concealment they gave us. We were in a horseshoe bend when a machine pistol *b-r-r-ted* and Carlton slumped to the ground. We hit the ground and scanned the undercover angrily and anxiously, but could see nothing.

I crawled up to Carlton, who lay on his back in the trail, blood oozing from his chest and belly. "Carlton, Carlton, where'd you get it?" I asked frantically. His bad humor was gone. He fixed his calm grey Texas eyes on me and smiled sweetly. "Pal, I've made my last jump. I've cussed out the old man for the last time. Tell the boys I wish them luck." And he died without another word.

Donlevy ordered. "Moving out, moving out, let's go!" And we came away and left Carlton there in the trail.

Oldring, Hastings, Carlton . . .

We never found any trace of the killer. We marched out of the woods to a long, boulder-strewn slope where the column stopped and took cover. Something far up on the crest of the slope moved. *Spang* went Big Rodger's rifle. A man leaped over the crest of the hill in an obvious hurry. A helmet emerged from behind a rock. *Spang, spang, spang.* Another man disappeared over the top with a great clatter of rocks. An angry voice hailed us, "Hey, down there, you stupid bastards, quit shootin'. We're you're own men!"

We moved on when darkness began to fall. As we rounded a curve Krauthead machine gunners killed two men and wounded one and then fled before we could attack them. Karnap, who tracked them over the slope, picked off one in the dusk. Late at night we dug in on a vast, bald, rocky knoll that reminded us of Hill 424, and prepared for a possible attack at daylight. We were far in advance of the 5th Army on our left and the 8th Army on our right, with only two 75 pack howitzers and scanty ammunition.

When dawn came we saw a complete German armored division quartered in a deep, long valley. We watched them all day. Since it would clearly have been suicidal for a few hundred mountain troops to attack an armored division, we only sent patrols down to harass them.

Big Casey woke up the next morning, cleaned his rifle, and climbed a bushy tree for a look over the country. About eight hundred yards to the rear and off the trail he spotted a Mark V tank. He put his hands up to his eyes, simulating binoculars, and we handed him up a pair. He saw a soldier climb up on the tank and begin to eat something out of a can. Casey looked down at us with his pale eyes gleaming and asked if he could shoot him. Toland went to the captain, who radioed the little colonel, who went to his 81st mortar crew and climbed a tree to have a look. He sent word that Casey could fire one shot when the mortar got ready to fire at the tank. We all began to dig like hell, for when you shoot at tanks they usually shoot back. Casey dusted off his rifle again, set the sights, checked the windage, got a comfortable position in the tree, and waited for the word. When it came, Casey's pale eyes squinted confidently down the barrel. He fired. The Krauthead dropped his chow, grabbed his chest, and fell off the tank to the ground. Casey skinned down the tree, and as he ran a patch with borecleaner through his rifle he remarked. "That was for Carlton."

12. Gruening's Grenades

That night a march memorable took place. The battalion
was ordered to sneak down into the valley, pass through the
armored division, and take some hills on the opposite side.
It was to be at least a fifteen-mile march over the worst possible terrain under extremely hazardous circumstances. If
the Krautheads surrounded us in the flat valley, we would
be slaughtered.

The air was frosty. A chill wind blew from the north.
High up the stars twinkled dimly and far off to the west, where
the 5th Army was raising hell with the enemy, lightning flashes
lighted up the peaks. To the east, perhaps twenty miles away
where the 8th Army was fighting, lightning also flashed. We
were in the middle, pushing the Krautheads over the bony
spine of Italy, a terrain that they never expected anyone to
climb.

Slipping, falling, cussing muffled cusses, the battalion commenced the descent. Gruening still clutched his shopping bag
of rifle grenades, which he had grown to hate worse than the
Krautheads. He was stocky, rocky-faced, square-jawed and
cranky. At twenty-nine quite a little gray hair showed on his
temples. When he didn't cuss the grenades, he cussed the
Arab for making him carry them.

Duquesne, his bosom pal, in the seventh heaven of glee,
walked along behind him nodding his old gray head, grinning
and talking about the important duties of a rifle grenadier.
Old Duquesne had spent nine years in the army and worn
stripes seventeen times. Now he was again a private, busted because he got drunk with two Italian prisoners in Sicily.

Thus Duquesne wagged his hoary head wisely and spake
winged words to Gruening: "Wan't like this in the old army.
They never got nothing done there. Now in this here new
army we go prepared. We got machine guns, BAR's, rifles,
and we got antitank guns. I reckon you're proud to carry one
of these modern antitank guns on your back, Gruening?
Yeah, you cud knock out a pillbox with that thing. Igod, I
wish the Arab would let me carry it. I like to go armed,

dammit, and a rifle ain't enough to fight with." And he would gouge Gruening in the ribs and laugh.

The harassed Gruening would snarl, "Yes, you gray-headed son of a bitch, you can talk, damn you, 'cause you're a scout. I wish by God they'd tie a 75 on your dam' back, and make you lug it to Rome. I ought to wrap these dam' grenades around your goddamned, beer-funneling throat. You two-bit bastard." And Duquesne would hold his sides in bubbling glee.

We reached the valley by eleven o'clock and after numerous false sallies started across it. Each of us was weighted down with his equipment and fighting specialties: mortars and ammunition, rifles, tommy guns, pistols, machine guns, BAR's, bazookas and assorted ammunition. We climbed onto the silent valley road at one thirty. Two, three, four o'clock. We kept stumbling along. I followed the man in front of me, looking at his back. He turned into a shapely girl wearing slacks. I rubbed my eyes, thinking I was crazy. I walked up close and reached out my hand to touch her. She turned into Gruening, a man with a horseshoe-shaped bedroll on his back, carrying a sack of grenades in his left hand.

On the right of that desolate road suddenly appeared a big white green-shuttered house surrounded by a well-kept, shrub-filled lawn. It's strange, I reflected, to see a fine house like that in this wilderness. When abreast of it, I turned my head to get a good look. The house had vanished.

With our leg bones become rubbery, our flesh numb, and our semiclosed gluey eyes seeing mirages, we were about done, and no one more so than Gruening. He finally dropped his grenades in a ditch.

Duquesne, staggering along behind him with his rifle and two boxes of thirty caliber ammo, picked them up and whispered to the Arab, "He thinks he is through with them. When we stop and he goes to sleep, I'll place them by his head so he'll see them first thing when he wakes up."

Combat humor, merciless and kind at the same time, is a hard thing for a civilian to comprehend. It is useless to try to explain it to those who have not been there how a little speck of laughter at someone's expense can save men from cracking up.

We stopped on a bridge for five minutes. Almost all hit the ground, asleep before they could stretch out, unbothered by the entrenching tools and canteens gouging them in the back. They could have slept on needles. Duquesne kept awake long enough to creep up to Gruening and put the grenades on his rifle. When the column was roused to continue the march, Gruening reached out for his rifle, touched the bag of grenades and cursed incredulously. He picked them up. Although swaying on his feet, Duquesne walking close behind kept up a needling line of chatter.

"God, what men! They could march ten more miles. Look at Casey back there, look at Rodgers, and Larkin, the Arab and Wild Bill! Look at you! You're as fresh as a daisy. I wish I could stand up as well as you. Igod, they grow *men* on the New York Central!"

Gruening gave out an inarticulate snarl. "You ignorant son of a bitch. I wish youse wuz in hell with your guts burning. I'm dying and you know it."

Duquesne gouged the Arab and lurched on in silently sadistic comradely glee. Again the grenades thudded into a ditch and Duquesne picked them up.

Dawn was breaking. The battalion selected a thicket in which to hide out for the day, but for some reason we staggered around it three times before we entered it. Gruening blew his top.

"These goddamned, hammerheaded, stupid, intercoursing, crazy, addle-brained bastards leading a battalion! They couldn't lead men to a beer in a saloon. I'd like to have 'em for one hour on the New York Central. I'd break their dam' backs and feed 'em to the hawgs."

Duquesne said that he didn't know of anything he would rather do than walk around in a thicket in enemy territory at five thirty in the morning. It showed how much the old army had to learn from the new army, he remarked.

When we finally stopped, every man, except those of us picked for guard duty, blacked out. I sat at the edge of the thicket and smoked under a blanket. If roving Krautheads got close enough, they would smell the smoke, but the night being foggy I knew I could hear them before they got close enough. As I sat there nodding, Berkely came up to me, lit a cigarette under my blanket, and we talked.

"Mac," he said, "remember the time we took part in that riot at the Town Pump in Fayetteville and the cops threw tear gas on the crowd?" I looked around with a start. Berkely was not there. Then I recollected that he was in the hospital with jaundice. Another mirage.

At daylight I went back and woke up Duquesne. He rubbed his eyes, picked up the grenades he had carried with him, put them by Gruening's cheek, took his rifle and went on post.

Later in the day when I woke up, Gruening sat staring with a dazed look at the bag of grenades. He looked at them for a long time, then woke up the half-dead Arab, who got up growling "Whatcha want?"

"Arab, how do I look? Do I look crazy? Have I lost my nut? Twice last night I know I dropped these damned grenades in the ditch, and every time I wake up, they're right by my nose. Igod, I'm headin' for a section eight."

The Arab grinned and blew smoke into the air. "Hell, Gruening, you got as much sense as you ever had. Course that ain't a hell of a lot. Your pardner in beer carried them whenever you dropped them. Laughing at you was all that kept him from passing out on the trail. Don't be too sore at him. He meant to do you a favor, and besides we need the grenades. I'd a helped you myself, but I was carrying some mortar shells for Pip, who's got bad feet."

Growling, Gruening hunted up Duquesne, and for ten minutes we heard suppressed laughs and strangling oaths.

13. Mission to the Ghost Town of Eighteen

Nazi Overcoats

A fifty-man combat patrol under the command of Lt. Gunnigan was recruited one afternoon to go to a mountain village north of Colli on the Volturno, near which the Nazis had their so-called winter line. We went into Colli, a little town beneath towering mountains, late in the afternoon. While Carey, the Arab, Nixon and I crouched in a doorway to get out of the freezing wind we heard the distant boom of an 88 set in the pass between snow-capped mountains, throwing trouble at the parachute engineers busy constructing a bridge just outside the town. The Italians left their houses when the shelling began, so we went in. A big pot of beef, potatoes, and garlic stood simmering on the kitchen stove. "Igod," said the Arab, grabbing a long spoon, "a man might as well die with a full belly." The rest of us got spoons and joined the Arab, who lay on the floor shivering and eating. We emptied the pot like a bunch of hogs.

The shelling stopped and we pushed north along the road toward a blown-out bridge across the Volturno. The Krautheads spotted us. Carey and I lay face to face in a rock-walled ditch, faces six inches apart, looking into each other's eyes, listening to the shrapnel whine. A smoke shell ten feet away covered us with white smoke. They had the range. If they kept firing, some of us would get it. Carey, his eyes milk-white, gulped, "Mac, they've got us dead to rights."

The shelling stopped. We chose to wade the hip-deep Volturno in freezing weather rather than risk stepping on S mines which covered the ground for a hundred square yards around the bridge. An S mine is a little metal container about the size of a big baking powder can filled with two or three hundred ball bearings. It is buried in the ground with three little prongs sticking up which are very difficult to see. If a man steps on it, the secondary charge of powder in it ignites, throws it into the air three to six feet and the container explodes, hurling the ball bearings all about with deadly effect for a hundred yards and more.

By the middle of the night the rain had stopped. A brilliant moon hung over the three old houses we selected as sleeping quarters. At dawn when Price stepped out, rifle in hand, he saw an armed German leave the room adjoining the one where he had slept and proceed to answer to the call of nature. They saw each other at the same time, but Price had the drop since the Nazi was in a disadvantageous position. The sniper was already asleep in a pile of straw when the patrol arrived.

It began to rain again. Our mission being to establish contact with the Krautheads, we couldn't return to Colli until we found them. We sneaked up the valley through vineyards, often wading little streams of muddy water, until we reached a little town hidden under a bare, gray, triangular-shaped peak. Friendly residents informed us that the Germans were a mile or so to the north. We left the town with our pockets bulging with bread, nuts, and apples.

Finally we sneaked through vineyards to another little town set against a rocky, snow-capped mountain. The strong glacial winds blowing off it banged shutters and doors on the deserted houses in this weirdly creepy, empty, lonely village. We couldn't see a bird, a chicken or a human being. In some homes plates of half-eaten food were on the table, in others the table was set and the food served but untouched. It reminded me of Pompeii. Since the town had not been shelled we could not imagine why the inhabitants had fled.

Gunnigan stationed Casey, Nixon, the Arab and me on the second floor of a house to serve as a reserve force if any of our boys ran into more trouble than they could handle. The Arab and I wiped the mud off our guns, oiled them, and went to sleep between two mattresses. In the meanwhile, Lt. Gunnigan, after kicking heavy doors into deserted rooms

all over town, finally found a house containing eighteen
Krauthead overcoats, newly dampened by the morning rain,
numerous S mines and Teller mines, barbedwire, and an MG
34 machine gun field-stripped, that is, taken apart for cleaning. Gunningan made the MG 34 useless by throwing away
essential parts and sent an ambush to watch for the absent
Krautheads.

Sewell killed the two first ones with an automatic rifle. A
third stuck his head out of a doorway and was peering up
and down the street when Gunnigan shot him between the
eyes: he slumped down in the doorway with blood spurting
onto the sill. Big Murray, sitting back from a window watching the street, saw a man wearing the familiar coal-bucket
helmet lead a donkey up to a building. He fired at him and
missed. The man ducked out of sight, then hurried back to the
donkey to grab a rifle off its back. Murray shot him in the leg
and he crawled out of sight in a hail of bullets. Judson pressing his face against a window pane, was shot at from across
the street. He ducked so fast that he beat the glass to the floor.

Nixon, who had climbed to the highest point he could
find in his building, detected a platoon of Krautheads to the
northwest moving in battle formation to our rear to cut us
off. Looking southeast he saw another enemy platoon cutting
in behind us. We were four miles ahead of our troops and in
serious danger of being hemmed in and annihilated. By glid-
ing unobserved through heavy foliaged vineyards and squat-
walking at a fast clip down a gulley we gained a little slope to
the rear of the platoons only five minutes before they con-
verged. We had accomplished our mission: contacted the
enemy, inflicted casualties but sustained none.

As we headed back to Colli in the rain, all miserable, wet,
cold and tired, I noticed that red-headed, lanky Nixon was
frowning.

"What's the matter, Nixon?" I inquired.

"Mac, that man Gunnigan is a good officer and he handled
this patrol well. But, damn his intercoursin' soul, he should
have let us carry off those Krauthead overcoats to keep those
bastards from being warm tonight. To think of a Krauthead
bastard being warm while we are cold and wet!"

We waded the Volturno, which was waist deep due to the
heavy rains, and rejoined the remainder of the company in
Colli, where we were soon sitting by a warm fire, toasting
cheese, browning corn pork loaf and drinking strong coffee.
We thawed out and slept well.

14. First Sergeant Henry

One afternoon when the rain was driving down in sheets, my company got orders to cross a gorge on a crude bridge consisting of two Manila ropes with planks tied between. There were no wires or ropes to cling to. The Volturno churned through the gorge as if speeded by hydraulic pressures. If a man tumbled into that angry stream, nothing could save him from drowning.

We were going up a mountain called Hill 1017 to relieve a company of the Legion that had been on duty for a week. We had to stick to the center of the path because the S mines were still planted on the sides. When we rested, we had to sit in the center, down which a fair-sized stream of water was pouring, or else run the risk of springing a mine. The rain trickled down our necks and into our boots. We didn't mind the rain though as much as usual since our tails were continuously wet anyhow from sitting in a brook.

At three in the morning my platoon was ordered to take up positions near the crest of the hill. As it had quit raining, Old Duquesne, Wild Bill and I spread out our shelter half and lay down to sleep. At four it began to rain again. We rigged up a crude tent in the dark and crawled into it. By this time the water had soaked through even our epidermis.

Wild Bill started to cuss. He was seldom moved to blasphemy and invective, but when he got going his artistry made the best of us take off our hats in admiring astonishment. As Duquesne and I lay shivering and grinning and listening approvingly my mind went back to the time gentle, rosy-cheeked Wild Bill McMurty joined us in Africa.

He seemed to look trustingly and with benevolence through his mild blue eyes at mankind and the wicked world. His Alabama drawl, which unlocked men's and women's hearts, gave a man ample time to empty a mess kit of Spam and grits before it crawled into a complete sentence. We feared lest this innocent-appearing youth, so patient, tactful and diplomatic, who never cussed guard duty, noncoms, officers, or slimy C rations, would become the victim of every sharper in the Legion and every wily Arab in the desert.

One dusty afternoon Wild Bill and Duquesne went to the

town of Cudja, where they made the acquaintance of two
dusky Arabian maidens. Duke returned with amazing tales
of Wild Bill's prowess as a ladies' man. Winters, one of the
best sergeants in the outfit, who journeyed with Wild Bill to
a little wine shop near the mountains along the Spanish
Moroccan border, told in pop-eyed astonishment of Wild Bill's
capacity for cognac. We began to wonder about Wild Bill, who
continued to remain rosy-cheeked, mild-eyed and modest.

One Saturday afternoon he holstered his pistol and made
his way to an Arab peddler noted for sharp dealing, who
practiced his swindling far out in the desert. Wild Bill returned with a full hamper of plums which, he reported, the
wily Arab had given him through compassionate goodness
of heart. Again we wondered.

One day we were in the desert on a problem, short of
water, fed up on C ration chow, tortured by heat, de-
voured at night by mosquitoes, hounded by officers and
sergeants. Wild Bill, sitting beneath a cactus plant, a half-
smoked fag dangling from his lip, eyes seeking the ground,
suddenly erupted, "These goddamned, half-witted, dirty, one-
way, lying, ignorant, sonova bitches, sitting in their goddamned big tents drinking ice water, while we beat out our
brains in this hellhole of sand and cactus! Colonel blank
down there, sitting on his tail, drinking ice water and eating
steak! That two-bit sonova bitch oughta be in hell with his
back broke. That goddamned, brass-hatted, brown-nosing,
bucking old general blank, that sonova bitch oughta have
to jump without a chute. These stupid, military-minded, salu-
tin' shavetails riding our sweat to promotion, I'd like to feed
to the goddamned sharks!"

We listened in admiration, our doubts resolved. Wild Bill
was one of us. . . .

Duquesne nudged me as Wild Bill crescendoed his itch-
battery of four-letter words to a cymbal-banging finale, paused
and with the dignity of British understatement anticlimaxed:
"The bastards!" Apparently the heat of Wild Bill's epithets
dried the atmosphere and relaxed us enough to sleep. When
I awoke it was daylight. We pitched pup tents in the cover
of some small trees and shrubs and prepared for a long stay.
The German winter line lay just beyond the big snow-capped
mountain at whose foot our patrol had contacted the enemy
in the deserted vilage.

For six days the rain never stopped. The tents sieve-
leaked and mildewed. We loathed diving into our muddy
water-filled slit trenches, but we dived in just the same. Our
skin commenced to rot. Little patches of fungus formed on
our bleached hands and toes. Sunny Italy!

But one day the sunlight glittered on the snow-capped peak, the bushes dried off, and the ground commenced to dry. We hung our blankets out in spots where the Krautheads couldn't see them and cleaned the rust off our guns. We spent the morning talking and laughing and congenially sunning ourselves.

In the afternoon Wild Bill and I took our rifles, canteens, and a five-gallon glass jug and went down the trail for some water. After we left shells began to hit the mountain behind us. We'd left just in time. Seated by a little spring near the foot of the mountain, we watched the Krautheads blow hell out of Colli for the hundredth time. On the way back we stopped to rest with some B Company men who had dug in in a small hollow less than acre in area. We stood there listening to shells hitting up on the mountain where we had to go. When the big guns on the north began to spit out stuff packaged for us, Wild Bill dived into a hole on top of a guy and I into a junior hole so small that my legs, rump and back stuck out. When a new cluster of shells cut down little trees all about me and shrapnel broke our water jug, I flopped over on my back and feverishly tried to lengthen my groove by kicking the end out of it. Four more shells screamed into the hollow. I commenced to kick harder than ever. A lanky guy nearby stuck his long neck out of his deep hole and allowed that he wouldn't give a plugged nickel for his chances. The cheerful son of a bitch! But the shells cut the trees around us only twice more and then stopped hitting as suddenly as a school of crappies. Wild Bill and I smoked a Chelsea to quiet our screaming nerves and then went on up the mountain.

Bad news awaited us. A captain and two radio operators from the 376th Parachute Field Artillery Battalion were on top of the mountain observing for their guns. Since Krautheads were not firing at the mountaintop, the captain is reported to have said, "Hell, I'll give them a target so I can find out where their guns are." He stepped out into an open space where the Krautheads could see him. They dropped a mortar barrage that killed the captain, Lt. Nightingale, our first sergeant, one radio operator, and severely wounded three other men.

Next afternoon donkeys were brought up on the mountain to carry off the dead men. The wounded had been carried down the night before. Ernie Pyle wrote about the beloved captain who came down the mountain on a donkey with his men hating to see him go.

First Sergeant Henry, the last to be carried down, was one of the best men who ever served his country. He was always fatherly and thoughtful of his squad's well-being.

We stood looking at Henry, whose short, black, curly-haired, blood-matted head hung on one side of the donkey and his shrapnel-mangled legs on the other. More than one man had tears in his eyes as Henry disappeared around a bend.

Berkely, who had been eating his heart out for fear we were killed or wounded, returned to us the day Sergeant Henry died. As he clattered up the little trail he met the Arab going down as a litter bearer. They instinctively spotted each other in the dark and, voiceless, shook hands in a grip of steel. Berkely cleared his throat, swore, and said, "You bastard, a man down below said you got it up on this godforsaken hill."

"Well, joker, you can put it in your dam' book that they tried like hell. Shrapnel flying low sounded like a bevy of Piper Cubs on parade. I was a popular man with those Krautheads today."

He stuck out a grimy paw to his pal. "I'll see you tomorrow. I gotta help wrangle this guy down the hill."

"Okay, pal," the giant growled.

The Arab and the litter party lurched on down the slick rock trail. Berkely came on up to the platoon and took over the squad that the Arab had been leading in his absence. I thought he would cry when he learned what had happened to Carlton. We were all overjoyed to see him. In a few minutes he was thumping away with his pick and borrowed shovel digging himself a hole.

It was a treat to watch the giants dig in. Little Finkelstein only had to turn out a few shovels of dirt to be underground. His crack completed, he would look jeeringly around at the bigger men still digging and then hit the sack. Presently the average-sized men would also jeer at giant Casey, Berkely, Rodgers, Nixon and Duquesne. Then they too would fall into their holes and snore away. Thirty minutes after Finkelstein had cuddled into his slit, the giants would finally be ready to crawl into the ground.

15. Thanksgiving with Lice and Socks in a Sheepshed

On the twenty-ninth day after we climbed the first big mountain, we were relieved from duty at Colli and on Hill

1017 by the 100th Nisei Battalion of the 34th Division. Some of our boys had been killed or wounded and a great many hospitalized with trench feet, pneumonia and dysentery.

When a mission is officially over or finished for a while, every additional moment in the danger zone is spent in an agony of fearful suspense. After the job is done and when zestful relaxation is an immediate possibility, no one wants to have the bad luck of getting it for nothing.

The Krautheads still shelled Colli at eight sharp and there we stood, five minutes to eight, on the very damned section of street where the shells would fall. At three minutes to eight we started out of town. At eight the barrage came whistling in and every man dived into the deep gutter along the road. My rifle went one way and my five gallon can of water the other. When the barrage was over, somebody was yelling "Medic, Medic."

We walked five miles in the rain, piled into open trucks and then rode in a downpour until five next morning. We stopped on some terraces at the foot of a mountain, piled on the ground and slept sounder in the rain than some people back home would in feather beds. At dawn my platoon found a leaky stone shed full of sheep, manure, fleas, lice and putrefied rain water. We hardened our hearts, chased the sheep into the rain and moved in. Thanksgiving Day, 1943!

We had licked the Germans in every fight, but during the two weeks we warred with the lice we lost every battle and even the skirmishes. Our entomologists identified three species of the vermin: a long, grayish louse with a spot on his back; a short, broad specimen that bunched up on us in black slimy knots; and the other, more familiar type, *Phthirius Inguinalis*. At night the gray lice and the black lice would engage in terrific struggles. We'd help one or the other army out, depending on which we could catch. Old *Phthirius* held aloof, tending strictly to his excavating projects. If we had had sterilizing facilities, we could have wiped them out. If we'd had insect powder, we could have decimated their ranks. Having neither, we indulged in philosophical speculation as to why the Creator made them and even made bets relating to the fertility and romantic angles of their love life. Strangely enough, the sheep lice preferred sheep. The preference disturbed Duquesne, who concluded that we must smell worse than mutton.

One day the men of the "Wild Blue Yonder" got messed up and bombed our shower bath at the foot of the mountain. Olson and the Big Polack had to dash naked out of the shower tent in freezing weather, hell-bent for a foxhole. The

Air Corps apologized to us, explaining that they'd mistaken us for Krautheads, but the dead men couldn't be present to acknowledge or to receive the apology. The Big Polack never forgave the incident. Every time he got drunk he would seek out the Air Corps boys, tell them their error, and wait for them to apologize. If they sassed him, he'd lower the boom and come back to us contented.

Through some fortuitous circumstance a letter from his wife was delivered to the Big Polack while we were living in the sheepshed. His name was too long and too filled with consonants for us to try to pronounce it; so we just called him the Big Polack. He was a good guy and a good soldier but at times as hard to dislodge from his stubborn eccentricities as a black snake from a knothole.

Since we had nothing to do but fight lice and reminisce, the arrival of the letter gave us old boys something to talk about. We recalled how back in the States he wangled a three day pass from the first sergeant so that he could go home and get married. He spent two of the three days making preparations (including the purchase of $99 worth of whisky) for the wedding which took place on the third day at seven in the evening. The guests invited to the big feast departed at one, which left him three hours for honeymooning before train time. But instead of billing and cooing he spent the three hours arguing with his brother-in-law, whom he finally beat up until he had to be hospitalized, and returned to camp, his wife still a virgin.

His lamentations shook the barracks. "I never spent a minute alone with my wife! Why was I such a fool?"

His jeremiads grew even louder when the first sergeant refused him another pass. He moped in the barracks, shirked his duty and made a nuisance of himself. The Arab solved the problem by suggesting to him that he have his wife come to see him.

The Big Polack had spent most of the day reading his letter.

"Does she still love you?" Duquesne inquired.

"Duke, she worships me. She's even sending me some socks."

The Arab scratched his head. "That reminds me. I have five pair of socks to distribute. I'll go get them."

Socks were precious objects for mountain troops because of the long hikes and wet weather. We had been ordered to carry extra pairs and to take care of them. No one heeded this advice except the Big Polack, who liked to have plenty of everything.

The Arab returned and asked, "How many men have socks?"

The Big Polack answered, "I got socks."

"Anybody else got socks?"

Silence.

"Okay, Big Polack, having socks, you don't need socks. The rest of us will draw straws to see who gets them."

The Big Polack blew his stack. "Listen, Arab! Orders were given for every man to carry extra socks. I carried extra socks. The other guys were too damned lazy to carry extra socks. Now I got socks and they ain't. I wash my socks when they're dirty. The other guys were too damned lazy to wash their socks. So I got socks. And I want another pair. I obeyed orders. I took care of my socks. I'll see the lieutenant about my socks. I'm gonna have a pair of socks. I earned 'em by obeying orders."

The crafty Arab was up against a situation that the guile of reasoning couldn't handle. The Big Polack was reasoning within the righteous framework of a logic-sealed syllogism.

"Big Polack, I know you got socks. I know you carry socks. I know you wash 'em. I know you deserve a pair. The rest of these ignorant dogfaces don't have socks. I don't have socks. We can't hike without them. And by jumping hell we are going to draw straws for them and you can't draw 'cause you got socks. It ain't fair, but it's the best I can do."

"Now listen, Arab! I got socks, I always got socks. And why in hell do I have socks? I carry extra socks. I wash my socks. These lazy bums sit on their tails and laugh while I wash my socks. Now I got socks 'cause I obeyed orders and I deserve more socks. They disobeyed orders and now they'll get socks. I want my socks. I'll see the lieutenant . . ."

The Big Polack argued all afternoon and well into the night. The Arab stuck his head out of the sheepshed at daylight, stretched and walked down the hill to the well, chanting, "I got socks, I want socks, they ain't got socks, but I got socks!"

He said to Berkely, who was combing infiltrations of dried sheep manure out of his hair:

"For years I've been trying to find words which translate the noise made by a flat wheel on a train coach. I've finally found 'em. You want to know what they are?"

"What are they?"

"I got socks, I want socks, I got socks, I want socks, I got socks, I want socks, I got socks, I want socks."

"How did you finally solve the sock problem?"

"I gave him my pair."

16. Hill 1205

The gods of war became irritated at us for living like sheep up there in the leaky, lousy sheepshed. One day we were told to roll it up and get ready to go. Since we hadn't been re-equipped we thought, and rumor confirmed it, that our mission in Italy was completed and that we were going to England to rejoin the 82nd. Rumor was wrong as usual. Although we didn't all have entrenching tools, and our shelter halves were worn out, and some of our guns were in bad shape, we got into some trucks and went driving through the rain. It always rained when we went anywhere. If the Legion would drive through the Sahara in the driest season, I bet a cloudburst would fall on it. We got off the trucks under the rocky slopes of the biggest mountain we ever saw in Italy and set up a bivouac in some olive trees. Dozens of 105 howitzers and 155 long toms and other breeds of howitzers were all around us. They fired day and night. A man had to be stone deaf to get any sleep. Plenty of tanks were all around. It looked like something big was going on, something bigger than anything we'd seen so far.

We were about two miles from Venafro. The 5th Army had pushed up to the peak, which was 3,613 feet high, barren of vegetation and composed of tricky masses of rotten stone given to easy landsliding, boulders and cliffs. The 36th Division, the 1st, 3rd, and 4th Ranger Battalions, the 1st Special Service Force, and the Legion took the hill. I don't want to leave any outfit that was there out of the story because any man who lived through that scrap ought to get credit for it. Hill 1205, called Monte Samucro, turned into one of the bloodiest hills seen in Italy up to that time.

We stayed down in the olive grove a couple of days. I talked at length with artillerymen in the 84th Chemical Battalion, which had been in action there for some time. Their 4.2 mortars weighed three or four-hundred pounds, were rifled like cannon, and propelled twenty-five pound high explosive phosphorous shells for about 4,500 yards. When the shell hit, the explosion dusted flakes of phosphorous into the enemy's foxholes. A flake as big as a nailhead would burn all

74

the way through a man's leg. Only water arrested the burning and then only for as long as the water was kept on it. It was a hellish invention which the Germans correctly called a hellbomb.

A veteran hellbomb thrower named Joe Dishner told me about Rudolph. For a long time the Krautheads had directed artillery fire on our troops from an observation post on the mountaintop located in a jumble of boulders with a cave leading back into the hill. At seven o'clock, a Nazi whom his victims nicknamed Rudolph the Gallant Bastard came outside his cave in his shirtsleeves and took setting-up exercises for ten minutes. The jokers watched his precise movements with admiration. Finished, he would smoke a cigarette, airily wave his hand at his audience and call on his big guns to start their rain of death.

Naturally the jokers tried to blow his cave down on his ears, but it couldn't be done. When they began to shell, he would dart inside and wait until it was his turn again. Krauthead infantry protected him from dogfaces who tried to sneak up and kill him. Thus Rudolph the Gallant Bastard had become a legend to the poor devils he shelled all day and all night.

One day an expert 4.2 mortar gunner showered Rudolph with phosphorous flakes. He danced into his cave and never came out again. The peculiar atmosphere of sad-gladness which settled over the artillery unit paid tribute to his talent as an entertainer.

Personal past experiences filled us with dread and foreboding as we sat scrutinizing the gray, weathered, rotten, landsliding, precipitous, ledge-covered, waterless, barren mountain. On the peak Krautheads were hidden in the caves, grottoes, camouflaged pillboxes, foxholes and behind the rocks. Big artillery sat leashed like giant dogs awaiting the signal to tear us to death. The Rangers who had fought their way to the top in a few spots had suffered 50 percent casualties. We were going up to relieve them. It was clear to us, as we sat amid the reverberating thunder of our own artillery, that we would die in heaps on that hideous pile of elevated stones.

Early one afternoon we began the seven hours' climb, our hearts as heavy as our backloads of ammo, guns, and rations. After two hours of steady climbing we reached a small rocky plateau. From this point we followed a shepherd's path along which lay blood-stained bandages, belts, mangled boots, abandoned stretchers and helmets with holes in them—a veritable trail of blood. Farther up a dead trooper (3rd Battalion man) lay by the trail, his skin a waxy yellow, his eyes sunk back in his head. He lay flat on his back with his right hand, like a yellow claw, reaching for the sky.

A few hundred yards above us the trail, which wound between high, narrow, crooked cliffs and could be seen, as we learned later, by the Germans from a secret cave, and become a belt of fire. There was no alternate route and the Krautheads were dumping a mortar shell on it every thirty seconds. The shells came plummeting and screeching, blasting splinters from the rocks, and in such rapidity that the dying echo from the last one merged with the borning echo of the new one. The clangings and clamors of battle in the Arab's Homer didn't stand ankle high in this technocratic hell.

A shell burst at the head of the company, killing two men and lacerating the hand of another. The wounded man, exuding triumph tempered by trepidation, passed us going down the trail, a white blood-soaked bandage around his hand. If he dodged a few more shells, he would be safe in a hospital for most of the winter. We looked at him envyingly, gripped in a mind-numbing fear, our entrails dissolving in acid anguish.

Halfway up the trail the entire company gave out and stopped for a ten-minute break. The troopers crawled beneath boulders, lit cigarettes and shuddered as the fearful echoes leaped from cliff to cliff. Lifting my head above my ledge, I saw a tiny black object speeding down the slope barely ten feet above the ground. I outducked the mortar shell before it burst five feet above me, but got smoke and dust covered. I stuck my head up again just in time to see Lindell and then O'Connell plummet whirling-swirling over the rock shelf. The latter bounced to his feet bellowing, "I'm hit, I'm hit, I'm hit all over!"

He rushed over to a medic, who was gingerly poking his head above a boulder, jerked up his jacket and roared, "Ya wanta look at me?" The medic assured him it was not serious.

Satisfied that O'Connell would live, I again looked up the slope and saw lanky Donlevy flopping like a half-cut-into snake. I rushed up to him. Simultaneously Berkely came leaping down the trail, crunching the rotten rocks and unloosening small boulders at each bound. Donlevy, bewildered by unbelief, shock and fear, turned his pallid face toward us and whispered feebly, "I'm going, I'm going, I'm going fast." Berkely inspected a two-inch rip in his bloody jump pants just below the left hipbone, laughed and said, "Donlevy, you lucky devil, you're going all right, but to the States. Die, hell, you're too mean to die."

We carried him under a sunken ledge, cut off his trouser

leg with a bayonet, poured sulfanilamide powders on the wound, bandaged it, gave him his sulfadiazine pills, held a canteen to his lips, yelled for some litter bearers (stationed along the trail to act as relays for carrying parties from above), shook his hand and left him. He made the States, recovered and got a medical discharge.

Berkely had dropped his rifle when he ran to aid Donlevy. While he looked for it I went on up the trail slowly to give him time to overtake me. Two hundred yards above him I stopped under a protruding rock, looked back and saw him disappear in a cloud of dust and smoke just as he started to climb over a ledge. I peered down, my guts tensed in a knot, expecting to see his big form in a tangled mess. But he rose and plunged on midst shells banging off boulders at ten-foot intervals. Indomitable and formidable he surged under my ledge with geysers of smoke and dust spouting above, below and to his sides.

We got our wind back and toiled upward to rejoin the company now far above us. The trail got steeper as we went, the precipices more dangerous. At last we were climbing the sheer cliff. It was dark when we tagged onto the end of the company.

All through the night the Krauthead machine-gun fire lashed the crest of the peak. A man who stuck his head above it was lucky to fetch it back down in one hunk. Sometime shortly before dawn, an enemy sharpshooter crawled to a point where he could snipe down the slope at us. Berkely and I crawled over the rocks to spot him. He escaped, but we found a dead Ranger on a litter, with a dead Nazi at each end. The Ranger was minus a leg. It was hard to figure the little drama. Either the Ranger had died while they were carrying him, and his buddies, having no further use for the prisoners, had shot them, or a shell had killed all three.

The dawn came cold following a night torn continually by the whizzing and awful crack of shells exploding on bare rock and the roaring guttural sputter of machine-gun fire. Fleecy clouds, pushed by a swift wind that blew under, lifted up and sucked back our helmets, speeded along beneath. I could understand their haste in getting away from such a man-made hell. The sky was clear and of a cobalt blue. Fifty-five miles away old Vesuvius blew its perpetual column of white smoke far up into the sky. Range on range of mountains stretched north and south as far as the eye could reach. To the west we caught glimpses of the Mediterranean.

The Krauthead planes flew through the pass to our left, dropping their bombs, and flew back in a hail of ack-ack through the pass to our right. One plane passed beneath me so close I could see the helmeted pilot grinning, no doubt, over the success of his mission, as he neared the northward pass and safety. In the valley our big guns maintained a constant roar. All day and night shells showered over our heads into Krauthead positions. Those from the 155 rifles passed over us high in the air and emitted an intense, cold, hollow moan.

Carrying parties, each paying a death toll, shuttled water, ammunition, food and supplies up the trail increasingly scattered with new dead men and their equipment. The living, far too tired to pay attention to the deceased, merely stepped across their bodies and pushed on with their loads.

The living robbed the dead to live maybe just a few hours before dying and being robbed in turn. We prowled around the cliffs like ghouls peering for a stray K-5 cracker or a dropped tin of corn pork. Since most of our food had to be carried up the trail of blood, we ate little. I eased my hunger by smoking a dead man's pipe. The half pound of Sir Walter Raleigh pipe tobacco that Carey had given me was worth more on that peak than a half-pound diamond. Sitting near the top in my little rock cleft, I blew puffs of smoke into the wind, watched them flicker out and dissolve.

The lean Arab, rifle on shoulder, was always searching for a stray mouthful of something. Gruening seeing him upturning stones accused him of being a beetle eater. His heavy black beard and a handlebar mustache whose tips almost switched his ear lobes made him resemble an outlaw in a dime movie. Casey sat patiently in his hole under a cliff, his yellow eyes sighting off to the far gray peaks, boding ill to the Krauthead that might come into his hands.

The Master Termite, anxious to get some wood for his incisors, sat wiping his gun behind a boulder. Larkin, never the same since Oldring died, had agreed that black was black ever since we had been on the peak. Finkelstein was the luckiest man in the platoon. Being able to fit into cracks where Big Rodgers couldn't slide his boot, he resembled a big lizard dressed as a combat trooper. Sheraton said the goddamned shells shatter-banging on the rocks reminded him of a honkytonk in Gallup, New Mexico.

One afternoon the sun came out and the wind died away. Troopers crawled from their hiding places to sit in the sun like woodchucks on a spring day. Berkely, Lopez, the Arab, Carey, Duquesne and I had gathered in a little flat space for a conference. Mortar shells were falling here and there on the peak, but being snugly comfortable, we decided that on such a big mountain only the freakest of accidents could plop a shell down on us. A number of subjects had been kicked around on the rock carpet, such as when ve'd get off that mountain mortuary, when Duquesne would get a beer, women round the clock and back again. Carey was in the midst of relating with great gusto how he made a dame in old Mexico when suddenly we heard a clatter about ten feet above us. A mortar shell, gleaming and aluminum-hued in the sunlight, fins sticking up, had just landed and buried its nose in some small gravel. So far it was a dud. But as we looked at it in fascinated gaping horror, too terrified to move, some gravel slid from under it, and it began to roll slowly and deliberately until it finally halted in the middle of our little circle. Any instant it might explode. Its seven pounds of metal would kill us all. Suddenly in his inimitable accent Lopez sang out, "This is no place for me," and in a flash he was deep in his hole with the rest of us giving him getaway competition. Only a bad fuse had saved us from death.

17. Olson and the Master Termite Make Plans

for the Future

The 2nd Battalion got orders to go over the northern slope one night and dislodge an enemy unit that was holding up our advance. Our company drew the assignment to guard the right flank until they took up positions. Then, when things were well in hand, we were to return to our foxholes and rock piles and leave the 2nd Battalion to fight it out.

We made it across the peak and down the side about three hundred yards before anything happened to break the tension that gunned our blood. Suddenly a battery of flares outlined us and we telescoped for safety behind rocks and boulders. Almost immediately fire from mortars, rifle grenades and MG 42's ricocheted sparks from the rocks, on which they exploded and banged, into intermingling streaks of red and silver tracers.

First advance squads crossed grenades and bayonets with the Krautheads and then soon the entire battalion moved into the fight. If they failed to stampede the Krauts, we would be lucky to hold out even briefly behind the thin rib of rocks which shielded us.

Below to the left we could hear an officer call to some of

his men who apparently had got lost. When he shouted, a happy Krauthead machine gunner would answer:

"Vot you vant, captain, vot you want?"

The officer would yell back, "Shut up, you son of a bitch, we'll take care of you in a minute."

Then the Krauthead would laugh and send a hail of death at the sound of the officer's voice.

Berkely, Nixon, Ciconte and I, lying behind a ledge waiting for the men in front to take care of the Krauts, hoping they wouldn't call on us to help, lay shaking with laughter at the verbal exchange.

Wounded men moaning and falling from weakness streamed past us up the hill. The medics had more business than they could handle. One was patching up a man's leg in a machine-gun cross fire when someone yelled, "Hey, you stupid obscenities, you're in a cross fire." The shot-up guy outran the medic up the hill.

A dimwit set up a 60 mm mortar a few yards from us and began to fire. The ten-foot flame that shot from the tube made a target the Krautheads could see clear to Cassino. They lobbed in more rifle grenades, mortar shells and bullets than hell could hold. We were losing men left and right. Down over the rib of rock two squads were shooting it out with machine guns. We heard our powerful little grenades exploding, the slick *putt-putt* of submachine guns and the heavy reports of Garands. Somebody opened up with an automatic rifle. A Krauthead cut loose with magazine Schmeisser ammo. The MG 42's never let up for a minute. Then heavy artillery began to pound the peaks behind us.

Things were in a bad way. We just lay low and hoped and wondered how the poor taxpayers and the bobby-soxers back home were making out and whether anybody in the States knew what we were doing.

Berkely and Ciconte went to sleep with the tracers streaking six inches over their noggins. I crawled over to Lopez who cautiously raised his head, scrutinized me, and said, "I may be prejudiced, but I don't like this place. A man could ketch his death of cold in a spot like this, and the skeeters'll give a man malaria. The army oughtn't to put a man in these unhealthy places."

His Spanish-accent twist on the words made me grin.

I found the Arab nearby. The Big Polack and he were lying on their sides making a rock pile to ward off machine-gun bullets. The Polack was wearing his overcoat and bitching steadily. Casey and Rodgers lay silently on the bare ground, awaiting developments with their usual patience.

Nixon was lying flat but contriving to scoop out a little trench behind two big rocks he'd pulled together as lead and shrapnel stoppers. The wounded men worked their way slowly and painfully up the hill, some of them getting hit and killed.

In due time we got word that the 2nd Battalion was ready for us to leave them. But just as we got started, a machine gun moved into position way up the hill on our right and opened fire where the rib of rock couldn't help us. Most of the men goat-hopped over the hill to safety in a split minute. A medic's bedroll and my own slowed me down to a near give-out crawl. Two wounded men behind a rock called for help. I put my bandage on one and gave the other some water. A man wearing a raincoat came strolling leisurely toward me not giving a damn apparently about whizzing lead and shrapnel. I covered him and said, "Speak up, you dam' fool, or I'll let you have it."

It was the company commander, as cool and gentle as if he were at tea, bringing up the rear of his troops. I showed him the wounded men. He sat down by them and told me to go over the peak and request that some litter bearers be sent down. From that moment I never doubted the courage of our CO.

The remainder of the night we crouched in our rocks thinking of the 2nd Battalion still down under the peak getting shot to pieces, and watching the walking wounded dribble by. Those unable to walk lay down by their fighting buddies who attended to them when they had time.

When daylight came, Colonel Tucker ordered that we ask for a truce so that the wounded men could be carried down. A big flag with a red cross was thrust above the peak's top and held there for a few moments. Then the two men holding it climbed up on the crest and thrust the flag higher in the air to make sure it could be seen. The sky was blue. The cold, brisk air whipped the flag around the flagstaff. The enemy soon agreed to the truce. All shooting stopped and quiet reigned along the trail of blood and midst the crags. The calm made us realize all the more the kind of fantastic hell we'd been living in.

A large party of unarmed litter bearers came for the wounded. The Krautheads left their hiding-places and climbed on ledges to witness our discomfiture. They sat and smoked and the Nazis among them guffawed at seeing our poor devils being laboriously and painfully carried up the rough slope. A few men died on the litters as they were being carried.

We took advantage of the unexpected truce to remove our boots and rub our feet to restore circulation and to build little fires to make hot coffee and cook up some X rations. The Big Polack changed and washed his socks. What a luxury to be able to perch on the boulders without fear of sudden death!

The Arab, gravely impressed by his close shaves of the night before, emerged from his hole, abysmal gloom written on his scurvy features, sighing and smoking his pipe and meditating upon the shortness of life on Hill 1205. His gloom thickened and clabbered into dejection when word came that his company was to cross the peak to stay. The Master Termite, also jittery, plodded over to join the Arab, Berkely, Duquesne, Gruening and Larkin, who took advantage of the truce to relax. The Master sat down on a stone and spoke of Angel and their plans for a house by the side of the Bay at Hoboken.

"Boys," he said, "I'm gonna put a bar in the wall of my parlor. All I'll have to do when I get it fixed will to be to press a button in my easy chair, and the whole bar will swing out and stop in easy reach. I'll have bottles of all the best whiskies and wines. Me and the Angel will sit there and drink and invite all the hoboes in to have a drink. I've been on the road and I know what it is to be cold, hungry, and wet, with no place to lay my head. Anybody who comes along will be welcome to what I'm gonna have. I read a poem once and this is the first line or the last one, I dunno which, 'I'm going to build a house by the side of the road, and be a friend to man,' and being a friend to man is giving him a drink when he's in low spirits, and giving him a hand-out when he's hungry, and putting him in a good bed for the night when he's homeless. I'm a bum at heart, but I'm gonna settle down with Angel . . . she calls me Wings, you know, and we'll be happy together."

Olson, who had his head stuck out from a nearby hole, took up the conversation: "I'm gonna buy me a saloon in Newark, New Jersey, and I'm gonna serve good liquor to everybody that needs a drink. All you guys can buy your drinks at cost. If I didn't know you so well, I'd give you the run of the joint, but in two days you'd drink me dry and outa business. But you can ask for Olson's joint and anybody'll point it out."

Two jokers who had joined us after we left Naples, Donald Pierson and Santos Sheraton, both battle-fractured into veterans on Hill 1205, crawled out of their holes and came down to visit. On the reasonable assumption, I suppose, that he might need it, Pierson carried enough equipment on his belt to start an army store. Shovels, picks, trench knives, wire cutters, a compass, hand grenades, a 45 automatic and other stuff, clanked and rattled on him as he walked. A few nights before we infiltrated Hill 1205 Winters heard a melodic tinkling outside his tent which he took to be a bell on a cow. It was Pierson's trench knife banging on his shovel. Larkin, who had been to Honolulu, said to him when he came up:

"Pierson, if you added a few spatulas and dippers to that outfit you'd resemble a hula dancer!"

The sun came out for a moment just in time to shine on his gold tooth as he grinned at Larkin.

"The sun shining on that peg tooth, Pierson, makes me think of a one-eyed car coming out of a dark alley."

Pierson didn't want to grin but he did. He didn't feel in a mood to risk a fight with Larkin.

Pierson turned out to be one of the best fighters, and luckiest men in the Legion. Everywhere he went he was always barely escaping death. After a close brush he would flash his gold and say, "The whole German army has it in for ole Pierson, but I don't mind." Or when things were rough: "I'm tired, sleepy, mad, hungry, thirsty, scared, and with no choke in my reed, but I don't mind." When he talked like that and flashed his gold, he made us feel better.

"Sheraton," began Duquesne in a tone that foretold a long string of nonsense, "I dreamed last night that the New York Central had given Gruening a Cadillac to get rid of him and me and him with him driving went down to Newark to 'Olson's Joint' to have a beer. Olson was too tight to give us one so I says, 'Gruening,' I says, 'We'll just go down to Hoboken and see the Master and drink his stuff 'cause the Master's got a heart and a house by the side of the road and a bar that follows your chair around and funnels it down your throat.' And Olson, he says. 'I'll lock up and go with you.'

"So we all goes to the Master Termite's house, but we can't find it. We drives around through the park for a while looking for him and finally finds him and Angel asleep under a newspaper. 'Master,' I says, 'Master, you got guests! Here's Gruening and Olson and me, Duquesne, your pals, and we want that bar to git after us you got in your house that's a friend to man.' And the Master Termite begins to cry and Angel, a purty fair tomato she was, she begins to cry and Gruening starts to cry and then me and Olson, we git to crying and the Master says:

" 'I was a real Termite on Hill 1205, but in the States, I'm just a make-believe Termite and I just got a make-believe bar.'

"Olson said, he says, 'Let's take the Master and Angel on their honeymoon. I'll pay for everything! We'll take 'em to the Grand Canyon!' So we buy Angel a dress and the Master a shirt and tie and off we take. We stopped at every honky-tonk,

Sheraton, and played every jukebox between Hoboken and Winslow, Arizona. When that mortar woke me this morning, we were in Winslow in a honky-tonk and a voice said. 'We're playing this number for Santos Sheraton, the best honky-tonk-and the biggest friend of juke-boxing west o' the Mississippi.' And they played a tune by Al Dexter called 'Pistol Packin' Mama' which the Master and Angel went to jitterbuggin'! And that's the way things stood when the shell went off and Olson yelled. 'They got me!' That was a helluva good dream, eh, Sheraton?"

Sheraton's smile faded into sadness as Duquesne talked. He was a honky-tonk devotee who had made the rounds from Houston to Frisco. For him the war was a simple affair. One time I asked him why he joined the paratroops. "So I can kill off these Krautheads faster and get back to honky-tonking!" He was an expert soldier and could have been a sergeant had he cared to, but he preferred just to have Sheraton to look after. When he dispatched an enemy, which was often, he'd grin and say, "One more step toward Texas!"

Sheraton was a slim, lithe, tough, calculating cool fellow of medium build with bright curly red hair, brick-red skin, sparkling white teeth and eyes of a mountain-lake blue. He never lost his temper or quit smiling what was probably the handsomest smile in all the Legion.

The Arab, who had listened enraptured to Duke's improvised dream, asked, "Where did the Master and Angel get married?"

Duke looked perplexed for a moment, then turned to the Master.

"Where did you get married, Master?"

The Master shook his head sadly and wiped the tears out of his eyes.

18. Hill 687

The enemy retreated before the 2nd Battalion's attack to positions on ridges jutting into the Liri Valley in the direction of Cassino. We spent the afternoon witnessing our artillery attack on San Pietro. At twelve sharp six hundred pieces of artillery began to spurt projectiles into the little town and they kept up the barrage until eight that night. San Pietro and the Liri Valley were pulverized, utterly devastated. Yet when our infantry attacked, the Nazis crowded out of the debris-covered cellars and caves and kept us from gaining more than a half mile.

Shortly after dusk, we went over the north side of the slope and hid around in the fairly thick brush on the lower parts of the mountain. Our new replacements, Moore and Parsons, beheld our bearded jowls and bloodshot eyes in wonder, and we their civilized freshness in astonished incredulity.

Later that night, Sgt. Winters took six men, among them Sheraton and Pierson, and went over to a little ridge that stuck out toward Cassino, Hill 687 by name, with the intention of occupying and holding it. While still some distance from the crest, the patrol sighted a number of men on it standing in a semicircle. Winters hollered, "Who in the hell are you?"

A little silence ensued, and then a voice replied, "Fifth Army."

Winters yelled back, "You're a goddamned liar, you're sonuvabitchin' Krauthead bastards."

Another silence took place and then a voice began issuing orders in German. Winters opened fire and his men followed suit. To avoid encirclement, the patrol dropped their bedrolls and shook it speed-haste back to the company.

The next night Lt. Toland went to the Arab and the Big Polack and said, "Tonight the platoon is going over and occupy Hill 687. Winters says the place is infested with Krautheads. We'll be careful, but regardless of how many Krautheads are on it, we're going to stay there. Arab, you are first scout, and the Big Polack is second scout. Aim for that pass you can see over there. Before you get to it, you'll run into some terraces with grain growing on them, and nearby are some little shepherds' huts. Those are your objective. We'll take the top of the hill which is two hundred yards north of the huts, and set up a defense, using the huts as a platoon CP. I saw the spot with field glasses today, and you should be able to find it easy. Arab, lead off, and take your time, and the Big Polack will follow right behind you."

The Arab sighed. He had been expecting to drag along in the rear of the column. He took the Polack aside and told him to move when he moved and for God's sake to throw away his inevitable overcoat, which would scratch and drag through the bush and perhaps get them both killed. The Polack refused on the grounds that he was cold, would rather be dead than cold, and that the Krautheads and the Arab could go to hell.

The Arab, his rifle at the ready, stalked through the darkness, like a soft-footing panther, with the Polack following him like a charging moose. The Arab wanted to live; therefore the noise put him in a deathly rage. The memory of Carlton was with him as he led the way expecting a machine pistol to empty itself in his guts at every step. Whenever the Arab stopped to listen, the Polack stopped, and Toland stopped, and the man behind him stopped, and so on until the entire platoon stopped.

Presently the Arab halted the column, told the Polack to stay put, and then went on ahead for a hundred and fifty yards to listen. He heard a column of fifteen or twenty men come down the mountain below him and move out of hearing. The platoon waited a few minutes before going on. Just as the Arab had discovered his first objective, a line of high, narrow terraces with grain sowed on them, a Krauthead MG 42 sprayed the middle of the platoon from the right flank. No one was hurt. Again the Arab led on. Suddenly someone in the rear yelled, "Halt, who is there?" and simultaneously opened fire. Grenades began to thump into the column.

A trigger-happy patrol from another company had ambushed us. It was a mistake, but Olson was shot through the hips and groin with a 45 slug and died in agony without saying a word. His struggles with the 60 mortar, which he was still carrying when shot, were ended. The weapon had worn the hard muscle off his legs, slimmed off his broad hips, put lines in his square face, and shadows beneath his bright blue eyes. He died like a dog all because the officer leading the patrol failed to wait until his challenge was answered. We left him there in his gore, his dream of "Olson's Joint" in Newark with drinks at cost for the Legion forever a dream.

The Arab continued on to the huts, his heart heavy. Olson had been a close and loyal friend. He crawled into the huts one at a time, prodding the darkness ahead of him with his bayonet and getting generously smeared with sheep and goat dung. In the last hut his keen nostrils scented fresh warm wood-smoke. He went back and got Berkely, to whom he always turned when he needed help. Berkely stood by and growled, "*Kamerad,* you dirty bastards!" and two Krautheads came out with their hands high. The platoon came up and deployed among the rocks while we questioned them. They said there were no other troops nearby and told us they knew

where some water was in a well. Having lived on half a cup
of water per day for sixteen days, we would have braved semi-
certain ambush for a drink. The Arab volunteered to take two
men and the prisoner and fetch a supply. The Arab stalked up
to the prisoner and thrust a bayonet beneath his chin to let
him know the result if he led them into a trap. Then they gathered up the canteens, tied them together to keep them from
banging, and disappeared into the night.

Lt. Toland dispatched some men to occupy the hill. The
remainder of us got busy building pillboxes behind a stone
wall that ran east and west near the top of the hill. The situation looked pretty fair.

The prisoner led the Arab and his party to a rock-walled
well deep among some terraces and began to draw water in
an old cracked jug. The troopers lay on guard behind the wall
while the Arab, stretched on his lean belly, kept his gun on the
captive. Presently the German let a canteen fall on a stone.
The loud tinkle brought fire from a Nazi machine gunner who
knew the location of the well. Bullets popping off the walls
imperiled the prisoner, who started to crawl for safety. The
thirsty Arab, however, thunked his bayonet into the Krauthead's rump and croaked, *"Wasser, Wasser."* Thus the unlucky prisoner was made to realize the importance of drawing
water even under the most hazardous of conditions. The
machine gun kept shooting and although the prisoner kept
wanting to get in a safe place, the implacable Arab kept
gigging his smarting buttocks until all the canteens were filled.

It is difficult to imagine a more miserable group of men than
we were. For seventeen days we had existed on the peak in
freezing weather, in constant rain, icy winds, and inconceivable danger. In all that time we had never washed our hands
or shaved or taken off our boots more than three times. Lice
were eating the hide off our bodies and desperation was eating
out our hearts. Each of us expected to die any second and
many of our comrades did. Rations, ammunition and the
wounded had to be carried seven miles over the mountain on
men's backs and on litters. A seriously wounded man couldn't
live through the terrible, jolting trip. We all preferred instant
death to a slow croak in horrible pain on jolting stretchers. The
Legion was at no more than half strength. My platoon alone
faced two hundred men on Hill 687, being outnumbered more
than five to one. Our odds were no greater than in some other
units of the Legion. Only a miracle of stubbornness and forti-
tude permitted us to win the battle of Hill 1205 and its adjacent area. I do not claim, of course, that we won the battle
alone, because several other units endured the same conditions

as we. Men died in blood, sweat and tears on that battlefield. And yet to Churchill and others Italy was the "soft underbelly of Festung Europa"!

The Krautheads pushed the boys off the hilltop in the middle of the night. Lt. Toland had the notion that the Krautheads didn't stay on the hill during the day. Berkely volunteered to go up just before daylight and take a look. If they were gone, it was Toland's plan to set a trap for them when they came back in the evening. I mentally said *adiós* to the giant as he passed by my outpost with Big Rodgers, for I had the feeling the enemy was up there day and night.

Berkely and Big Rodgers had been gone for about ten minutes when I heard three rapid rifle shots, an MG 42, growling, and the screech of a machine pistol. "They are gone," I said to myself. "Berkely and Big Rodgers have joined Olson, Oldring, Hastings, Carlton." In the midst of these melancholy reflections I heard a tremendous clatter of rocks, a mighty stomping like two Percheron horses running in perfect step, and then two voices chanting in frantic cadence, "Medico, medico, medico." The clatter and chant pursued by tracers kept crashing our way, reached the three-foot wall and swept through it like a tank. As the two giants hurtled past, their thundering feet unloosening an avalanche of rocks, I conjectured reassuringly that men who could run that fast couldn't be hurt bad. I followed them down, reflecting that this incident was something to laugh at in better times when we would be sitting around a blazing campfire with a pot of coffee brewing.

I found Berkely lying on the floor of a hut with a little white-haired medic slitting his pant leg to find the wound. He rubbed his hand over the afflicted knee and said in indecision, "Berkely, I can't find no wound." In anger the giant roared, "Well, feel of the other leg then." I laughed until my sides hurt.

Berkely had left Rodgers halfway up the hill to cover his retreat and had walked up to a Krauthead sentry leaning out of a stone pillbox. The sentry saw him, yelled an alarm. Berkely threw three quick shots at him. Then he threw a snap shot at a nearby machine gunner who began to cut the rocks all about him and took off like a big woodcock. A Krauthead rose up from somewhere with a machine pistol whose squirting lead knocked his rifle from his hands, causing him to plunge into some rocks. His knee was numb and paralyzed, but he made it work well enough to storm off that hill like a wild bull. He picked up Rodgers on the way down, both spurred on their flight by the singing bullets of the MG 42. Berkely had gravely injured his knee on the rocks. It swelled up and ached for months. He never admitted that he ran through the stone wall, but around many a campfire in later days we continued to insist that he did.

At dawn we saw the Germans piling up stone pillboxes about five hundred yards away on a little spur of Hill 687. It began to rain in great sheets, but stopped about two o'clock and a thick fog floated down from the pass overlooking Venafro. Lt. Toland recruited half a dozen volunteers to go out into the fog with him to see if some excitement could be stirred up. Sheraton, a lad we called "Destiny's Tot," Winters, the Master Termite and I went with him. We slipped down a draw and slithered up some terraces which extended down under the north side of 687. We lay down along a terraced terrain behind the Krauthead defenses. I was posted as a rear guard to keep a lookout for encircling maneuvers. The fog lifted, leaving us completely exposed in the middle of the enemy lines. It was a tense moment until another wave of fog covered us up again. Visibility was about ten yards. The boys rose up for a look. Just in front of the Master Termite was a pillbox and standing on it with a rock in his hands was a storm trooper ambitiously engaged in building it a little higher. In front of Winters, a soldier was shaking the water off a shelter half, and another was sitting on a rock smoking. Just then the pillbox builder saw the Termite looking at him with his rifle lowered on his middle. The bearded-face and glittering-eyed Master shot him in the stomach. He swayed a second on the pillbox, then toppled to the ground where he lay jerking his legs until he died. Winters pinged the second and Sheraton shot the third one through the heart. A machine gun started to pour a leaden hail over the terrace. We got the hell out and back to the huts late enough to miss an artillery barrage directed at them. Berkely, who had been sleeping all through the episode, was aroused by the artillery fire and raised hell because no one had asked him to go.

Next night we prepared to drive the Krautheads off the hill with an all-out attack. It was Christmas Eve, 1943. Twenty men from another company came down to help us out. They were to attack on the left side of the hill to create a diversion while one of our squads attacked the now familiar machine gun nest. At this time we had only two squads left out of the platoon. One was to remain in reserve to repel a possible attack by some Germans who had been annoying us from a ravine. The artillery support we were supposed to have proved ineffective because the observer didn't direct it correctly.

Berkely, with the Arab second in command, was to lead the

squad that was to attack the machine gun nest. Indefatigable
Feroni and Berkely were leading the way, the Master close behind, with the squad following in single file and the Arab
bringing up the rear. Homer trailed along with the Arab, his
assignment being to carry a message back to the huts if
necessary.

About four o'clock in the morning of Christmas Day, 1943,
Berkely and Feroni walked up to the machine gun nest.
Berkely tossed a grenade at the panicky hollering Krauthead.
Feroni opened fire and then Berkely charged the pillbox. A
Krauthead rose up from behind it and shot the Master Termite
full of holes. Then the grenade exploded and killed the German who had shot the Master. Another Krauthead mowed a
swath around Berkely with the machine gun, which had just
got into action, and he had to drop back for a few yards. Our
boys, although lying in the path of machine-gun fire, continued
to hurl bullets at the pillbox from behind which the Nazis were
shooting up flares which silhouetted us in bold targets. Enemy
machine guns from the reverse slope pattered lead along the
crest to prevent anyone from flanking the pillbox.

The Arab had jumped into a 105 shell hole to the left of the
other boys and about twenty-five yards from the machine gun.
He was on the alert to keep the enemy from getting flanking
fire and to prevent the twenty men who were to attack from
the left from getting shot by some of us. We kept waiting, but
the main attack never came. Rumor had it that the officer was
chicken and didn't have the guts to lead it.

Berkely, the Arab and the others laid down a devastating
fire on the Krauthead machine gun, which soon fell silent. It
was impossible to advance any farther unless the men attacked
on the left, because two machine guns located where we
couldn't see them crisscrossed fire just in front of the pillbox.
After a suitable wait Berkely, disheartened and disgusted, ordered the boys back to the hut.

It was just breaking daylight. Artillery fire was falling
around the huts. The Arab, safely out of it in his ample shell
hole, felt no inclination to withdraw immediately. Soon he saw
an enemy rifleman crawl up on the crest about twenty yards
from him and begin to fling bullets in the direction the boys
had taken. The Arab watched the muzzle-blast of the rifle and
reflected, "Oh, yes, you ambitious murderer! Just stay there
until it gets a little lighter, and I'll give you absolution."
Finally the increasing light turned the lead-throwing Kraut
into a clear target. With a cold eye and a colder heart and the
spirit of the Master Termite directing his aim, the Arab put
four bullets through him. The rifle fell from his hands and the

body sagged on the rocks. The Arab threw a salute in the direction of the fallen Master and ambled back to the huts. Christmas Morning, 1943.

About eleven o'clock the little colonel with one man as a bodyguard came down from 1205 wanting to know why in hell the attack failed. The battalion medical officer who came with him brought one bottle of whisky for the entire company! It was the best he could do and we appreciated his good will. Although every man thirsted for the whole bottle, no one more than touched it to his lips for fear the next man wouldn't get a taste. Some of the drinkingest men in the army refused it entirely so that their buddies could get a drop.

The little colonel took two men, walked to the pillbox, caught the Nazis cleaning the machine gun and took eleven prisoners without firing a shot. He made us look silly.

Four prisoners came carrying the Master in a shelter half and put him down at our feet. A hole was above his left eye, one in his throat and several in his stomach and chest. We stared down at his blank eyes fixed on us, fingered our guns, and looked at the Krautheads and then at the colonel. He shook his head.

We could have no greater reason for not celebrating Christmas than the death of the Master. We mourned him with aching, hating hearts. He was one of those great, original characters that command love and devotion. We thought of Angel and the hospitable house, never to be built, overlooking Hoboken Bay. "The House Overlooking the Bay" joined "Olson's Joint" as battle dreams killed in battle. Platoon phantoms marching at our sides were now almost a squad: Oldring Hastings, Carlton, Olson, the Master Termite.

As the little colonel started down the hill, he called back to Toland to send three men after him as a bodyguard. The Arab, Rodgers and Nixon drew the assignment, but they couldn't catch up with him. Before they had gone very far, however, Nixon captured two Krautheads in a little pillbox, left Rodgers to guard them while he and the Arab went on to look for the colonel. Rodgers was told to shoot the prisoners if he heard any firing in the direction the two were going. He said, after a little pause, "All right." The Arab saw helmets pushing up a shelter half that covered a pillbox. He went over, stuck his rifle in the front and yelled, "Heil Hitler, you ignorant devils!" They soared over the side of the pillbox with alacrity and stood there eying him. One prisoner was a tough-looking corporal wearing only one shoe. He asked if he could go into the pillbox and get his other one. The Arab nodded and the guy reached into the pillbox for it. His hand quivered with

desire to get his rifle leaning within easy reach against the wall.
He cast a quick glance at the Arab who, ostensibly busy
watching the other prisoner, would not see him. He reached,
but when he saw the Arab grinning at him out of the side of
his mouth he jerked his hand back in a flash. Then he realized
the Arab was wanting him to grab the gun!

They took their prisoners back to Rodgers, who said simply
in his serious way, "Arab, I thought I was gonna have to shoot
these guys. One kept wanting to stick his hands in his pocket
for a cigarette, and I didn't know how to tell him to stop, and
I was gonna shoot him if he did." He meant it. Big Rodgers
never joked.

In the meanwhile, the colonel had personally chased the retreating Krautheads far up the valley toward Cassino. He later
told us that if we had caught up with him we could have shot
hell out of a big bunch of them. I guess maybe he was right.

The day ended the battle of Cassino for the Legion. The
mountain was ours. It was somebody else's turn to carry the
ball. The regiment was shot all to pieces. Many men, including
Winters, who had got shot above the knee, were in the hospital
recovering from wounds, trench feet or pneumonia. We were
under half strength. For sixty days we had been fighting in a
terrain that God must have made when He was mad at somebody and forgot to improve after He made it. And we were
half dead.

19.   Meditations in Hot Water

We climbed back over the mountain to the olive grove, shaved
and slept in big tents and ate steaks and potatoes, gravy and
toast, pie and chicken, turkey and dressing. For two months
we had lived on K ration. Our appetites were too big for our
stomachs, which had shrunk to half size. After we ate a big
meal, we would roll on the ground in agony, clutching ourselves in the middle. We would again eat like a hog at the next
meal, however. In about a week we were in fine shape. When
we shaved, none of the replacements knew us. They would
walk around and around us, trying to pick out something
familiar by which to identify us.

In a few days we went to a little place not far from Naples

called Villa Ricci, which was full of apples, nuts, good food
and pretty girls who wouldn't look at us. We spent the days
sleeping and the nights in Naples drinking and making love to
any *signorinas* who were willing.

Wild Bill McMurty and I got a room in a house occupied by
a widow and her three daughters, two of them grown. The
eldest was named Italia and the one next to her Carmelina. I
latched onto round-faced Italia, who weighed only ninety-five
pounds. At eighteen her lover had been killed in one of Il
Duce's imbroglios. She had worn crepe for four years and was
still wearing it. After a few days she decided to talk to me.
Each night we exchanged lessons in English and Italian. Wild
Bill lost his heart to sixteen-year old Carmelina and talked of
marrying her. With her soft, dark skin, softer black eyes,
little pearly teeth and dimpled cheeks, she could have charmed
a harder man than Wild Bill, who had the habit of falling in
love wherever he stopped.

The sisters were nice girls and couldn't be had for flattery,
marital promises or money. We passed many delightful hours
with them before the big open fireplace hung with pots and
cooking equipment. Whenever I desired it, they would fill a
big cask with hot water and shut me up in the room by the
fire to enjoy a wonderful luxury. There was room in it to sit
cross-legged. I would sit in it until the water cooled, trying to
forget the dark bloody battles still raging at Cassino, speculating about our uncertain future as front line combat troops
and dreaming of the day when the mess would be cleaned up
and the world would be at peace.

As things now looked I would probably cash in my chips in
battle and dissolve into soil and air in some place no one in the
States had ever heard of. But what the hell! Men had been
dying like that since the days of the Arab's Homer. After all,
a man's life is essentially but a trifling thing, really important
to almost no one but himself. I reflected that a man who is
really a man has to slug it out to a finish even though he senses
that in the end there won't be enough of him left to make a
soupbone. I had also learned that boys who wanted to live to
eat steak and drink Scotch and feel the firm breasts of giggling
girls could die with a smile on their lips. Oldring, Hastings,
Carlton, Olson and the Master would never march, camp, eat,
drink, love or talk with us again. That they wouldn't wouldn't
matter a damn to anybody much except those of us left in the
platoon. My life wasn't any more important than theirs and
my number would no doubt come up, sooner or later, just as
theirs had. But somehow I felt that comradeship with them
and with jokers like Duquesne, Big Rodgers, Berkely, Finkel-

stein, Casey, and all the others had about it a value that in itself geared me to face whatever lay ahead as well if not better than my hatred for the enemy and his philosophy. I owe more to that cut-in-two cask than cleanliness and comfort. I am indebted to it for helping me to arrive at a philosophy which carried me through the dark and bloody days that followed.

One week after our arrival at Villa Ricci, we were being re-equipped. New guns, belts, ammunition, clothes, boots, medical supplies, knives and replacements added to the regiment, had brought us almost to full strength again. Once more we sparkled and shone. A man new to combat would have reason to think that we were a brand new regiment in the PBSI—the Peninsula Base Section of Italy. The veteran or anyone in the know would have observed the boys' young-old faces, the manner in which they walked, the careless ease with which they handled their guns, how they drank, how little they slept, how fast they spent their money, and would not have been deceived. They knew their destiny and accepted it. However bitter the pill of death, and it is bitter for youths in their teens and twenties, they were prepared to swallow it, knowing that they had been set apart to die if need be.

When I was a child I looked at doddering old men, tottering about the country bearing their feeble weight on a cane, with their graying hair, their toothless mouths, their vacant eyes, peering into a past known only to them, and I wondered how they felt, being so near to their graves. I knew now. I too lived in the past. There was no perceptible road to life visible for the front line men in Italy in 1943 and 1944. To be *wounded, killed* or *captured:* these were the three roads to our destiny.

20.   Finkelstein Bubbles onto Anzio Beachhead

It was first decided that we would make another combat jump in Italy. We were shown sand tables of the jump area and briefed, but at the last minute instead of boarding planes we loaded in LCI's and other landing craft. All that afternoon and night we sailed smoothly in the blue water of the Tyrrhenian Sea, embarked upon an adventure that staggers the mind.

Now this Anzio deal was a battle that went down in history

and any man that was in it got it seared in his brain like a burn with a blowtorch. It was on the Anzio beachhead that the Legion fought what was perhaps its hardest battle and it was here that the Krautheads definitely began to fear the paratroops.

The Legion went in toward the beach about eleven o'clock on a cold, windy day in January. The American Rangers, 509th Parachute Infantry Battalion, and the ordnance division were already on the beach and we were going in to help them. One of our battalions, the 3rd, was attached to a British division on the left flank and wasn't with us then, but the 1st and 2nd were. We pushed toward the beach in a few LCI's to unload. Everything seemed quiet and it looked like a good deal; therefore we were nervous, for good deals are what get men killed in the army.

The deck of our LCI was crowded with troops standing around waiting to unload into the icy water and wade the three hundred yards to the beach. Just as Berkely was reaching for one of Pierson's cigarettes a dive bomber came in and hell opened it doors. The bomb missed the bow five feet or so, but the explosion lifted the boat clear out of the sea and blew a column of oily water into the sky which fell back on the boat and left us oil-coated for several days.

The nervous skipper of the LCI refused to take us any closer to land. A man swam ashore with a rope, one end of which was fastened to the unloading ramp, and tied the other to the strut of an amphibious Piper Cub that was sitting on the beach. We clomped down the ramp, grabbed the rope with one hand, and committed ourselves to the sea, loaded with mortars, machine guns, bedrolls and other equipment. The water was eight or ten feet deep and icy as a spinster's heart. By holding onto the rope and pulling like regatta rowers we all got ashore, but some had difficulty.

Finkelstein, who because of a superfluidous boil had been absent during the recent battles, had rejoined us. He missed the rope on sliding into the water and was pulled under by the weight of his equipment. A stream of salt-water bubbles progressing toward the shore from the spot of his disappearance informed us that he was headed in the right direction. Forbes, an incurable gambler, watched the bubbles for a few seconds, then hollered, "Five to one, jawbone, that he never comes up." "Done," yelped mortar sergeant Dolan as he too entered the salt water. At that moment, Finkelstein's little egg head, buried to his nose in an enormous helmet, broke the surface minus his bedroll and box of gum ammo. "Help!" he squeaked in a voice that brought Big Rodgers to the rescue. The giant seized him by the collar and carried the gasping little man to the shore like a half-drowned puppy. He grabbed Rodgers by the hand and looked up at him in gratitude. Then he waded out and got his bedroll.

Wet, cold, miserable, mad, disgusted, and laughing, we crossed a level space into a wood, hung our clothes on the bushes and began to get settled for a brief stay. Several pictures of wives and sweethearts were ignominiously hung on bushes to dry alongside thousand-lira notes and small change. The water filled the holes we scooped in the swampy soil as fast as we dug them. Soon a plane swung low to strafe us and we splashed into them like a bunch of frogs.

Duquesne, wounded but not seriously a few hours after the truce on Hill 1205 and now back from the hospital, informed his pardner and boon companion Gruening how ludicrous he looked in his wet drawers, which dramatized his stocky legs and angular kneecaps. Gruening scowled and commented sourly that the loon-brained, addlepated bastards of the old army never had had any sense, never would have any sense, and never would have children or grandchildren or great-grandchildren to the sixth generation with any sense.

While an officer was explaining to us in an authoritative manner that the Legion was in reserve and would not fight for a spell, the first sergeant began to bellow orders to get ready to move. The sun beat down so hard on the asphalt road along which we marched that the tar was melting. There wasn't any noise. Except for two dead Germans, one slumped in the seat of a motorcycle, the other in the sidecar, we didn't see much evidence of battle. We looked at the cadavers as we marched by, each drawing from the spectacle a different set of mental images but probably about the same reflections.

The night, which came rainy, windy and cold, passed without incident. The next morning we outposted some houses still occupied by the Italians. They took off, leaving behind several plump chickens, tubs of lard, sides of bacon and sacks of flour, when they learned that all hell was about to break loose. Toland prepared a breakfast of hot cakes for the boys. For lunch we had chicken and dumplings and a pot of strong coffee with fresh milk to go in it.

21. "Arab, We're Looking for Trouble!"

In the afternoon orders came for the platoon to abandon the outposts and to rejoin the company now a mile or so distant. We were in a flat country, a few miles from Colli Lazuali, a steep mountain with an extinct crater on the summit. From it the enemy could observe nearly every movement made on the beachhead. A narrow valley leading to Rome lay near the mountains. The Alban Hills were only a few miles away.

The air was too clear and crisp and the day too beautiful for people to kill each other. Just the same, word came that following a barrage to be directed against a canal we were to attack and take it. After the shells had chewed up the banks of the objective, the battalion went forward. As our platoon started to move, a fall of shells that ripped up the fields killed Pompey, Brooks and two new replacements. Clark, the supply sergeant, and Corwin, although seriously wounded, eventually recovered.

The channel of the canal was about twenty feet wide, but the banks, approximately thirty feet high, were at least a hundred yards apart and formed an ideal defense against tank and infantry attacks. Called the Mussolini Canal, it was one of the hot spots of the Anzio hell.

The project had been launched a few years before by Il Duce as a means of utilizing some of the Pontine Marshes for agricultural purposes. He had drained the swamps, helped to provide good machinery and livestock, built model farmhouses and settled loyal Fascist families in them. It was our privilege to eat their livestock and food and live in the houses until the Krautheads toppled them down on our ears.

One company of the battalion which fought its way across the canal ran into Krauthead self-propelled artillery pieces consisting of armored cars shooting 20 mm machine cannon, which we encountered there for the first time. With these guns they so shot up that company that thereafter we could walk through its ranks without seeing almost any of the old boys.

Our platoon settled down to outposting some strongly built Italian houses, spaced about three hundred yards apart, some distance up the canal on the enemy side. We put six men to a house. To draw an assignment in those houses, located six

97

hundred yards in front of the main lines, was the same as holding a lightning rod on a hill in an electrical storm. You could almost count on getting struck.

Our company had got off to a bad start in the battle of Anzio. A few days before we lost Brooks and Pompey, a foursome we called the "Air Raid Wardens" (because they woke us all up when they came in drunk), which included Bailey, Brooks, Dolan and Johnson, had made the prediction that none of them would come out of it alive. Bailey said, "Hell, they'll never stop sending us up 'til we are all dead. Every man in the 504th is doomed. We're a Legion of the Doomed. Look at Carlton, Olson, Oldring, Hastings and the Master Termite and all the rest. We're as good as dead, 'cause we're going up again, and all four of us'll get it this time.

"Drink up, Chet," he said to Brooks, "you won't be drinking long." The Wardens clanked bottles in somber acquiescence.

That night following Brooks' death, the old boys in the platoon at the suggestion of the Arab rounded up the gloomy Wardens to drink a toast to his memory.

Berkely had a quart of scotch he had won in a dice game. He held it at arm's length before him and said, "Here's to you, Brooks, old fellow," and then took a drink and passed it to the trooper next to him. Thus the bottle passed from one to the other of us until empty and each had made the toast nearest to his heart or that he happened to think of.

The three Wardens then prepared a special toast. They poured some Chianti into four small glasses, Bailey handed one of them to the Arab.

"Arab, here's a drink for Brooks. He always liked Chianti. When we finish our toast, throw the glass into the air as high as you can. Okay! Here's to you, Brooks, we won't be drinking long!"

The Arab said solemnly, "Brooks, we dedicate this comradely libation to thy spirit," and launched the glass skyward; the mournful Wardens watched it ascend and vanish from twilight into the upper darkness.

Someone produced a gallon jug of Chianta, which was soon emptied in toasts to Brooks, and then we returned pensively to our foxholes. . . .

Since it was still the first week of the invasion, naturally the big shots wanted to know what the Krautheads were doing. They called on Lt. Toland to take some men on patrol and find out. He was very much aggrieved and so were we that he had to leave his kitchen. But orders being orders, he chucked another pancake down his gullet and began to hunt us up.

The lieutenant found Berkely playing poker with three of the replacements who had money to lose and nabbed him. They found the Arab squatting on his heels trying to read a love story written in German and between words (the Arab was what the experts would call a "retarded reader" in the language) attending benevolently to a cup of heating coffee. He was now a squad sergeant, Berkely a platoon sergeant. He looked up inquiringly at them. Berkely pointed north. The Arab understood, sighed and put down his book.

Because of his utter fearlessness, tempered by good common sense in handling men and situations, Berkely had acquired the reputation of being the best noncom in the company. His keen brown eyes searched his friend's face.

"Do you feel like going?"

The Arab nodded and stood up.

Toland said, "Arab, we're going on a patrol. We're going to take five men besides us and go down to that road about 1,800 yards from here."

"What are we looking for, lieutenant?" the Arab asked.

"Arab, we're looking for trouble, any kind of trouble. We are taking a bazooka along. Maybe we'll ambush a tank or armored car. We leave at eight o'clock."

"Berkely," said the Arab after the officer left, "if a man hunts trouble with those truculent bastards, he'll find it. We'll go easy tonight."

The giant laid his hand on his shoulder in reply. Then they both grinned.

At eight o'clock, the Arab, Berkely, Casey, Duquesne, Pierson, Sheraton, Toland and I, all wearing dark clothes, stepped onto a road which about 1,800 yards distant ran into a main road leading straight to Rome on the left and toward Cassino on the right. Called Highway No. 6, it was a main supply artery for the enemy.

We moved silently down the little dark road into no man's land with the Arab and Berkely serving respectively as first and second scouts. I marched just ahead of Casey, who brought up the rear. We had progressed about 800 yards when the Arab stopped the patrol. From thirty yards away, in a small grove of trees, came the sound of picks and shovels striking the hard ground. We moved on, leaving the Kraut-heads to their digging. Casey soon stopped the patrol and his report, "Man following us," was whispered up the line to Toland. We tried to capture him, but he kept warily behind.

The panther-footed Arab halted the patrol when we were

1,700 yards into Krauthead land and but one hundred yards from Highway 6. Going on alone, he discovered well-dug holes on both sides of the road, with belts of machine gun ammo, jackets, shovels, and other German equipment. No guns were around, but it was apparent that the holes were being used inasmuch as straw was in the bottom of some of them and a telephone wire led away toward Highway 6 on the left. When Toland received the report, he instructed us to cut across the field to the left until we reached Highway 6. The Arab, with Berkely and the others trailing him, entered the field and sneaked toward it. They had advanced but a short distance when a guttural voice said in German, "Halt!" The Arab hit the ground and the rest of us followed suit. The order was repeated twice more, each time in a higher pitch, and then the man behind the voice opened fire. To our surprise no bullets came near us. Obviously someone else farther to the left was annoying the uneasy sentinel.

A brief battle started during which we wriggled into the deep ditch by the side of Highway 6. A tank opened fire on the beachhead from just over the road. We could see the powder ring flash outward from the muzzle. The powerful *whoosh* of the projectile passing overhead set our heads to ringing. A hundred yards to the left a truck drove up and unloaded a lot of men who went into the field and began to dig holes about fifty yards from us. The murmur of conversation, thud of shovels, and rattle of equipment were plainly audible. Dark figures could be seen moving about the field. The tank across the road clashed its gears and noisily moved to a new place from which to fire. At that moment one of the Germans digging in, hearkening, I conjectured, to a call from nature, left his group and had the bad luck to pass near the end of our patrol. Casey, tensely coiled like a great snake, enveloped him, slit his throat with his eleven-inch dagger and silently stretched him on the ground. "Casey cut one's throat! Casey cut one's throat!" went whispered up the line until it reached the Arab. The latter whispered, "I always feel safer on a patrol with Casey!" Berkely nodded.

Toland crawled up to Berkely and the Arab for a conference. The malicious Arab queried in a soft whisper, "Lieutenant, are we still looking for trouble?" Before Toland could reply a *sh-sh* came up the line. We heard the tramp of approaching hobnail boots and lay frozen in the ditch, our noses even with the top of the road, fearing someone would sneeze, cough or break wind. Berkely gripped a grenade and readied his rifle, the rest of us our tommy guns. Four soldiers walking in perfect cadence, one carrying a machine gun and the others machine gun ammo and machine pistols, hobnailed past us, the nearest within ten inches of our heads. They halted at the crossroads and sent up a flare that lit up the whole area. The fact that they used a flare so far behind their own lines made it evident that they knew a patrol had infiltrated their positions. Fortunately, a deep bend in the ditch shielded us from the light.

The three now resumed their deliberations in earnest. It was impossible for a patrol to be in a more critical position. We were entirely surrounded. If captured we would be executed, perhaps tortured first, because of their comrade's cut throat. After various counsels were whisperingly proposed and rejected, the wily Arab offered a stratagem well worthy of artful Ulysses. "They're looking for men sneaking back to the canal like whipped dogs and they'll stop anyone trying to sneak back. I think we ought to stomp down the damn road like we own it. They will mistake us for their own men long enough to challenge us, and while they're halting us we'll cut 'em down."

Toland agreed and said, "Okay, Arab! Lead off. We're right behind you."

The Arab led off, tommy gun pointing forward from his hip, and the rest of us followed four and three abreast so that our marching would resemble the cadenced pace of enemy troops. We German-stepped, our guts and saliva frozen, up the ditch road to a little bridge which we crossed and then continued down the main road till we reached the prepared positions. So far so good. The collectionist instincts of the Arab were pushing his hand toward a jacket in a foxhole, when Berkely tapped his shoulder and thumbed his attention across the ditch where the four aforementioned Nazi soldiers, one leaning on a machine gun, stood looking at us. Heads up, eyes slanted towards them, we clomped noisily on, trying to keep on dirt since rubbed heels on gravel don't sound the same as hobnails.

Our boldness had fooled them at this point. If we could make it past the woods where we had heard the enemy digging in, we could reasonably count on getting to the canal. Had they found the man Casey had killed? This was the question uppermost in our minds as we neared the spot. If they had, we could expect them to be more on the *qui vive* and more likely to cause trouble. My breathing almost stopped when a Krauthead left the wood and stepped onto the road. The Arab started to shoot but changed his mind and we kept stepping it off toward the canal, which we soon reached and crossed, our breasts bursting with excitement and thrilling

with exultation. By God, we'd done the kind of thing the
story books tell about! We shook each other's clammy hands
and kidded about the condition of our baggy pants.

As soon, however, as we were back in the houses, drinking coffee and opening some rations, our exhilaration changed
to exhaustion. We sagged in our chairs, our nerves limp, and
could do no better than sputter in aimless conversation. Only
Casey remained emotionally undisturbed, his feral eyes glowing a palish yellow in the firelight.

That night's doings of our patrol made the *Stars and Stripes*.

22. Duquesne Leads the Platoon on a Rampage

At one o'clock one cold, rainy morning our battalion with
the 2nd Battalion following, pushed across a little canal running at right angles to the Mussolini Canal and entered no
man's land. My company was the lead company and my platoon the lead platoon and Duquesne with six men (Gruening,
Big Rodgers, Larkin and three replacements) was the point
or lead man.

He headed off on a certain compass reading with orders
to kill every German that offered resistance. We never again
found it so easy to kill and capture Germans without suffering casualties ourselves as we did that night. They seemed
too dazed to fire except very spasmodically. It was a rare
opportunity compared to the rock-to-rock fighting we were
used to, and we made the most of it. Big Rodgers fired one
round into a hole and captured two Nazis. He shot another
who was sighting his gun at Finkelstein and then captured
him. Gruening, on the prowl like an old gray wolf, was fired
on from a foxhole and he tossed in a grenade that accounted
for two more. Duquesne shot two more who fired at him
from a pile of straw. The old lumberjack and his men shot
two motorcycle riders who came chugging up to the crossroads from the north after a brisk exchange of fire. Big
Rodgers saved his own life and that of the Arab by beating
an enemy who lay hidden in a ditch to the draw. Larkin
captured two Nazis and had a fist fight with each as he and
Wild Bill were marching them back.

A Sherman tank, which had come roaring up to see if we

needed help, swung its guns onto the top floor of a house where we had some Krautheads covered. The tank commander said, "Boys, that house is my meat and I'll tear it down for you." The first armor-piercing shell went clean through the house. When the second one hit it in the middle, a medley of voices yodeled *"Kamerad"* and twenty Germans swarmed out.

We knew we were surrounded, but from experience we also knew that we were too hot for the Krautheads to handle. We set up a circular defense in the ditches and little canals and dug in. Five tanks which had reached us were ranged about the crossroads ready to take on all comers.

When it became light enough to see, the boys sprawled behind their rifles, cuddled the stocks to their shoulders, and made bets as to who would get the first shot. A Czech-American named Sokal spotted the first Nazi, but his rifle being full of mud wouldn't shoot. Carey began to pot at him with a carbine. The Krauthead and his hidden buddy sprang up and dashed across the field. Carey, a rotten shot with a carbine, galloped after them, taking snap shots as he ran. One disappeared in a ditch, but the other fell on his knees and begged for mercy. Carey triumphantly prodded him back to us and we razzed him for being such a rotten shot that he had to run them down. The Arab told him he would certainly win a letter in track if he lived and went to college.

A tank commander spotted a 76.7 mm antitank gun sitting camouflaged near a house and with one round blew the breech block out of it. The Arab and his mortar gunner spied some helmets bobbing about three hundred yeards away in a ditch and let them have it. As the soldiers dived out of the ditch, our boys calmly rifle-potted them as they ran. It was still a one-way battle.

The Arab and Berkely, their nostrils swollen with the scent of combat, recruited Ciconte and waded down a canal to do some flanking. They stuck their heads up through some grass and discovered three 20 mm ack-ack emplacements about fifty yards away. The muzzles were depressed for use, but some parachute engineers apparently had the Krautheads convinced that it was better to remain in their emplacements. The Arab asked a lanky engineer how many of them there were.

"One bastard poked his head up and I put a slug through his helmet and I've seen no more," he said.

The Arab scrutinized the emplacements, noticing that the gun mounts were above the ground and curved up to the gun. He recalled a western story in which a cowboy ricocheted slugs off rocks into the villain's hide-out and killed him. The wily Arab began to bounce bullets off the curving mount into the gun pit. After eight rounds he let out a stentorian yell, *"Kameraden, heraus!"*

A pair of hands and a white face appeared followed in quick succession by twenty-nine others. The first captain, a young fellow with down on his cheeks, came up to the Arab and said in good English, "I am wounded." Blood was seeping out of his shoulder. The Arab thoughtfully acquired his pistol while an accommodating engineer lifted his binoculars. The engineers marched the prisoners away and Berkely, the Arab and Ciconte, well satisfied with their flanking maneuvers, returned to the platoon.

The 2nd Battalion leapfrogged through us on the way to an objective farther on and captured a complete company including the captain. As the battalion sat deployed in some ditches with the captured company under guard, the enemy began to lower the boom on them with heavy artillery. Men were being hit on all sides. A major called the German captain and ordered: "Fall your company in on that road and give them close order drill!"

The captain demurred because of the shells.

"You damn fool!" roared the major. "Drill them or die."

He made his company fall in and drilled them up and down in the midst of the shelling. The German artillery observer saw them and called off his guns.

One Company of the 2nd Battalion pushed across the level fields at a great pace popping off Krautheads en masse as they went and having everything their way until some tanks counterattacked them. Having no bazookas, and being too far in front to get protection from our own tanks, all the boys could do was lie in the ditches and hope for the best, which under such conditions nearly always turns out to be the worst. The enemy roared up in their Mark IV's and Mark V's and depressed the tank guns until they covered the sweating jokers in the ditches. A German opened the hatch on his tank, stuck his handsome blond head through it and grinned devilishly, said in English, "Come on out of those ditches, boys. The game is up." The Krautheads marched them away and we never saw any of them again. A trooper hidden beneath some brush saw the fifty of them captured and told us the story.

My platoon occupied the house where the smashed anti-tank gun was. In it we found eighteen Krauthead rifles, machine gun ammunition, mess kits, blankets, personal equipment, cheese in little metal tubes that squirted out like toothpaste, margarine, honey, a mess of cooked but still warm sausage and hamburger, dark brown bread, crackers so hard it took a bayonet to split them, and a mess of beef and potatoes still bubbling in the pot. We sat down, recalling that the spoils belong to the victor, and began to eat. It was a nervous meal, for the Germans, peeved and for good cause, were trying hard to lower the boom on our house. They were mad at everything and they laid it on. The front line on the northeast was only a few hundred yards away. Snipers potted at every man they saw and even shot at the doors of the house for luck.

In the back yard was a big half-truck still intact, containing blankets, a big, well-stocked modern medicine cabinet, boots, bolts of looted fine-woven cloth and an excellent little pipe which I secured for myself. Berkely, puzzled at first by the ten forward and reverse speeds, after crashing through a wall and backing over a small shed, finally succeeded in driving it down to the Company Command Post. With a flourish and a roar he stopped on a bridge just above the captain, who was huddled in a ditch. Right off the Krautheads began to shell the vehicle. The captain howled, "Move that thing the hell out of here."

Berkely, disappointed, drove it off and gave it to a supply man.

23. The Strangeness of Coincidence and of Toland's Foxholes

A platoon of our company which had dug in on our right flank several hundred yards to the east had just got settled when a terrific barrage of 88's shrieked in on them, killing one man and wounding four. Then on the heels of the barrage fourteen Nazis with machine pistols burping charged over the bank and pinned the whole platoon down. A hundred others followed the fast-shooting fourteen, now reduced to ten, thanks to the heroism of a trooper named Glutz, who died with his gun blazing, and to two other boys who succeeded in escaping.

An artillery officer named Jordan, who was directing fire from the second-story window of a house nearby the breakthrough, discovered a bunch of Nazis crawling into the yard through a hedge just beneath his window. He grabbed his telephone. "In thirty seconds fire concentration 52 and throw the book at it." Jordan dropped the phone, jumped out a back window and anteloped it to hell away, concentration 52 being the house he was in. He barely got out before the artillery fire leveled it.

Our platoon was chosen to go over and kick hell out of the Germans who made the break-through. We slid into a deep canal containing two feet of water and began to walk sloshingly down it, cussing the ice floating in it and the month of January every step we took. The muzzle blast of a tank sitting on the bridge behind us and firing over our heads knocked us to our knees each time it fired.

A little slim-faced, blond kid named Johnson, a recent replacement, slogged along in the ditch fairly close to Berkely. That morning he had given his partner, Alexander, five thousand lire, saying, "Today I'll get mine. I won't be needing this money, Ted. I want you to take this money and get stewed in Naples. I want you to take this money and spend it on yourself, and each drink you take have another one for your pal, and I'll be watching you do it." Alexander reluctantly took it.

Johnson was sloshing through the water, an arm's length behind Berkely. The tank fired a round that exploded when it accidentally hit a tree branch over our heads. A piece of shrapnel hit Johnson's neck and broke it. Another man took his bazooka and the column sloshed on. Berkely was knocked down and stunned. He walked a hundred yards before he knew what he was doing. My heart pinged as I looked at the little kid lying hunched up in the water, colored red by the diffusing blood, and I wanted to walk on the bank to keep from walking in it, but I couldn't. I recalled his prediction and pondered the strangeness of coincidence. Alexander carried out his instructions to the letter.

By the time we moved in to attack, the enemy, having had enough for one day, lit out for safer territory. It was raining and we had no raincoats; it was freezing and we had no dry clothes; we were hungry and our rations hadn't caught up with us; otherwise, we were living the life of Riley—whoever the hell that much-talked-of contented bastard was.

Officer Toland sat calmly by and watched the Arab and his mortar corporal energetically shovel out a large pit to sleep in and fire the mortar from. When they were finished and made a move toward settling down for the night, he spoke, "Arab, your hole is too far forward for mortar position. Tomorrow the Krautheads will pin you down with machine-gun fire from the notch in the canal bank so you can't fire the gun. You'd better take your men and move back two hundred yards and dig in again."

The Arab, totally worn out from burdens packed and holes excavated, recalled that Toland hadn't dug a hole for himself yet. He choked with rage and said, "Lieutenant, igod, why'd you sit there and watch us dig this damned cave if it was in the wrong place? It would take five hundred dollars to move me out of this hole if I were my own boss." The officer persisted and the fuming Arab, his fuming corporal and his fuming squad moved back a couple of hundred yards.

They dug in, named a guard and got settled down. Again officer Toland came and stood over the Arab. "Arab," he said, "tomorrow the Krautheads will pin you down with machine-gun fire from the notch in the canal bank. You ought to move farther back."

A hush like the quiet before a hurricane stuffed the atmosphere with destructive menace. Toland, sensing impending mutiny, hurriedly withdrew, but trailed a final sentence over his shoulder as he went. "You can stay there if you want to, but don't blame me if you can't move all day tomorrow."

"Move, hell. Who in the hell will want to move," snarled the corporal. "I could sleep for a week and I'm going to."

At daylight the squad fell asleep. At ten o'clock Berkely strode over and awoke the Arab. "The Krautheads have pulled back from the canal bank and we're moving up to it at eleven. You're not pinned down any more."

The Arab cast a jaundiced eye up at the giant and yelped malevolently, "But, dear, I wanna be pinned down, I wanna be pinned down, pinned down, down." The grinning squad took up the chant, "I wanna be pinned, pinned, pinned, I wanna be pinned down, down, down." The chant was loud enough to be heard by Toland, sitting snugly on the side of the Arab's ex-foxhole, eating some corn pork loaf.

24. By the Banks of Il Duce's Canal

The 1st and 2nd Battalions of the Legion moved up to the high banks of the Mussolini Canal and there they stayed until sixty-three long, weary days had passed. The Kraut-

heads sat up on the Alban Hills comfortably eating wieners
and sauerkraut, peering through their top-quality range
finders and spotting scopes, and at their leisure focused accurate fire at all points of the beachhead. We were surrounded
on three sides with the sea at our back. It was no unusual
thing for artillery men to fire a barrage west, then north and
finally swing their guns to fire due east. For the first time in
the Italian war there were no safe back areas. The rear
echeloners, who used to gloat because they had a gravy train,
were under heavy fire day and night from the biggest caliber
guns the Krautheads had: 150, 170, 210 and a larger caliber
gun nicknamed the Anzio Express. The front line (where a
man never felt safe) was about as safe as the beach. On our
infrequent trips to the rear to take a shower we were always
in a sweat to get back to the front line. We felt safer up
there, where we had to endure only machine gun, machine
pistol, rifle, mortar, small antitank gun, 75, 105, 88 and oc-
casional 150 and 170 mm fire. Infantry on the front line offered targets that were too scattered to be worth throwing
many extremely heavy shells.

The banks of the Mussolini Canal became the center of
intense earth-moving operations. We tunneled holes that
baffle description, and strangely enough we never did get
through digging. A joker would dig five feet and be content
until a mortar or 88 barrage tore holes all around. Then he
would sink his hole down to six and after the next barrage
to seven and so on till an artesian well stopped him. Finally
he would drag up heavy timbers, cunningly erect a roof and
shovel dirt on it.

We set up a platoon headquarters in one of a group of
three houses which were about three hundred yards from
the Mussolini Canal. The squad leaders set up housekeeping
in the other two. By day most of the men stayed in the houses,
leaving a strong outpost to watch out for surprise assaults.
Old gray-headed Duquesne, on approaching his house for the
first time, inspected it with a critical eye. No prospective
renter could have scrutinized its advantages or disadvantages
more closely. He pounded his fist into the mattresses to see
if they were soft; surveyed the burnable fences and doors;
looked over the dairy herd like a discerning cattleman and
then appointed competent chore boys to feed and milk them;
gazing humid-eyed and moist-lipped at the flock of plump lay-
ing hens; searched and found tubs of lard and barrels of flour.
Only then, these many things done, did provident Duquesne
move his men in and take over.

Duquesne summoned an old peasant still living in the

house to come to the henyard. Pulling his 45, he calmly shot the head off a fat hen and informed the stupified old fellow that he wanted it for breakfast at eight next morning. Next he found three bushels of potatoes which had escaped detection on the first scrutiny and set his eager jokers to work peeling them for supper. Lovable Duquesne knew how to enjoy life and get the most out of any situation. But luck could be against him.

For example, while he was solemnly lecturing his satellites on the proper distribution of eggs, the correct manner in which to parboil an old hen, and instructing Sokal to feed the chickens, gather the eggs and guard against chicken thieves from other squads, a basket of eggs from 88's fell on the estate. When it was over, Sokal investigated and returned to report in a choked voice that a shell had landed in the henyard and that but one solitary hen, with most of her feathers blown off, had survived. Chicken feathers, entrails, feet and heads were scattered over twenty square yards. The old soldier's swearing was colossal, adequate, and to the point. Tears flooded his eyes as he shook his fist northward at the inconsiderate bastards who had wrecked his poultry yard.

Casey and Big Rodgers carried a hind quarter of a cow into the house which Winters bossed. Meekly and timidly Rodgers explained that a shell had killed the cow and that they hated to see good meat wasted. In a few seconds jokers covered the bleeding carcass like jackals and in ten minutes late-comers were scraping the bones. T. L. spent considerable time cleaning his 45 that night. . .

Of all those days spent on Anzio, which filled our minds with gruesome images, our hearts with death, and sandpapered the din of mechanized battle into our tangled nerves, I retain but one set of tranquilly contrasting remembrances.

Among forty Italians occupying one of the large houses was a sixteen-year-old girl whose pure, noble, sweet face evoked the artist's representation of the Madonna. She conducted nightly religious services for her people. The ragged mob, obviously inspired and soothed by her calm dulcet voice, drank in the words she read from a prayer book and repeated them after her. When the shells whined over the house or exploded nearby, her voice grew firmer whereas that of the listeners hushed to a frightened murmur.

Any hard, crude paratroopers, for whom religious sentiment was something mysterious or meaningless, who happened to be present during her services removed their helmets or woolen caps and sat looking silently and sadly at the floor. Newcomers erupting into the room, immediately captured by the atmosphere of piously hungry sincerity, removed their helmets and stood their tools of war in a corner.

We looked upon her with a reverence foreign to our natures. We made licentious remarks but never about her. I think that she brought to our minds the face of a younger sister or sweetheart whom we might never see again. As long as we lived those days of crowded terror on Anzio we revered her as a symbol and connecting link to another world and another way of life.

Our front line outposts being as much as two hundred yards apart, the Krautheads, armed with machine pistols, easily passed through our lines at night and prowled unmolested for hours. Our front positions were so well camouflaged that they ran into them only by accident. If the two or three men on an outpost detected a twenty-man patrol, they let them pass but telephoned the information to a small reserve of tommy gunners located back a few hundred yards, who would sally forth to shoot it out.

It must have been very disconcerting and was certainly misleading to the enemy to prowl behind our lines for an hour and find nobody. When enemy patrols returned to their company commander and reported that the line was weakly held, a counterattack took place at the presumed weak spot. They came storming over almost every day and were always surprised when the boys rose out of their gopher-hole hiding places and scattered the ground with them. In a few weeks they held us in healthy respect. We captured a Krauthead once who complained about us in very flattering fashion, "We've got plenty of men and equipment," he said, "and we're full of fight and we don't mind tangling with most Americans, but you *verdammt* people are crazy. On that attack last week our patrols reported beforehand that only a handful held that line and we called on our artillery and then attacked. From somewhere you mowed us down and wiped us out by scores. Our dead filled six ambulances. We don't mind fighting the regular infantry so much, but deliver us from those devils in baggy pants. You don't fight a fair war."

The shellfire competed with the rain in dependable frequency. We came to take both for granted. On waking up in the morning the Arab would look over at the Alban Hills and comment, "The bastards shelled us six times yesterday and the 1st Special Service Force on our right seventeen times. We are way behind and ought to get our share today." Or, "They poled in twenty-one separate barrages on our positions yesterday and slighted B Company, which got only nineteen. They'll even up the score today." Or, "They blew the roof off our house yesterday killing two men and three of our milk cows. Today they'll shell Gonzalez' house."

When we weren't being shelled or attacking or repelling attacks we watched the aerial activity over the beachhead, particularly the harbor. The 99th Negro Fighter Squadron, known as the Flying Mustangs, had at that time some of the hottest pilots in the Mediterranean theater. We delighted in seeing them in operation. At night the enemy dropped long-burning brilliant parachute flares over the harbor. Night after night we watched the awesomely spectacular fireworks and shivered at the sight of burning planes falling to the earth or into the sea.

We felt naked and defenseless, with our lives dependent largely on luck. The soldiering skill which stood us in such good stead at Salerno, Volturno and Cassino could do little for us at Anzio. In one of his poems Victor Hugo describes the futile efforts of Cain to escape the accusing and punishing eye of the Creator. It was equally useless for us to try to hide from the evil eyes of the Alban Hills.

25.   Nine Hundred Nazis Came Marching

Some of us had just returned to our houses for a breakfast of "blowout patches" (pancakes), steak (cows died regularly in shellfire) and coffee, after a night spent on outpost duty. I was reaching for my cup when a terrific screaming and exploding of shells brought me to my feet. Berkely ran in breathless and exhorted, "Run like hell to the canal bank; the Krautheads are only two hundred yards from it." We grabbed our guns and loped out of the house putting on our belts as we ran.

Artillery shells bigger than any we'd yet dodged were falling with amazing rapidity, sending up mighty geysers of dirt, spraying shrapnel high and wide and leaving holes big enough to hide jeeps. I'd rather have taken a chance on swimming the Niagara above the falls than to run through that barrage to the canal bank. Halfway across a shell thundered close enough to knock me down. My right hip, leg and foot went numb. Concussion numbed it, I suppose, for it got all right after I massaged it. I managed somehow to hobble across the canal to my outpost hole. How in quadruple-hinged hell we managed to get to our outposts without losing a man is a mystery.

By the time I reached my outpost position Berkely, Casey, Finkelstein, Wild Bill, the Big Polack, Parsons and Sheraton were already in theirs. Duquesne, Gruening, Pierson, Winters, Luciano, Bledsoe and others were ready with machine guns on the rear bank in case of a break-through. The mortar corporal, also in a rear position, sat by his mortar awaiting fire orders from the Arab.

I looked over into the level plain that led to the little town of Cozano. What I saw still remains the most vivid recollection I have of the entire war. Four or five hundred yards away, marching steadily forward in four broad skirmish lines, with an interval of twenty feet between each line, came approximately nine hundred Nazis. Their bright metal belt buckles glimmering in the sunlight, high soft-polished jack boots and gray-green uniforms contrasted strikingly with the brown fields behind and in front of them. Noncoms or officers giving orders in loud, guttural-bradded tones, walked just in front of each wave to keep it in perfect alignment. The gray-green uniforms, geometrically massed for attack, an unheard-of tactic in World War II, continued to advance toward us across the meadow. My reaction was one of absolute amazement—and wounded pride. To think that the Nazis could have the brazen effrontery and suicidal stupidity to attack *us, us, us,* who feared nothing on earth or in hell, in any such manner! I guess we had about the same feeling a lion would have if assaulted by a rabbit gone crazy.

The foolhardiness of such an attack was inconceivable. Although numerically strong, well disciplined, backed by plenty of artillery, brave and willing to die, they were deliberately marching into the never-give resistance and deadly fire of men armed with machine guns and automatic weapons, who could call on forty-eight artillery pieces from the 3rd Division, a battalion of 4.2 mortars, their own parachute pack howitzers and battalion mortars.

For a time, then, we were so petrified by astonishment that no one moved or fired a shot. Our inaction was of short duration, however. We began to pour a devastating mortar, rifle and machine-gun fire into their ranks, which they reformed without pause over the bodies of their dead and wounded. The voices of their officers giving orders rose above the lulls in the firing. The powerful, stubborn, brave gray-green mass moved on inexorably.

Berkely's machine gun mowed them down until it got so

hot he couldn't touch it. Casey took less than his usual me-
thodical aim, sure of scoring a hit anyway. Wild Bill, Honky-
tonk Sheraton, Parsons and the Big Polack burped their
automatic weapons with veteran efficiency. None of us heeded
any longer the continuing barrage of enemy explosive. Hypno-
tized to murdering action, we all fired with deadly precision
at the iron-nerved, obedient men walking across the field to
the certain death of sheep following the leader to the slaugh-
ter pen.

Only a minute or so passed before a tremendous volley of
shells poured into the Krautheads like a waterspout. Forty-
eight guns, plus mortars and tank guns, dropped an arsenal
into their ranks. A shell exploded in every five yards of the
enemy formation. It seemed that not even a fly or cockroach
could survive in that hell of shrapnel. Down to the left in
front of the 2nd Platoon, the first wave broke into a trot
and then into a run, leaning forward as it went. I saw men
fall and others run forward who in turn spun round and fell
on them.

The 2nd Platoon boys were having the battle of their
lives. Moore's rifle smoked in his hands. Fox, the best rifle
shot in the battalion, saw a big Krauthead lead his squad
out of a ditch, turn around, and wave to the others to follow.
For a moment the big man stood motionless, and then with a
spasmodic fling of his arm threw his rifle far over his head,
spun on his heel and toppled to the ground. The troopers
killed all who staggered through the dark swirling horror of
that shell hell.

In ten minutes nearly every enemy soldier participating
in that brave, foolhardy attack lay on that brown meadow
shattered or ripped or decapitated or torn in half.

A tanker guner could see the helmet of the Arab bob up
and down as he, short pipe in mouth, observed for his mortar. The enemy gunner, who had already killed two of our
boys, set his sights on Homer's disciple. Presently he crashed
a shell into the bank that knocked him out cold. But when
Casey crawled up the bank to have a look, he found the groggy, dazed Arab placidly smoking his pipe with his eyes closed.

Pierson, who had already had a phenomenal run of good
luck, was the next man the Krauthead turned his gun on. The
shell lifted him to the top of the hole, mangled his automatic
rifle beyond repair, and left him dazed, shocked, pale and
dusty but otherwise unhurt. He lay in the pit for forty minutes just staring at the walls. For once Pierson had nothing to
say. Even to this time his narrow escapes were the talk of the
Legion.

Berkely seeing a squad intent on escape, swung his gun and smoked up 250 rounds on the hapless running, diving, crawling, rolling enemy soldiers. The Arab, now observing from a spot farther up the canal bank amid some briars, thought he was in a safe spot. The Krautheads made a thirty-yard error in leveling eight rounds of 170 mm stuff on Berkely's machine gun, with the result that it thundered just behind the Arab, cutting briars all around him. He felt a tingling in the little finger of his left hand. Soon a tiny trickle of blood began to flow. "A briar scratch and nothing more," he thought. But no! A shell fragment or dislodged rock had lacerated his fingernail. Grinning he loped down to Berkely: "Mother, kiss it and make it well. I got a purple heart at last."

In disdain the giant wound six yards of bandage around the scratch and kicked the Arab's buttocks.

We had won the battle, but had paid the price. Bailey, Dolan and Johnson, the three surviving Air Raid Wardens, got it that morning. Bailey's toast to Johnson, "Drink up, Chet, you won't be drinking long," had achieved its tragic significance. A 47 mm tank gun shot a lieutenant's head completely off his shoulders. Judson, chosen to go home on rotation, and his buddy H. D. Rodgers killed by his side, his tommy gun blown to bits and his binoculars broken, but escaped untouched and made it to the States. Lowry, although wounded in six places, made it home and recovered. In all, thirteen comrades paid for our victory with white crosses and seventeen others went to the hospital.

26. "Our Day" on the Anzio Beachhead

The average soldier, much less a civilian, can form little concept of the scope of a battle. For us it was the part we were mixed up in. Over a large area little scraps are taking place with men suffering, fearing and dying in them, and the loosely connected little scraps taken together constitute a battle. The war, to the dogface dodging mortar shells, is concentrated on him. He judges the nature of combat by his own relation to it. Thus battle becomes a very personal thing. If he gets killed, the war is over; if he lives, the war goes on. It becomes personally important therefore to the front line infantryman that the war for him continue! He will not cease to be in it until he is either dead or seriously incapacitated. War gets to be the one permanent value in his being. After one or two battles time comes to mean nothing. A day may seem longer than a week, a month or even a year. He divides time into two parts: before entering the war and after engaging in battle. The only time-point that has meaning exists in the brief intermissions between battles. I think I aged as much in ten days on Hill 1205 as I would in ten years of civilian life. Any veteran who fought six or seven campaigns in the infantry will know what I mean.

A typical day for an infantryman, the Arab for example, on Anzio went about like this:

Before daylight he is awakened in his hole in the bank by a fall of mortar shells. They shoot out their shrapnel like tentacles feeling just for him and nose into the surrounding dirt like a giant barking hound. After digging ten or fifteen holes around him the enemy mortar man stops probably for breakfast and the joker lies and trembles until daylight. Then he gets out and starts toward a house after some coffee. On the way he is shot at three times by a sniper in a church tower three hundred yards away. He dives into the house and makes himself a cup of coffee, but before he can drink it a shell blows off a corner. Just the same he finished his coffee and starts back to his hole. Halfway across the field he runs into a bevy of screaming-in 88's.

He is lucky enough to make it to a small ditch that runs through the field. The shells land on all sides and one covers him up with dirt. With his knees knocking, he barrels into his dugout and lies there chain smoking. It is now quiet outside, so he decides to write a letter home: "Dear Mom: I am well and in pretty good circumstances considering. Don't worry about me. I'll make out okay." He writes a little more, but he has said the important thing. Details would bother her and besides the officer would delete them. He grimaces at his promise to make out okay. Jim Smith, who promised his mother the same thing, got a fragment in his guts last night and he isn't any safer than Jim Smith.

He picks up his rifle and field glasses and goes over to an observation post to have a look-see. He slides into a hole with a buddy. While they are smoking and beating their gums, an enemy tank gunner throws in a shell to get the range and then begins to level in air-bursts timed to explode above the holes. Shrapnel rains obliquely into the banks above theirs. Sizable pieces even ring off their helmets, but neither is hurt. The gunner moves his aim thirty yards up the canal and lets go another volley of thunderclaps. The shells continue to burst farther away, but they are too wise to feel safe. The bastard may backtrack. . . .

As he scurries back the Arab wonders why he ever left his dugout in the first place. He decides to take a nap. Being a squad leader, he has a field telephone in his burrow. It rings and he recognizes Carey's voice: "Mac, I hate to tell you this, but I thought you'd want to know. Jernigan and McDonald got a direct hit on their hole awhile ago. Both dead'ern a mackerel." The Arab puts down the telephone, pulls out a fag and blows smoke slowly at the side of the dugout. He recalls the time he got drunk with Jernigan in Atlanta and that McDonald is an only child. He met his mother once. The poor woman's heart would be broken. Then his thoughts become dull, apathetic, wooden. He thinks of the Krautheads and without getting up a sweat about it, promises to take it out of somebody's hide if he lives long enough. To take his mind out of the present, the Arab pulls out his Homer and rereads the passage in the Iliad describing the sacking of Troy.

The joker gets hungrier. He is always hungry. He drags a supper ration off the shelf of his dugout. Although he knows the lettering on the box by heart, he reads it again to pass the time. He even counts the words that begin with M and then those that begin with N. He pries the end off the box with his bayonet, tears the waxed paper off the crackers, surveys the corn pork loaf with hatred, and puts the stick of stale gum and small chocolate bar in his jacket pocket to chew on outpost that night. As he starts to eat, a bevy of shells rings his dugout and contracts his stomach. His expert ear detects from the ringing stamp of the explosion that they are 88's. No longer hungry, he peers out to see how close they came. Two holes just twenty-five yards away give him the shivers. He munches the crackers slowly in his salivaless mouth and stares straight ahead with the vacant expression of a cow.

Toward dark, the Arab goes over to platoon C to see if a *Stars and Stripes* has arrived. A barrage of 20 mm fire from armored cars escorts him in. Inside, he leans his gun in the corner, lights a cigarette and leans over a buddy's shoulder to look at Mauldin's cartoon. He looks at it and grins in sardonic approval. He likes Bill Mauldin. They speak the same language. The buddy looks up at the bearded Arab and says, "You old reprobate, how you doing?" He grins back, "Oh, so so. You guys got any of that chicken left you stole from Big Nose?" "Hell no! Casey ate the whole damn platter and has gone to steal some more!"

He steps from the house and looks around. To the south the darkness is punctured by a series of rapid flashes. Our artillery, to avoid easy spotting, has learned to fire twenty or thirty guns by one order. As he looks, the enemy begins to use counter battery on the guns. Heavy shells whine over his head. As he turns to go into the house, he hears a shell bearing his number. Flashes of light blind him; the concussion deafens him. Red spots float up and down in his eyes. He gropes for the door and stumbles in over his buddies who are just getting off the floor. They ask him how close they were. "So damned close they knocked me down." The Arab smokes a cigarette. Then when it burns down he lights another from the butt. His rusty hands tremble. He feels cold all over. Casey brings him a sip of coffee. He drinks it and lights another cigarette.

The Arab gets his rifle and takes his squad down to the canal bank. Our shells are still falling in enemy positions. A mile down the line he hears an MG 42 cut loose and listens attentively to the long bursts. Then he and his five men talk over their outpost. He puts two men in each of the two holes on the bank and he and the fifth man occupy one slightly to the rear. After a while the Arab goes up to relieve one of the other men so he can come down and smoke. The relieved man relieves another man and so on until all have had a chance to relax.

A cold rain begins to fall through the tar-black night. The rear hole, having a roof over it, provides more protection and warmth than the front ones, which have to be open since there is nothing between them and the enemy. The Arab takes a raincoat to a joker who has none and relieves him for a while so that he can return to the rear hole, get under some blankets and warm up. In the front position, he can't wear gloves because he has to keep his trigger hand unencumbered. To do so, he sticks it successively under his raincoat, jacket, sweater, shirt, undershirt and finally under his armpit, the only place where it always thaws out. Then he pulls it out to get cold again.

The Arab has been on outpost one hour; it seems like a week. He pulls out his chocolate bar, breaks it in half, and splits with his pardner. They munch slowly, prolonging the action of their jaws and taste ducts. They don't want to get through too quick and have nothing to do. He then takes out the stick of gum and splits it too. Later his buddy will share his chocolate and gum.

The Arab, his sharp senses vibrating for danger signals, visits the boys in the front holes.

"Okay, boys?" he whispers.

"Yeah, we're okay. I like the damned rain. It saves me the trouble of washing my face."

They feel each other's grin.

A nervous Nazi sends up a flare which illuminates the soupy field in front of them. An MG 42 begins to stutter; long, looping tracers pass thirty yards to the right. Usually when the enemy sends up a flare it can be taken to mean that none of his own patrols are out. But the cunning Arab, knowing only too well from experience that it could have been a blind, does not temper his vigilance.

The circular flash of mortar fire crouches them in their holes. The shells explode fifty yards behind. The Arab lines his compass on the flashes, gets the approximate reading, goes down to the telephone and whistles into it. A voice answers: "This is Charlie Three, what ya want, Mac?"

"Homer, that mortar again, same location. Those misbegotten sons of bitches are playing with it again."

"Okay, Mac, we'll have it shelled again for you. Is it still raining?"

The Arab snorts his answer. He lights his pipe under a blanket, hoping the smoke will warm it up, but it only makes him cough. At eleven he starts to climb out of his hole, but a shell falling into the canal thirty yards behind tumbles him back. When he finally sets out again to relieve a man in second hole, he has to walk sideways through the wind-blown rain. It is darker than ever. He reflects that such a night is ideal for an enemy patrol wishing to penetrate the lines, take prisoners or simply butcher the boys in their holes. The troopers finger the neat rows of hand grenades lying in front of them; each one holds one in his hand. Their guns are handy. By now they are soaked through and through. "Somewhere in the world," the Arab reflects, "there are people who sleep in warm beds. They do not know, do not wish to know and will probably never know how we lived." The thought makes him sad but not acid bitter. The Arab is a philosopher.

The mortar flashes fourteen times. From the bottom of the hole they can see the blinding flashes of shells plunging into the earth all around them. One is almost a direct hit. The Arab, spitting poison every leap, races to the telephone and contacts Charlie Three. He snarls: "What in the goddamned, hammered-down hinges of hell are you son of a bitching goldbricks doing back there? You promised to put artillery fire on that dam' mortar. He almost put one in our lap a minute ago."

The joker at Charlie Three drones soothingly: "Now, Mac,

don't get hot under the collar. We're cooking up some steak for you boys when you come in and we got a pot of coffee on the stove. As soon as we' re done, we'll lower the dam' Kraut-head line a whole foot."

"Okay," growls the mollified Arab, "but be dam' sure you send our relief out on time. It's twenty to twelve and it takes time to get out here." He hangs the phone up and climbs up to tell the boys about the steak and coffee.

The minutes drag by on lead weights. The closer relief, the leadier they hang. They damn a Krauthead gunner to hell for a million years who just for luck fires a long burst of bullets that flick past their heads with a little popping sound. Artillery shells begin to pound bridge No. 5 two hundred yards back. They duck just to be on the safe side but so clumsily that the bank of their hole breaks loose and tumbles on them in a muddy mass.

Twelve o'clock finds them clawing out of the cold, cling-ing mass as Duquesne and his men slither up to the out-post on the dot. Since the old gray head is in a bad mood, they take off for their house without tarrying to visit. More-over, they don't want to visit. Before they reach the house, they have to hug the ground a few times to let the shrapnel from a bunch of mortar shells whine over them.

Carey and Toland, who are sitting by the stove, move aside so that they can warm up. They sit on benches and soak up the heat, cigarettes dangling from the corner of their mouths and with identical harsh, bold, hard, firm lines on all their faces. For the moment their minds are blank. The heat thaws the unconscious weariness riding their shoulders. Their heads droop. By the dim light of candle and the splinter of firelight seeping through a crack in the stove, they look like brothers.

They drink the black, bitter coffee and chew the steaks slowly to savor each bite like a rare luxury. The Arab picks up a paper and by the candlelight reads about a congressman who wants to limit overseas duty to eighteen months. "Some son of one wanting to curry political favor with the dogfaces. Only this and nothing more," comments the Arab as he throws down the paper. They go to their dugouts. The Arab crawls into his, gets under the blankets and tries to sleep. He can't. Dark shadows dance beneath his eyelids; he feels like he is sitting on a slope watching molten lava race down to cover him. For hours he lies open-eyed, smoking one cigarette after the other, staring into the black. Finally he falls asleep cer-tain of but one thing: tomorrow today would be yesterday.

27. Life in Reserve at Anzio!

One morning we were told that the company was going into reserve about a mile and a half behind the front line. On scrutinizing the maps we saw that we would be very near to the artillery, which took a hell of a pounding from enemy big stuff. Many of us bitched long and viciously because we preferred the battle up front to shells in the rear. It was the only time in the war we didn't especially care about being sent back from the front. But what we thought didn't matter. We went into reserve and that was that.

The houses that were supposed to be waiting for us turned out to be mirages in the rain. We found some holes half full of mud and water along a secondary canal running into the Mussolini Canal and tried to bed down midst doleful laments and vicious profanity. Gruening's tongue was bouncing vitriolic words off his leathery gums as he pawed around in the mud looking for his missing raincoat. Finkelstein found a little square of canvas on the ground and handed it to him. Gruening fell into a muddy hole while trying to put it on and had to be helped out. He vituperated the great-grand-mother of every brass hat since the battle of Waterloo.

Sheraton, Pierson, Duquesne, Carey, the Arab, Brownell and I went beneath the arch of a nearby bridge, climbed upon the level strip of soil next to the bank foundation, put down our blankets, spread a shelter half over us and were taking a smoke when Berkely came down to tell us he had found a shed. We preferred to stay where we were.

Shells were falling all around the bridge and a few into the canal under it, but being beneath the heavy concrete arch, we felt rather safe until a kill-joy engineer gave us the bad news. "I hate to tell you jokers this," he said, "but there are 1,600 pounds of dynamite with the fuse set ready to blow up this bridge if the Krautheads break through. It's down among the piers where the shells are landing. If they hit the dam' stuff, there wouldn't be a greasy spot left of you guys."

Sheraton and Pierson left precipitately for safer places. "Hell," we thought, "if they hit it, we'll never know it." We

120

slept therefore the sound sleep of the don't-give-a-damn on that powder keg until long after daylight.

On the afternoon of the second day of our reserve status the platoon jokers had a weapons inspection out in an open field which the Krautheads had the habit of shelling whenever they saw as much as one man. Thirty of us lined up in three ranks, snapped to attention, and stood fully exposed to their malevolent gaze while Toland carefully inspected each gun. We were ripe for an artillery target, yet there we stood for a dam' trifling inspection. It was a miracle every damned one of us didn't get sausaged.

We had moved into a house after the first night. To keep us from relaxing, however, they made us pick up tin cans and paper boxes and even talked of giving us close order drill. To amuse or make us mad, nice young, inexperienced shavetails gave us lectures on scouting and patroling. Well, we listened to it part of the time because we had to, but spent our other hours carving foot-long steaks off some unlucky cow, making coffee, playing poker on credit, talking about whisky and women or just ribbing one another.

A good kid from Delaware, who had been with us since Hill 1205, still believed, in spite of his associations with a bunch of roughnecks and the horrors of war, that people were good to know and could be trusted and taken at their word. We resolved one day to set him straight about the ways of the world by brown-nosing him out of a box of chocolate bars his mother had sent him. First the artful Arab came up to him and spoke winged words of beguiling kindness; "Mortimer, I have developed a great affection for you. You're the sort of lad I'd want for a son. You're the open-hearted, generous sort of joker that makes the American soldier well thought of all over the world today."

The Arab then patted the sleek-jawed kid on the shoulder and went to sit in a corner, obviously spiderwebbed in meditations.

Duquesne wandered in and gazed affectionately at the lad: "Mortimer, I said to Lopez here, the day you got wit us, I said, that is a fine litle joker, a credit to the troops. Mortimer, if I got anything you need, let me know."

After a ten-minute lull, Berkely came in: "I just thought I'd tell you, Mortimer, that I'm gonna have you made PFC. You're a damned good dogface, though little, scurvy, and light in the conk."

Much amazed and gratified, the little joker dug up his box of candy from beneath the straw: "Jokers, have some candy bars. I am among friends. I'm in the best platoon in the 504.

Here, take two." With extravagant praise, the lusty jokers shared the candy until it was gone. Then, Sokal, who was in on the joke, asked for another bar.

"Sorry, it's all gone," Mortimer replied.

"Why, you one-way, half-witted, ignorant, scurvy bastard!" yelped Sokal. "Keeping all that candy to yourself. Igod! That I should have to go into battle with a such a depraved nitwit."

And the Arab sadly said, "Mortimer, I had hopes for you. I knew that you were a selfish, hardhearted little scrub, but I didn't know you ain't fit to live with us."

Duquesne: "I been in the damned army nine years and I never saw a guy as one-way as you. Don't ever ask me fer nuthin' . . . I'm through with you."

Berkely: "And I was gonna make a joker like you a PFC!" And he stomped out shaking his head.

Mortimer looked at the stony-eyed troopers with incredulous dismay flooding his little face. How people could manifest such friendship and appreciation for generosity one minute and then insult him the next because he had nothing more to give them was without the orbit of his experience and comprehension. He sat in dejection, disillusion and despair sagging his eyes, as he meditated on the perfidy of man.

In two hours, however, a procession filed into the little room: Sokal put down a package of cookies; the Arab opened a carton of cigarettes; Duquesne tore the paper off a box of candy; and Berkely opened a box full of fruit cake. The jokers laughed at the look on his face as they filled up his musette bag and stuffed his pockets to overflowing, Mortimer was riveted to the floor, filled with a great peace. He knew that he really belonged in the most exclusive fraternity in the world. And he did become a PFC.

We got many replacements, all fine boys with strength of mules and the ignorance of old maids. We pitied the scared, bewildered, shy, eager youngsters who acted awestruck around us old boys. We felt sad when it became our duty to lead them into battle, because a large percentage of them got killed before they learned how to woo the narrow percentage of safety accorded by lady luck to discerning and sagacious warriors. They would die in the damndest ways: One would trip over a mine and get a leg blown off; another would shoot himself or get shot accidentally, a third would let his foxhole cave in and smother him. And in the first battle they usually died in heaps. I must say though that those who didn't get it the first time wised up, husbanded their chances like the rest of us, and soon acquired the sixth sense so present, yet so intangible, in all veteran soldiers. Although the veterans died separately and not in bunches as replacements often did, they too would in time ride out the law of averages and go west in spite of the best of soldiering.

My platoon managed to find space in the house for its new men. Seven young replacements in another platoon, unable to find room in the house, had taken up residence in a strawstack in a shed covered with a straw roof. One day I strolled by, recognized the danger they were in, and advised them, since the ground was too marshy for trenches, to erect dirt-covered log bunkers on top of the ground as a shelter against flying shrapnel. Filled with the bravado born of ignorance, the youngsters didn't think the danger justified the trouble and continued to make coffee and be homesick. The next afternoon a mortar shell crashed through the thatched roof.

On hearing the explosion, we rushed out of our house and ran to them. They lay dying around the gasoline stove, their fourteen legs scattered all over the shed. Of all the gruesome images etched in my mental cells after 340 days of front line combat this was the most horrible and the most pathetic.

Later I went out to a strawstack adjoining the shed to get some stuffings for my bed. A stolid, solid, unimaginative trooper who was trying to match the amputated legs with the owner bodies, was engaging in a weird monologue which went as follows:

"Let's see now, this is a size eight boot for the right foot. Yeah, it fits him. Cut off at the same place. Here's his left foot. Now what about this blond kid? His leg is missing at the knee. No, this'n don't fit.... I'll try this leg ... no, it don't fit. Good, it matches. Hell, I can't find this guy's foot. Oh, it's under the straw. Well, that's a dam' good pair of boots to bury on a man. Poor devil, he deserves them though. One more kid now? Yeah, that's right."

As I listened to his stream of consciousness, I began to pull straw from the side of the stack. Something slippery and sticky came off it. Then I observed that blood clung to the straw in drops like rain to leaves and that the sunlight turned each drop into the likeness of a ruby. I got my straw elsewhere.

Sokal and I emerged with shining faces and feeling uncommonly clean from the shower tent set up down in the town of Nettuno. Sokal wriggled into his clean drawers with a bashful air. "Igod, Mac, I feel like a sixteen-year-old after his first kiss. Let's go find a drink ... we ain't had one lately, you know."

As we shagged up the battered street, the tantalizing aroma

of food exuding from a big building still unroofed, set our nostrils to vibrating and we followed to it. We addressed discreet inquiries to a big staff sergeant leaning against a beat-up lamppost. "Sergeant, reckon a pore starved dogface would rate a handout from the mess sergeant? These intercoursing K rations get old." He nodded us in.

The deep-voiced, calm-demeanored, leonine-headed sergeant had the daredevil job of exploding duds and time bombs. As we ate he told us about it.

"It takes a natural-born gambler to get in this outfit. When a bomb is dropped and don't go off, they send for us. The guy whose turn it is to take one apart takes a telephone with him to the job. He crawls into the hole with it and looks at the fuse. He phones what he is gonna do first to the man back out of danger. Then he describes the fuse in it. He says, 'I am going to turn this little thing to the left.' He turns it. He then says, 'I'm going to take off this little so and so, meanwhile describing it.' He does so. If it goes off, the other jokers will know how far he got toward dismantling the fuse before he was blown up. The next bomb with a fuse of the same type should be a little easier to handle because of the little already known about the previous one. But the Krautheads rig up new type fuses all the time and they drop the dam' bombs so they won't explode just to try to get us to disarm them. If we touch the fuse, we are blown all to hell. Tricky bastards, those Krautheads. They get some of us now and then. It is my turn to disarm the next dud . . . a man never knows what will happen when he messes with a bomb."

At that moment a great noise, comparable to that of a freight train downhilling it round a bend, jarred us into the gutter.

"What the hell was that?" we inquired in weak voices.

"Oh, that was the Anzio Express coming in on time. They send one over every fifteen minutes. We're used to it. Don't let it upset you. Would you care for a Camel?"

We clipped our thanks and regrets at leaving so soon to phrases shortened to exclamatory briefness and fled that town as if ten thousand fleas were on our tails. To hell with getting clean in the future and mooching chow from crazy dud shell exploders! Give us nice deep dugouts and rain and mud and 88's and enemy patrols.

28. Farewell to Italy

From latrine to latrine, house to house, room to room, outpost to outpost, man to man, the rumor flew. Each hearer
wound his own string of details round the ball of the uncon-
firmed which rounded faster that the Mademoiselle from
Armentières.

First joker: "I heard a man say who talked with a man
who happened to be eavesdropping behind the sergeant major's
house that he heard Major Oppenheimer say that the colonel
says that our days in Italy are about over. No, I can't confirm
all this because it was passed on to me."

Second joker: "A joker in the 2nd Battalion told me that
he talked with a guy who had seen some papers in regimental
headquarters stating that the 504 is due to leave Anzio for
Naples pretty soon. From Naples we sail for England, maybe
the States."

Third joker: "I talked with a joker who is company clerk
for H Company and he told me that his captain was called
up to regimental headquarters to talk with Tucker. He is
going to have the advance details sent to England, so we're
bound to be going soon."

We cursed the rumors, but we listened all the same. It was
like believing in Santa Claus when we were getting a little
too old to put much faith in him.

The rumor began to turn into something solid when the
old man informed us the next day that we were to go down
to the beach that very night. Rejoicing grew faster than the
rumor had. If we could live another day or so, we would have
beat the rap! Our bones would not bleach in Italy and we
would get to see England. There was a great creaking of
vertebrae as men straightened up their shoulders for the first
time in weeks. A few rum basses burst into song. Thoughts
of back pay and Neapolitan fleshpots began to dim the horrors
and hardships of sixty-three days of Anzio.

Some of the jokers couldn't wait to celebrate. Shelton
made a liquid dynamite out of half a gallon of 180-proof
medical alcohol weakly diluted with synthetic orange juice
powder, sugar and water. In ten minutes Sheraton, the Arab

Smith and the drink's concocter were lying in a corner as white as ghosts with no sign of blood in their usually ruddy faces. It was just as well. They didn't hear the farewell barrage the Krautheads threw in so that the boys could have a final sweat and dodge before leaving the beachhead.

When darkness came, we lightheartedly picked our way across the fields to a road where transportation was waiting for us. Each stride, like a flat wheel on a train coach, beat a joyful rhythm—not the *I got socks, I want socks* of the Arab's Big Polack—which seemed to fit the words: "Leaving Anzio, leaving Anzio, leaving Italy, leaving Anzio." We piled off the trucks on the beach and rolled up in our blankets. Many alternating sad and happy thoughts crowded my mind as I lay smoking under the starry sky. Carlton, Oldring, Hastings, the Master Termite, Olson, the Air Raid Wardens, and many others in our company, merry and solid companions in celebration and tribulations, could not go with us. Through the smile of chance the majority of the old boys in my platoon had survived. I took confidence in the knowledge that scattered about me in pleasant sleep were Berkely, Duquesne, Gruening, Finkelstein, T. L. Rodgers, Casey, the Arab, Carey alias Homer, Pierson, Sheraton, Wild Bill McMurtry, Nixon and others. I felt proud to be the comrade of such men and proud to be a veteran of Company C, 1st Battalion, 504 Parachute Infantry of the 82nd Airborne Division.

When I awakened, the rising sun was sparkling on the thick frost crust on my blankets. Tin cup in hand I walked over to a transportation company mess hall and solicited a cup of coffee. I stepped and breathed to the tune of "We're leaving Anzio today, we're leaving Anzio today." And I must have smiled it into communicative meaning as I drank my coffee. Anyway some joker began to beef. "Oh, I wish I were a paratrooper! You guys fight a few days at a time and then you get relieved. You guys are the glamour boys of the damned army. You didn't fight much. Hell, I see you loafing about Naples most of the time. Igod! And you draw fifty dollars extra a month for it too!"

As I recall the incident, I cannot understand how I kept from batting in his teeth with the butt of my rifle. I scowled and stalked out, calling like a stationmaster as I went: "Sicily, Salerno, Shrapnel Pass, Plains of Naples, the Volturno, Cassino and sixty-three days on Anzio. Now go goof your gums on a clam, you silly bastard!"

As we loaded on the LST, new arrivals would comment, "How do those jokers rate a trip to England? Did they screw up on the front? Maybe they are being sent back for more training. Who in the hell are they to leave us here to fight the dam' war? We have fought two weeks on this beachhead, and no relief in sight. Why should they leave and us stay?"

A veteran 3rd Division man called the shot: "Jokers, quit beating your gums. That is the 504th Parachute Infantry leaving the beachhead. They got more combat than you got time in the army. They killed more Krautheads than you could add up with an adding machine. Be quiet or one of them hellers'll bat you in the teeth." Pacified, we filed onto the ship and settled down for the trip to Naples through the glorious Tyrrhenian Sea.

For two golden weeks we loafed in the spring sunshine of Naples, which, now that we were leaving it, radiated cultural charm and civilized *Gemütlichkeit* whose existence we had not even suspected. Some of us made the rounds of the museums, cathedrals and other points visited by tourists in peacetime. It was disconsoling to reflect on the gap separating what man had done and could do from what, in spite of his science and so-called progress, he was doing. I recalled how stupid I considered one of my professors who held passionately to the view that scientific progress in itself did not offer a solution to the human problem. Now I speculated, after living in the metallic hell of mechanized warfare diabolically contrived at great expense by scientific wizards the world over, that technological progress as used to date had probably retarded as much as it had advanced the real possibilities of western civilization.

But to front line men confronted with violent death in battle, the cultural manifestations of a society offer attractions incomparably inferior to those of the bar and the brothel. Most of us sailed away from Europe with no knowledge of what it really was. Some day I would like to return to pay homage to their monuments, artistic achievements and great men.

On a sunny morning we fell out, shined, polished, clean and neat, to receive Mark Clark's farewell. The tall lanky general, calm in voice and cool in action, spoke to us over a loudspeaker as we stood in formation in a large square. I cannot quote him verbatim, but what he said went something like this:

Men of the 504th combat team, you have fought for long months in the bloodiest battles of the Italian campaign to date. You have acquitted yourselves superbly. There is no better regiment in any army in the world than your regiment. I salute you. Now you are leaving my command to rejoin your division in England. Your division is proud of you, will be proud to have you back with them. Farewell and good luck." If Mark Clark should happen to read these words and they are not correct, I offer my apologies. What he said was well spoken and pleased us all the more because we esteemed him.

A few days later we marched aboard the *Dunbar Castle*, sister ship of the ill-fated *Morro Castle*, and soon were steaming towards England.

29.   A Pound a Week

The good ship *Dunbar Castle*, escorted by sleek British and Canadian destroyers, rocked us toward England through the blue waters of the Mediterranean. Aboard were superbly disciplined tall, lean, dry-skinned, powerfully built Scotch, Irish and Coldstream Guards, wearing standard British battle dress which they always kept neat and spotless, making the long voyage home after five or six years' service for the King in the far corners of the world.

By contrast the troopers resembled a mob of pirates. Nearly all of us, dressed in anything from fatigues to tan jump suits, wore a handle-bar mustache and shuffled around with a pistol or knife or both swinging on our shoulder or hip. I am certain that, in modern times, a more desperate-looking gang of ruffians had not sailed on a British ship.

The British Guardsmen, knowing us to be one of the crack regiments of the American Army, surveyed us with undisguised amazement and curiosity. To them discipline was an important factor in war and if we had any they couldn't put their finger on it. When they questioned us about the matter, they got an unsatisfactory answer which was phrased approximately as follows:

"Hell, yes, Colonel Tucker and I get along fine. He is just one of the boys. When Old Rube tells us to go out and kill off some Krautheads, we go out and kill 'em off for him. He tells us to kill some: he don't say how. He leaves the way of doing it up to us and we go out and do it. He is a hard old joker to get along with but he stands up for our rights and we fight like hell for him. Yeah, we salute our officers cause we're in the dam' army, but most officers in the Legion don't give a damn whether they're saluted or not. Discipline, hell yes, we got it, but not the lady-laced kind! We'd obey Old Reuben if he told us to jump into hell. What you mean . . . we ain't got discipline? We got more discipline than we need!" The British joker would walk away trying to puzzle out what made us a fighting outfit.

Early in May we pulled up to a dock in Liverpool. When all of us rushed over to the dockside of the ship to have a look, the ship titled. The British colonel pleaded with us to spread our weight to the other side to keep her from capsizing. We didn't hear or do a thing until Colonel Tucker grabbed the loud-speaker. When he said "Spread," we spread because for the colonel we always maintained the kind of discipline which only his kind of leadership can inspire.

It was a thrill to march down the gangplank and set foot on the soil of my ancestors. My parents had often expressed the desire to visit the Isles. Now I could at least write them a firsthand account of how they appeared and try to make allowances for the distortions of war by the discerning use of my imagination. I wondered from what port my forebear Thomas Carter, who reached Virginia in 1650, could have sailed. It could have been Liverpool. Idle thoughts.

We threw our "A" and "B" bags into trucks, but kept our guns, bedrolls and field bags. At strict attention we marched up the street, proud of our outfit and proud of ourselves, to a railway station. There we lightheartedly stowed our equipment aboard a crack British passenger train which we rode all night. At daylight we piled off at a quiet country rail stop to the tune of the division song, "We're all Americans and proud to be. We are the soldiers of liberty," played by the 82nd Airborne band. Generals Ridgeway and Gavin and hundreds of others were present to welcome us back. There was rejoicing on all sides, because the rest of the division was as proud of us as we were of ourselves! We all had a big head.

Exhilaration lifted our steps high as we marched the two miles to our quarters, consisting of tents already erected for us, at Camp Stoughton, Leicestershire, England. We relished the piping hot breakfast ready for us and went to sleep flooded by wonderful feelings of relaxation and anticipation of things to come.

After the stony slopes of the Italian mountains, green England seemed a paradise. The adjacent golf course, the hedges, shrubs, grasses, trees, flowers, vegetables and grains, all sporting different shades of green, enchanted us as did the cool climate. We didn't mind the rain pattering down on our tents in England, whereas in the water-filled foxholes of Italy we longed for Needles, California, at two P.M. in July.

When the British girls in Leicester and adjoining towns learned that one of the crack outfits of the American Army was close by and that we hadn't kissed an English-speaking girl since 1943, they moved in on us like Dakota grasshoppers on a garden patch in a drouth year. The sweet, rosy-cheeked darlings swamped to the confines of our camp by bicycle, pony cart, taxi, and on foot, and hung over the fence to sheep's-eye us. The guard around the fences had to be doubled to prevent our leaping them and taking off before class "A" uniforms could be found for us. We drooled, pawed the ground and shook the fences.

Finally we got bright new uniforms and swept through the gates. Wild Bill Murtry rode off in a pony cart with both arms around a spicy blonde and his toe in the pony's rump. Casey chose a big gal on a man-sized bicycle and pedaled away with her on the handle bars. Duquesne and Gruening piled into a taxi with two raw-boned flesh-pots whom they ditched when they got to Leicester in favor of beer and ale.

In due time, however, the old gray head fell for a girl he called "Jelly" and set up a *ménage à deux* somewhere in the city. I think he promised her every log in New England. One night when I made the rounds with them she talked about trees and logs and lumber in a vocabulary English-accented and army-spiced until I nearly split laughing. "What's so bloody funny, Yank? Duquesne and I have plans!" And I think they did. In later days and battles, we heard as much about "Jelly" as we once did about the beloved Master Termite's "Angel." Gruening changed women several times, but not because he necessarily wanted to. He just couldn't interest them in the New York Central!

Pierson and Sheraton drew a couple of luscious shakes and were getting into their taxi when Larkin decided to horn in. He kayoed both of them and invited Finkelstein to help him handle the situation.

Winters, Nixon, Brownell, Carey and the Arab licked their dry chops, clacked their parched tongues against their arid palates and decided liquids for the moment were more to their liking than caresses. T. L. Rodgers, himself a teetotaler, went along to look after them.

Berkely and I seeing no particular reason to specialize on drinks or women, decided on both but with beer and gin getting top priority. In the pub we agreed to try to date the first two women we saw on the street. We were successful and both thought we had made conquests of the two most beautiful ladies in England until we began to sober up. The beverages had conferred on the damsels the same kind of beautiful perfections that Don Quixote's chivalrous idealism had on the ugly country wench he called Dulcinea del Toboso. As the alcohol loosened its grip, observation of my lady led me to discreet inquiries about her age and past history. She blushed and blurped, "Why you blooming bloody Yank, I'm thirty-nine. I've got five children!"

Berkely took stock of his faded out, muddy-haired and foam-complexioned blonde, pondered seriously for a moment and commented, "Mac, it is getting late, very late, and we'd better get back to camp."

We pulled the same stunt once again and got stuck. After that we decided not to go out together, both convinced that we jinxed each other in things amorous.

We did many scabby things in England, for which I apologize to any Britisher who happens to read this narrative, but none scabbier than giving the scabies, commonly called the red itch, to the citizens of Leicester and environs. Almost every man in the 504th had caught it in Italy. Inasmuch as we would have to spend a week or two of our precious time in quarantine if the battalion and regimental surgeons learned about it, we enjoined our platoons medics under dire threats of retribution not to mention the matter.

They agreed, having scabies themselves and wanting to go to town as badly as we did. Since the itch didn't show plainly on our hands and necks, we could hobnob undetected with the innocent British people. We gave it to the British girls, who in turn gave it to their friends and families. I confess that it was an amusing thing to watch the young chicks surreptitiously giving themselves a dig in the flanks, or slyly scratching a shapely leg, or innocently giving their bosoms a scrape with their nails, never suspecting that we understood their plight only too well and scratched ourselves discreetly and indiscreetly when the opportunity offered. It was a filthy trick to play on the chicks, but I do believe that they'd rather have had the itch than have us shut up in quarantine.

Finally after the British had already got the itch we told the medics about our plight and a great battle was launched against the bugs. They didn't quarantine us now that the British had it too. Those of us who got well of it in a hurry expertly examined our prospective dates for itch symptoms, but in spite of precautions many caught it back from their victims. We were having an itching good time in Ye Merrie Olde England.

The mayor of Leicester had welcomed the coming of the

Legion, but in a few days I am certain he regretted his show of
hospitality. The truth of the matter is that we conducted ourselves like uncouth barbarians. Africa, plus the campaigns in
Sicily and Italy, had dissolved most of the thin veneer that
civilization spreads over the instincts. The boys simply went
wild in England and didn't give two hoots in hell what they
said or did. It is so easy to imagine how disconcerting it must
have been for the British, who have the custom of drinking
a pint or so of beer in an entire evening, meantime playing a
friendly game of darts and beating their gums in a mild way,
to behold the unsophisticated and inconsiderate exuberance of
our boys as they poured into the pubs, took over tables, which
they covered with twenty pints of beer, and invited all present
to drink, particularly the girls. They frequently started arguments which ended in tipped-over tables and spilled beer. The
scowling pub keeper would scurry over brandishing a mop
with a martial air and scrub the floor while the jokers stood by
waiting to sit down again. If he ordered them out, they
laughed at him and sometimes broke glasses which they paid
for, but in good-natured condescension.

Not all of our boys were so rude or got drunk every night,
but enough of them were and did to give many Britishers the
impression that we were a mob of cloutish rubes. I can understand why we acted as we did, but can neither condone
or justify it.

Within six weeks, pregnant women began to flock into
the regimental personnel section, wanting the erring jokers
to marry them or at least to make an allotment of a pound
a week for sixteen years for the upbringing of the ripening
love fruit. At the end of sixteen years, the youngster would
presumably be large enough to forage for its own living.

The erring lovers roared and bellowed at the thought of
being penalized financially over so long a time for what
they regarded as a trifling matter. "Little jokers," said the
wayward expectant fathers, "are born every day into this
hard world! England needs citizens so why all the hue and
cry. The nation should be grateful, not indignant!"

Bullom's coming fatherhood inspired the gleeful poets of
the platoon to disapear for an entire evening. Next morning
the results of their labors appeared on the company bulletin
board. I cannot remember the entire poem, but the punch
line at the end of each verse was: "For he's got the pound
a week blues."

Once he was happy, but now he's forlorn,
Now he's a pappy and we laugh him to scorn,

Soon he'll be a daddy, with diapers to do,
Once he was Lochinvar and his wants were few,
Now Bullom, O Bullom, why are you so blue?
Maybe it's 'cause you got those 'Pound a week blues'?
Yes, he's got those pound a week, pound a week,
Yes, he's got those pound a week blues.

He'll pay 'til he's a pauper, he'll pay all his life,
For a short minute of pleasure, he'll sign away his life,
Lawdy, lawdy, has he got, yes, he's got, man he's got
Those pound a week, weekly pound, a pound a week blues.
Those pound a week, pound a week blues. Pore man, for
He's got those pound a week, pound a week blues.

Bullom was a devil, with the women would be
A son of a gun was he.
Until he met a virgin both pure and elite
And now he's got the pound a week,
Pound a week, yes, pound a week blues.
Lawdy, lawdy, Bullom's got, yes he's got his just dues
His pound, his heavy pound, his pound a week blues.

Bullom went wild as a knob hare when he read the poem on
the bulletin board. But many who laughed at him laughed
bitter laughs. They too had erred and had to spend their share
of time sweating and meditating about pre-and postnatal
sons and daughters. They were learning that the seeds of love,
even for soldiers, could bear bitter fruits.

30. Big Rodger's Socks

The rest honeymoon did not last long. D-Day was already long
in the making when we reached England and naturally experienced soldiers such as we could not expect to be left out of
some phase of it. T. L. Rodgers and twenty-four more of our
boys volunteered for detached service in Normandy. We
gravely shook hands with the giant, a gnawing anxiety chewing
into our gizzards. Big Rodgers was more than just a member
of the platoon. He was a staunch pillar in our ranks both
morally and physically. He radiated a quiet encouragement

that sustained our confidence. In battle he manifested a courage that translated itself into deeds and a bulwark of security for us all. When on outpost or patrol duty with him, I always had the feeling that things were well in hand.

"Be careful, T. L.," I said.

He hesitated as was his custom before answering: "I'll be as careful as I can, Ross, but I may not be careful enough this time." Then he left us.

That evening we drank several bottles of ale and we toasted Big Rodgers on every bottle.

The 504th hadn't made a jump since Salerno. That was a long time to go without jumping. To me while still on the ground and out of sight of a plane or a parachute, a jump always seemed an impossible thing. The night preceding it we lay on our cots and sweated it out. I felt petrified by that wide yawning door, the swift-flowing ground, the tense wait until the chute opened. But next morning at the airport standing in front of the planes and the piles of parachutes, I felt that a jump was not an unreasonable thing at all. Then when the plane soared aloft, the terrifying impression of being trapped, an emotion verging on panic, gripped me. As usual I resorted to the reassurances of self talk. "It is simple. All I have to do is hop out the damned door. I have a good chute, good nerve, a good body and my buddies will jump with me. I can do it. It is simple." And now my time comes to leap through. For a second I feel the cold lash of the propeller blast in my face, then start falling, my body hunched into a knot, waiting, breathless, waiting for that vibrant jerk on my shoulders and legs. When it comes and I look up at the silk umbrella with gratitude, I feel the glow of beatific happiness. On the ground I head, sweating, beaming, in excellent morale, convinced that nothing is better than jumping and being a paratrooper, for the assembly point where I find the rest of the boys feeling happy too because they had also vindicated their reputations as men of steel and solid nerves.

The training schedule began to gather momentum after the jump, which was followed by several others. We did calisthenics, close and extended order drills, and drills with bayonets, mortars, rifles and hand grenades, pistols, tommy guns, automatic rifles, and machine guns. From short hikes of five miles we gradually toughened up to a forty mile one. Scouting, patrolling and map reading were emphasized and applied practically on large scale maneuvers. Little by little as the summer wore on our bodies got tough in spite of drunks, women and ornery carousing.

In the meanwhile D-Day, June 6, 1944, had come and gone.

Early that morning I heard thunderous roars, lifted my tent flap and saw hundreds of planes heading for Normandy. The scene brought sober reflections and reminiscences of our take-off in Sicily. No one knew better than we what lay ahead. I spent the day and night in nervous agitation, my mind filled with battle images and anxious speculations. I feared the worst for Big Rodgers and our other buddies. My fears were justified. Of the twenty-five, seventeen were killed, including Big Rodgers.

The news of T. L.'s passing rolled gloom through the platoon thicker than London fog. At the same time, we felt the elevation of spirit that comes with the confirmation of trust well placed. The giant had given a good account of himself. According to the reports we received, he slew forty Germans at the Eglise Ste. Mère before he went west. It had always been my personal hope to die fighting, if it were my destiny to die in battle, by T. L.'s side, surrounded by Berkely, the Arab, Duquesne, Casey, Gruening and the other stalwarts of the platoon. Perhaps if we too had volunteered and gone with him, we might have saved his life. I felt a certain sense of guilt and so did Berkely and many of the rest of us. Berkely, the Arab, Guitry, Duquesne, Winters, Gruening, Casey and I vowed to take terrible vengeance. Thereafter we never took a drink without toasting his spirit and his spot marked by the white cross somewhere in Normandy. If a man ever merited the DSC, it was T. L. Rodgers.

After he died a package arrived from his mother. Among its contents were several pairs of fine woolen socks. We distributed them among us and reserved them to wear only in battle. When we wore his socks, we had the feeling that Big Rodgers was with us in body as well as in spirit and could participate personally in his revenge. Oldring, Hastings, Carlton, Olson, the Master Termite, Big Rodgers, the Air Raid Wardens, etc., etc. The invisible members of our platoon nearly equaled the visible.

31. Take-off Eve

The battle of France continued to go in our favor. The fortunes of war had rolled on from Caen through Paris toward

Strasbourg and the Rhine. False rumor first had it that our
82nd would jump behind the Siegfried line in support of Patton's armored drive. Then we were briefed and prepared to
jump at Tournai, Belgium, ahead of the British Second Army
to seize canals and hold bridges. But at the last minute it was
called off. Finally our number came out, as indeed it eventually must, from the urn of chance: Holland.

Field Marshal Montgomery's 21st Army Group, already
through Belgium, was crashing on into Holland. The master
plan called for three airborne divisions to land simultaneously
and to grab all the important canal bridges, the huge bridges
over the Rhine at Arnheim and its Maas Waal branch at
Nijmegen and many smaller bridges. The Siegfried line ended
on the other side of this network of canals and rivers. If we
were successful in seizing the bridges, the British 2nd Army
would be in a position to break through to us and could then
dash on across the level country toward Berlin. It was a
masterly plan.

The 101st Airborne Division was to jump about thirty miles
and the 82nd Airborne fifty-seven in front of the British 2nd
Army. The British Airborne "Red Devil" division was to
jump eight miles farther inland from us and grab the Big
Bridge across the Rhine at Arnheim.

The 82nd was to grab an important bridge at Grave and in
addition to several others the big one at Nijmegen.

The men of the 504th had the specific task of taking the
bridge at Grave. If one of our regiments failed in its assignment, the entire division mission would be jeopardized inasmuch as the various objectives complemented each other. The
regiment missions were further subdivided into battalion and
company missions. My company was to jump about half a
mile from our bridge, assemble into platoons, the platoons into
the company which would then move toward the bridge and
seize it. The jump was to take place about one thirty in the
afternoon, Sunday, September 17, 1944.

We all studied maps, sand tables, aerial photographs, and
were given the usual briefiings and last-minute checks to see
that every man had all his battle equipment. In addition to the
usual jump load, we were to carry one or more grenades popu-
larly called gammon grenades. These gadgets, filled with from
one to three pounds of high explosive, detonated on contact
and were powerful enough to blow the roof off a house. We
called them "hand artillery" because they made a flash and
noise like a 155 shell.

As we sat in our tents at the airport, we recalled the pleasant
days at Camp Stoughton and particularly the poignancy of

farewell kisses and embraces. We took it for granted that many of us would never return.

The usual days of strained waiting finally shriveled into hours. It was ten o'clock. The eight of us lay on our cots, sometimes going several minutes without speaking but thinking the same thought: Tomorrow night at this hour some of us will be dead. Who will it be?

The Arab drawled in his easy, unhurried manner, "It is a dam' good thing I've read the first chapter of Hemingway's *Short Stories*. Now I can build a fire with that chapter. If I read fast enough, I can tear out and burn the pages as I go along to keep the fire going to read by so that I can tear out more pages. That's the way I've been living; burning my pages behind me. This Hemingway is a good writer. You guys want me to read to you? No, well, you are a gang of no good, illiterate bastards. You'll need to know about Hemingway tomorrow when we take the bridge. Igod, that a bridge should be so damned important!"

Sokal chuckled from his cot and threw a burnt-out fag into the muddy flood. "Arab, don't forget we're gonna break virgin Butler in tomorrow. You'd better heave that book away and give 'im a pep talk."

Butler thrust a scrawny chin out of his sack. "Tomorrow I'm gonna take the bridge by me lonesome. To hell wit you, Sokal." Butler, a dandy lad full of zip and tabasco, had been assigned to our platoon to replace the Big Polack, who had been wounded seriously enough on Anzio to get a medical discharge.

The following dialogue erupted between Gruening and Duquesne.

Duquesne: "Right now, next to a ride on the New York Central, nothing would please me better than a hug and kiss from Jelly and a bottle of beer for my thirsty belly. How do you like that poetry, choo choo train?"

Gruening: "It stinks worse than your damned feet. Why don't you stick them through the tent flap and follow them out? You smelled sweat-logged lumberjacks so long, that you don't hurt one bit when you brown-nose."

Duquesne: "Brown nose, hell! You've rammed it so much on the New York Central the top of it looks like a sausage!"

Gruening: "Ah, tie off that goddamned fungus-coated, beer-stinking tongue of yours so I can get some sleep."

Duquesne: "How can I sleep lying here thinking about my head resting on Jelly's soft belly!"

Gruening: "Jelly's soft belly, hell! It's got callouses and you didn't put 'em on it."

Duquesne: "Now, Gruening, that ain't no way to talk about the woman I'm going to marry. She's a lady. She's not like that easy-make you fell for. Jelly's got refinement and taste. That's why she chose me."

Gruening: "You go to hell!"

For a while the tent was silent.

Casey's love affair with a young widow in Leicester had mellowed him to the letter-writing stage. Larkin, who had kept his distance since the time Casey took him out in the desert and stomped him, watched him write, apparently with great difficulty, and commented, "Casey, why don't you boil it down to a few four-letter words such as . . . ?"

Casey pointed to the door. Larkin grinned: "Later. I don't want to miss this trip!" Casey nodded.

Berkely, who had some last-minute information, came in with Wild Bill, Sheraton, Pierson and Nixon. As he talked, Sheraton twirled Gruening's New York Central watch chain, which Berkely, as was his custom, unconsciously appropriated.

"Arab," said the giant, "how many of you are wearing Rodgers' socks?"

"Gruening, Duquesne, Guitry, Casey, Finkelstein, Winters, Carter and I," he said.

"Okay! Remember, boys, tomorrow we're fighting for Big Rodgers in addition to just fighting!"

They went out and we lay thinking of Big Rodgers.

The voice of Finkelstein cut through the darkness. "Jokers, it is a hell of a deal. We all want out of this damned mission . . . yet if any one of us got the chance to stay behind, he would bitch up a storm. It all proves that we ain't got good sense."

32.   We Jumped at One Thirty

Seated in the planes like grim steel-trap-jawed automatons, all softness, smiles and good humor vanished from our faces, we waited for the newest episode to unfold into the desperate bloody action that would take place in a matter of hours. The armada of planes representing the biggest airborne drop in history circled and roared and then formed into long curving

formations that darkened the sky for hundreds of miles. It was
ten A.M. We jumped at one thirty.

The good days were gone. Many of us would never see
England again. As we roared over the cities and countryside
the stouthearted citizens waved to us from fields, streets and
housetops. The thought that we were ridding them of the
dreadful buzz bombs added strength to our purpose. Soon the
cheerless waters of the North Sea swam into sight beneath us.

Most of us sat quietly and smoked cigarettes, trying as best
we could to confine our reflections and mental images within
the vacuum of nothingness. But in spite of my efforts I thought
of *after* the jump and *before* the jump, but did succeed in bar-
ring the jump itself from my conscious speculation. I let myself think of being *shot at*, but not of being *shot and hit*. I
knew that in that direction lurked cowardice and indecision. I
thought of the enemy and the damage I would do him, but of
his ability to wound and possibly kill me I wouldn't permit myself to think. Imagination given free play could ruin a man
under such tensions; therefore I kept tight reins on mine.

The drowned coast of Holland came into view. As we flew
over the front, I tried to picture the dismay of the Krautheads
at the sight of our armada which certainly must be drilling
doubt into their stubborn hearts. I knew them too well from
hand-to-hand experience, however, to let myself hope that
seeing us pass overhead in such numbers would be enough in
itself to make them stop fighting.

Before long we began to fly over the inundated area. Except
for ack-ack guns, set on the few dry spots, and the tops of
houses and windmills, there was no evidence of life or of the
regions of former prosperity in the desolate expanse of sad
waters. After we had left the Zuider Zee behind us, our formations began to draw plenty of ack-ack. Some of our fighter
planes, diving down to spray the winking semicontinuous
flashes of enemy guns, folded in the air like shot quail and fell
in flame and smoke. A shell rocked us. My God! To sit like
clay pigeons at attention in the belly of our big-tailed bird and
be shot at! I wanted to jump, to be on the ground. In the
plane it was *take* and I wanted to *give*. I wanted out so bad
that I would have jumped with a red-hot stove in my arms. I
had an intense horror of dying a futile death. If I had to go in
this war, I wanted to go giving a good account of myself.
Another ack-ack shook us.

"Ten minutes left to fly!" The crew chief was calm.

Two long minutes bogged their seconds through the tension
in our boiling brains. Each second wound our nerves a little

tighter. If we didn't jump soon, they'd uncoil and mess up like the spring in an overwound watch.

"Stand up and hook up!"

I was to be the last man out. If we were hit, I was sure to go down with the plane. Damn my luck! In Sicily I was the second man. The parachute, tommy gun, eleven magazines of 45 ammo, antitank mine, hand grenades, sleeping bag, ration-filled musette bag and other items gripped and strangled and oppressed. My breath came in short gasps. God! would they never start jumping?

We flew by Grave. The line began to shuffle up to the door. Everything fine. No more ack-ack. Then Peterson jammed his rifle crosswise in the door. His delayed jump threw the rest of us off balance and slowed us up. As I released my static line I turned to look at the crew chief standing teacup-eyed and hang-jawed in the tail of the plane. The whimsical reflection, "What in the hell is he scared of? He's not gonna jump," accompanied me falling, turning, twisting, waiting and hoping into space. Then I felt the snap-up pull of the opening chute and looked up gratefully at the billowing green silk.

The sputtering crackle of a fast-firing machine gun evoked the thought that because Peterson got jammed in the door I would fall much closer than the others to our objective. I gripped my tommy gun and looked down with the intention of trying to get a line-up on the terrain. Terrain hell! I was falling right into the middle of a lake that appeared to be about two hundred yards wide. I began a desperate manhandling of the chute risers with my aim set on the left bank. Right up to the edge, I thought that I would inevitably fall into that water and drown. The possibility of being the victim of such worthless luck embittered and angered me. I no more wanted my life wasted in a pond than I did in a transport plane. But chance had been with me. In a second I freed myself from the chute and was ready for battle.

A forest of evergreens, the tallest not over fifteen feet, had cushioned my fall and now provided protection. I got the direction of the bridge by observing the planes' line of flight. Then I pushed through the conifers until I came to a trail. A careful scrutiny of my position convinced me that the company would follow the trail toward the bridge. Since I was closest to it, I constituted myself as an advance outpost to guard against ambush and impatiently waited for my buddies.

33. The Bridge Blew Up in Our Face

The first to arrive was Berkely, who came waddling through the bushes with the awkwardness of a fat bear. We shook hands. The boys dribbled down the trail in twos and threes until the company was together. Nearly everyone had had a good jump. Within fifteen minutes after falling into Holland we were on the way to the bridge.

Soon we emerged from the comfortable cover of evergreens and hurried over mostly open country toward our objective. We were within five hundred yards of it when a tremendous explosion lifted the bridge high into the air and scattered it over a wide area. A few of us got bruised by the flying debris.

Weiner, the successor to Toland, had allowed himself to be pinned down by machine-gun fire. Casey, one of a small group with the lieutenant, spied an enemy across the canal hiding behind a low stone post. He shot him in the foot. As the wounded man squirmed, he bulged from behind the post much too small to conceal him. Casey shot him in the knee, in the rump and finally in the belly.

After destroying the bridge the Germans set up a stout defense in its ruins. With the intention of relieving the pressure on Wiener, Casey and Feroni, Berkely started to lead the platoon across an open space to the right of the demolished bridge, but got pinned down in a small ditch by machine-gun fire which shot a box af ammo out of his hand, put two bullets through Pierson's boot heel, and one through Sokal's arm just below the elbow.

The remainder of the battalion had seized their bridges intact though not without casualties. One company lost eight noncoms. Inasmuch as our objective had been blown up, it was pointless to risk our lives in daylight on the level terrain which could be machine-gunned from several directions. So we lay in the ditch and waited for darkness.

Any time some joker moving in the ditch shook the briars or bushes machine gunners trimmed them to stubs. Dusquesne and Gruening, feeling frisky, amused themselves by crawling up and down, shaking everything movable as they went, in order to draw fire deliberately. Then the laughing jokers lay flat on their backs to watch the banks get mowed. The MG 42 was located in a grove of trees across the canal, but we never succeeded in spotting it.

When darkness came, the company moved into a wood near the blown-up bridge. We put out sentries, sent out patrols and dug in for the night. Relative quietness settled down over the immediate countryside. Soon the rising moon burnished a mellow luster onto the trees and blown-up ruins. Later a patrol from the 505th, which had had one hell of a battle judging by the gunfire, contacted us from the other side of the bridge. The battle picture at midnight of our first day in Holland was roughly this: A sister company was a mile to our left, battalion headquarters a mile to the rear. The Red Devils were seizing the bridge at Arnheim; the 101st was holding the roads to our rear, awaiting the British break-through. The 82nd had taken and was retaining all of its objectives except the important bridge across the Mass Waal River at Nijmegen.

The next day we moved up the canal in the direction of Nijmegen with orders to attack bridge 10. The enemy had pulled out, however, by the time we reached it. As we set up a defense, the citizens thronged about us in such numbers that they interfered with the traffic. Oldsters, youngsters, fat women and plump girls formed a queue to greet us. We would pause in our defense arrangements, shake hands all around, and start back to work. But we barely had time to put in a mincing lick before another queue stood smiling and hospitably eager to press our palms. They further jeopardized defense preparations by stuffing our bellies with pears, apples, sandwiches, cakes, milk and beer.

Finally gray-headed Duquehne blew his top.

"These people ought to go away and leave us be. If they don't quit handshaking, I'm gonna start kissing the women. That'll break it up!"

The old soldier saw two beautiful Dutch girls, obviously twins and both slim, shapely, blue-eyed, full-breasted, red-lipped and sweet, moving toward him in the queue.

"Here's where I put a stop to Dutch cordiality!"

He pulled her off balance by his handshake, slipped his left arm around her lissome bodice and glued on as the bystanders laughed and applauded. When he released her, her sister held up her dainty mouth. Again Duquesne glued on. By the time he squeezed off the second kiss the first twin was back in line for seconds. The strategy had backfired—to Duke's satisfaction.

34. A Salute to Master Scout Bachenheimer

We had been at the bridge but a short time when the happy-go-lucky master scout, Bachenheimer, rode up on a bicycle. He looked over in the direction of Nijmegen, two or three miles away, which at the moment was being dive-bombed and strafed, and wistfully commented: "I ain't been over there yet."

He straddled his bicycle and started off.

"Bachenheimer," admired the Arab, "you're showing no more sense than usual. It's daylight, the Krautheads hold the town and it's being bombed. If you go over there by yourself, you won't come back."

"Ah, hell! I'm going over there to see what the score is."

The Bachenheimer legend started on the Anzio beachhead. Having left Germany for the States when twelve years old, this brown-eyed, rosy-cheeked, slightly built youngster of twenty-one spoke English and German equally well. His services to our armed forces began in Sicily where he had been captured, interrogated and put under guard near the German regimental headquarters. Somehow he managed to eavesdrop on a regimental staff meeting and to escape with important information concerning enemy plans.

One night accompanied by a buddy who spoke no German he sneaked up on a German having a supper of wieners and potatoes. The enemy soldier never suspecting that an American could speak such fluent German invited them to share his rations. The three sat in the darkness in convivial intimacy until Bachenheimer, tired of the game, suggested to the German that he eat well as he might not eat again for a long time. When the suspicious soldier reached for his gun, Bachenheimer shot him in the throat.

Once when Gutierrez, Kale and Tedeschi were with him, Bachenheimer seized a gunner out of a machine gun nest and withdrew with him in a hail of bullets to the cover of a ditch. Tedeschi, seriously wounded, had to be abandoned. Kale, a medic who was more familiar with Red Cross brassards than tommy guns, was lying with his gun pointing towards his own chest; Gutierrez, a daring youngster of Mexican

143

ancestry, had the job of keeping the prisoner within bayonet range. In the dark, the enemy succeeded in pulling the trigger on Kale's gun, which sent a burst of 45 slugs through the medic's side and chest. Gutierrez dexterously slid the point of his bayonet into the Krauthead's throat. A year later Tedeschi minus a leg landed in New York as a repatriate on the *Gripsholm*. Kale turned up as a freed prisoner at the end of the war.

Bachenheimer prowled behind the enemy's lines so much that he knew the location of the company, medic and supply dugouts, of the machine gun nests and of the various platoon headquarters. He even knew the names of the officers and their reputation among the men.

It is impossible to estimate the number of notches he could have cut on his gunstock. One night, the story goes, while roving the dark lonely trails of the Volturno country, he discovered a six-man enemy patrol climbing the mountains. He liquidated the rear man and took his place. One by one he did away with the man in front of him until only two were left. He shot them.

Such was Bachenheimer, whom we had come to look upon as a phenomenon of the first order. Casey watched him pedal off whistling a merry tune and exclaimed:

"What a joker!"

We looked at each other in astonishment. Clam-lipped Casey had been guilty of an exclamation!

A squad of Nazis kameraded Bachenheimer as he rode boldly into town around one P.M. He jumped from his bicycle and vanished—in a horizontal rain of bullets. His knowledge of German, cool nerve and ability to make decisions gained him the position as leader of the Dutch underground in Nijmegen. From his basement headquarters he directed the operations of three hundred guerillas, who hindered German troop movements, and collected much useful information for the Allies. It was a curious situation. The Germans held the town, but Bachenheimer administered it. When we finally moved in, we found Bachenheimer sitting in his headquarters issuing orders to his guerillas. Soon colonels and generals were seeking Private Bachenheimer's advice.

General Gavin is said to have asked Colonel Tucker why such a valuable man was still a private. The general ordered Bachenheimer to report to him, perhaps intending to give him a commission. The kid wore a jump suit, moccasins and a knitted cap to his interview! So far as we could learn, he was never given a commission, probably because he didn't want one. It was not in this careless joker to conform to conventional army regulations.

One day a British intelligence officer was tonguing his gums to Bachenheimer about a large prisoner-of-war stockade located eighteen miles behind the lines. The master scout suggested that they cross the river and have a look-see. The lad's guerrilla partisans strung a telephone line across the river and rowed them across. They were to use a telephone hidden on the bank to request a boat when they returned from their mission. They never used it.

The Krautheads had accumulated a large dossier on one-man-army Bachenheimer, who had plagued them since Sicily. They had every reason not to want him to live. For a while he was carried on regimental rolls as MIA, then as KIA.

Bachenheimer told me on the Anzio beachhead that he knew he would get it if he persisted in his spying, but he said that his sense of duty and the attraction of the perilous adventure magnetized him to it. Bachenheimer, gay young stalker of death, I take off my hat to you in deference. I wonder if adequate credit will ever be done your name. . . .

35. Nixon Outwitted Our Number

A brief interval of relaxation ended when an officer nicknamed Rateye called in the noncoms and passed out the bad news. With the help of the 307th Parachute Engineer Battalion and covering fire from British tanks and artillery we were to cross the Maas Waal in rowboats and land to the left of Nijmegen. Frontal assaults on the Nijmegen bridge having been unsuccessful, the decision was taken to cross the river, work down it and attack the bridge from the side and both ends. It sounded easy on paper.

It was a fine day. We ate the apples in our bulging pockets marching in boatload groups of ten to fifteen. We did not know at the time that Maas Waal was the Dutch name for one fork of the Rhine River and that our Legion would get credit for being the first American troops to cross it.

It was a fine day. We are the apples in our bulging pockets as we swung along and like big brothers threw the cores at the grinning youngsters. It was too cheerful a day to fight and there were far too many good-looking Dutch girls peeping at us to make us relish the prospect of being made into carp bait in a rowboat.

We passed a considerable number of British tankmen squatted in the midst of their armor having a spot of tea. A little farther on I came across three Britishers huddled around their tea fire, detachedly scrutinizing our actions. As I trotted by, my tongue pushed out by the A-6 machine gun on my shoulder and bespattered by shell-tossed dirt, one of the tea drinkers lifted his thumb, grinned and hollered: "A bit spotty, eh, old chap?" At that moment a shell scattered their fire and they took to the ditch. Good jokers, the bloody British!

Finally we reached a point, probably five hundred yards from the levee, from where through the trees and shrubbery we could glimpse a high bank and above it a tall modern building of stone which was the Nijmegen power plant. Several large Churchill tanks, maneuvering on the level ground next to the levees, were drawing armor-piercing shells which whistled over them and through and into our tanks as thick as pregame baseballs before the bleachers.

A sniper got a bead on little Harbin, who was loping along just ahead of me and was knocking up the dirt all around him. For a few seconds I scrutinized the direction of the fire and finally I spotted little puffs of smoke belching out of the control cabin of some overhead cranes to the left of the power plant. I crossed over one stone wall and was advancing toward another when a wailing voice from beyond it sounded off, "Hey, Nixon, Tom's hurtin'." I laid the machine gun on the wall and vaulted over. Tom Harbin was lying on the ground with a hole as big as my thumb through his shoulder. Nixon and I patched him up and got set to take off when I discovered that my machine gun was gone. How it vanished without a trace from that wall, I'll never know. I still had my tommy gun which Nixon had been carrying. As we galloped around the bank, kid Butler loped by, his face as bloody as a stuck hog, and grinning to set hell, I half heard his jocular passing yell: "Got my Purple Heart, Mac."

We rejoined the company behind the power plant. Lean, eaglesque, grim-faced Colonel Tucker, an icy glitter in his cold eyes and wearing a raincoat which dangled to his heels, observed me looking at the cranes and on learning the why of it sent Nixon and me to investigate.

After a reasonable search had convinced us that the sniper had left, we hastened on to overtake the company. Our first glimpse of the Maas Waal awed us. I don't know how wide it really was (probably a quarter of a mile at least), but a man on the opposite bank appeared no bigger than a postage stamp. By the time we got to the point of embarkation the company had vanished. We were in a helluva shape. Shells were plunging into the river and onto the banks and bullets were digging navels all over the belly of the mighty stream.

Up the bank about a hundred yards we saw Colonel Tucker and some other men loading into the only boat in sight. We made an eleven-second sprint and dived in with him. The old eagle snarled, "Hell might break loose any minute . . . row like hell." He steered, Nixon held the guns off the muddy floor and the rest of us smote mightily with our oars. We went straight across with only a few bullets hitting around us, beached the boat, grabbed our weapons and asked where the company was. No one seemed to know exactly. Numerous wounded and dead men lay about. An engineer buddy of mine from the Anzio days lay below a sand dune, shot in the throat. He signaled in answer to my inquiry that he would be okay. A captain in the battalion who was starting to lead his company down to the right told Nixon and me to stick with him as my company was down that way. With misgivings we followed him.

Down the river about a mile, I could see the giant span of the Nijmegen bridge. A hot fight was going on for it. Our pro tem adopted company strung out and trotted across a level pasture midst whistling and screeching bullets to the bank of the road about one quarter mile from the bridge. The captain, when told that a moated, drawbridged fort a couple of hunderd yards on the other side of the road sheltered numerous Krautheads firmly defending it with machine guns, lined up his men, drew his pistol and said: "Men, follow me. We'll rush them all at once.

Inasmuch as we did not belong to the company, Nixon and I rationalized ourselves into the roles of interested bystanders. Brandishing his pistol and bellowing like a bull with laryngitis, the captain, followed by his men, raged through the bullets to his objective, which was taken almost instantly with a loss of two men killed. One of his soldiers when halfway across the road was knocked back over the bank by a bullet which struck the rifle held in front of his body. He threw it down, pulled a 45 automatic and dashed out of sight. An officer stood beneath the bank by us waving reinforcements after the captain. A tank gun fired a flat trajectory shell which wounded three men, including the officer, and shrapnel numbed my leg. Sweating terror, I dived into a hole on Nixon who, using his head, had been in it all the time.

A lieutenant told us that our company was far up the road

to the left. In dismay we looked up the long bottom which, beset with snipers and filled with shot and shell, did not offer the prospect of safe or pleasant travel. A big gun was throwing shells far up it, spacing each approximately 150 yards apart and bringing them closer to us. There was a desperate fascination about our situation. Every thirty seconds the gun made a shell hole 150 yards nearer. Nixon calculated that within two more minutes the missile would explode at the spot where we were. He grabbed my arm.

"Mac, when I say run, you follow me like a bat out of hell."

"Okay."

A shell shattered the ground 150 yards ahead. Nixon yelled, "Run!"

We dashed to the new-made shell hole and tumbled in. From far up in the air a geyser of dirt began its downward rain on the very spot from where we'd started our sprint. Nixon wiped his freckled forehead.

"Son," he said, "I was a good guesser. It would have got us if we'd stayed there."

I shook his hand. "Yes, Nixon, you outwitted our number!"

36.   Five Mark VI Tanks

Nixon and I found the company digging in along a high road bank which curved toward the Rhine. Around the road's curve was a little town whose church steeple served as a spy lookout. It was a sensitive position to be in.

The boys had had an eventful day. They had bottled up 267 Germans on and around the bridge and accounted for them to the last man. Expert rifleman Fox added four notches to his gunstock. One of our chaplains got drilled through the buttocks as he crossed the river. Sheraton claimed he exploded in language unbecoming to a man in his position. "Those sons of bitches have shot me in the tail!" he wailed, "and I can't shoot back!" Truly a tough spot to be in. Pierson had his helmet shot from his head, but as usual escaped unscathed. Bolton wrecked eight enemy soldiers with a large gammon grenade. Iron-jawed Winters' patrol collided unexpectedly with three Krautheads. He shot one in the belly and another in the throat. The third cut the grass around them with an automatic pistol and escaped. Guitry, a member of the patrol, had been toting an automatic rifle for a year in hopes of finally getting to use it. He lowered it on three Nazis unlimbering a machine gun, but it jammed. The machine gun chased them back across the road. He confided to me that the failure of his gun was the biggest disappointment in his life.

All through the night we kept nervous watch. James K., curly-headed, freckle-faced, blue-eyed, nineteen-year-old, replacement, listened in jittery agitation to the sounds of the night from his hole in the road bank. He could barely read or write, never got any mail, didn't know what in hell it was all about, nor why or what he was fighting except that they were called Krautheads. These strange creatures could have had horns and a bushy tail for all he knew.

James K. had been forced to trade a carefree, vagabond existence for the circumscribed, harassed and inexplicable disciplines of the army. He felt trapped, persecuted, tortured and cruelly mistreated. In England he would sit around in his tent, head in hands, as completely miserable as a fox in a steel trap. He was in the Arab's squad. The wily old warrior, usually engaged in reading a few pages of Homer, sometimes lifted his eyes and smiled kindly at the miserable young fellow. James K. would scowl, eye him ferociously and growl, "Obscenity on you, Arab." Next he would observe the lanky Nixon, "Obscenity on you too, Nixon." Then he would say in rage, "Obscenity on the damned colonel, obscenity on the intercoursin' army and obscenity on Casey and Larkin!"

He uttered the last two names to climax his hierarchy of invectives, knowing that the Arab would always lift his finger and comment:

"James K., God and the colonel won't hear you, the army is too indifferent to give a damn, but Casey and Larkin would be willing to stomp your guts two feet into the ground! Ahhh! Don't even think, much less say, such sacrilegious things about old warriors!"

Whereupon James K. would slink from the tent, throw back his head and give forth with a wild, strange scream of helplessness and frustration. Upon hearing him, Knowles would remark. "Well, there's James K. giving up again!" Other men revolting against their hard lot occasionally let out strange, strangled expressions in futile anger, but the bitterly-lonely cry of James K., epitomized a desolate moral isolation belonging to a category supreme in its uniqueness. And now James K. was in battle—on outpost.

During the night evidently not knowing that we were there, two Krautheads came down the road pushing bicycles. James K. halted them and on recognizing them as enemies put two holes so close together in one's neck that a dime would have covered both. The other fled. Some of our jokers dragged the body to James K.'s hole. All night through the long, lonely hours of his first outpost in battle, he stared at the dead man, imagining that the sightless eyes focused him accusingly.

Berkely saw a head pop up in the shadows across the road, pulled the pin on a grenade, held it for two or three seconds and tossed it. For a brief time the night's relative quiet was made hideous by the screams of the mortally wounded man. Soon silence fell again.

At daylight Big Murray spotted a twelve-man Krauthead patrol coming his way. Aided by the Arab, Duquesne, Gruening, Casey and Finkelstein, he wiped it out to a man. Then he rounded up a few more jokers and led them into a little town, ostensibly to contact the enemy, but really in search of some brandy. They found three liters and were starting back when a column of Nazis came filing into town. He and his men scattered them, crossed the road in haste through swarming bullets and made it back without casualties.

From time to time our boys, lying in their foxholes, could see Nazis slinking through the orchards and fields which lay across the road. They picked them off coolly, unhurriedly, deliberately. Berkely shot one to pieces with an automatic rifle; tobacco-chewing Wild Bill McMurtry sniped purposefully and spat at random; Casey said nothing but drilled any head that he spied: Duquesne smoked cigarettes while he and Gruening railroaded round after round at unwary enemies. Big Rodgers' socks had brought him revenge and us luck. Everyone wearing them, with the possible exception of Guitry, had scored.

War with a stubborn and resourceful enemy, however, never offers a one-way advantage for long. Our successful rifle fire invited retaliation which came first as a heavy artillery barrage and second in the form of preparations for an attack with armor. Five Mark VI tanks, supported by numerous infantrymen, moved into the little town and then toward us. Behind the opposite bank of the road we heard them roaring and clanking. Then we saw the five great shapes lined up in assault formation. The long gleaming guns stuck up like vicious snouts of prehistoric monsters almost to the top of the road. Only the high bank prevented them from lowering the muzzles enough to hit us. The Krauthead infantry, full of respect for our unerring marksmanship, stayed out of sight in the ditches. They were waiting for the kill like jackals.

I had an intuition of the emotions which went into James K.'s strange screams. For the first time we were menaced by forces beyond the compass of our spirits and our fighting resources. James K.'s was the frustration rooted in a total environment, ours in specific objects: five monstrous Mark VI tanks. I suppose that cavemen threatened by the monstrous viciousness of dinosaurs had much the same feeling of terrified helplessness as we had as we crouched across the road, our eyes glued with lethal anticipation on the ends of those five metal cylinders being readied to destroy us.

Since the field behind us was perfectly level clear back to the river, if the tanks once got over the road, we were lost. Now it was only a matter of minutes until they would come, perhaps until most or all of us would be dead. We were conjecturing whether the Krautheads would wipe us all out or give us a chance to surrender when slim, youthful Towle, followed by James K. carrying some shells, came hurrying up with his bazooka. Towle, who had joined us in Italy, was a quiet, self-possessed, dark-haired boy whose fate and luck it was to be the only bazooka man in the company with any ammunition.

He climbed up the bank, took a quick peep at the tanks, then slid down and got his bazooka. He said ironically, "I see that I'm going to get the Congressional today." He crawled back up and set to work. He would fire his metal pipe, slide down to reload, then crawl back up at a new point. The Krautheads swiveled their 88's and tank machine guns to cover the different portions of the embankment; wherever he stuck his weapon over, they sniped at him at point-blank range. Towle was facing five tanks weighing sixty tons each. Three hundred tons of mobile metal forts were being opposed by one man and one bazooka! Finally the stout-hearted trooper forced the tanks to withdraw to the town. His bravery had saved our company and the left bank of the Rhine.

In a few minutes a mortar shell dropped on Towle and killed him. James K. saw him die and immediately blew his stack. It took four men to lead him to the rear. Towle got his Congressional posthumously—the only Medal of Honor granted in the entire division during the war. Sergeant York got the Medal of Honor for the 82nd in World War I and Towle in World War II.

We had an hour or so of respite from the tanks, but presently they began again to gun their motors. Once more the reflection that we would be dead or eating sauerkraut and

wieners by nightfall unless we got help, dosed our gloom
with additional melancholy. Word came down the line that the
captain had requested British tank support. We looked down
the road toward the bridge, hoping doubtfully that the British
would come in time since it was four o'clock. They never
passed up teatime to our knowledge. We listened to the tanks
growling in the little town and for the sound of British tanks.
We cursed the British Lion and Old Patton because his tanks
were elsewhere.

At last we heard the enemy tanks start moving. Our hearts
plummeted to our boots. Then far down the road we heard a
vast roaring. The British were coming. Soon six Churchill
tanks, followed by several Bren carriers loaded with British
infantry, came into sight. We hit the bottom of our holes
knowing that the enemy would redouble its shellfire. The British tanks came up and set to work in a most matter-of-fact
way. They knocked out three Mark VI's almost instantly and
machine-gunned everything in sight.

A machine gun in a big house across the road fired on
them. Immediately a tank shot an armor-piercing shell through
the house, followed by a white phosphorus shell which exploded inside. A hullabaloo started within, succeeded in short
order by a mass exodus in a mad rush. Next they blew a mortar position to hell. These helpful actions plus the *tac-tac* of
their machine guns beat the music of gratitude deep into
our hearts. They had achieved a Lone Ranger rescue in
grand style.

Their job done, the gallant tank cavaliers rumbled off the
way they had come. Since, however, the hour was well past
teatime, they pulled into a nearby wood to have their spot.

37. Six Men on a Suicide Stand

NEXT morning we were relieved by British infantry. As we
marched across the Nijmegen bridge into the city I had an
opportunity to get a close-up of the objectives which had

caused so much anxiety and bloodshed. Dead Germans lay and hung everywhere. Enemy equipment was scattered about in heaps. The town square was being systematically shelled. A bomb which exploded as we marched through gave Tom Lecesse his fourth wound. I observed a burned Bren carrier on the square and beside it the charred body of a British soldier. We passed near a little park where the Hollanders had buried some American paratroopers. They had sodded the graves with green grass and put fresh flowers around the helmets.

We rode on British trucks through magnificent resort country toward the German frontier. After crossing it some of us, as soon as we had the occasion, picked up a handful of German soil and squeezed it in gratitude. We had scarcely dared to hope that our lives would stretch long enough to permit us to wage war within Germany itself. The country seemed very prosperous. It always saddened me to see war's ruins in friendly poorer countries. I felt no particular glee in reflecting about the future we intended for the factories whose smokestacks stood haughtily in every direction. I wondered what Germany might have been today if her imperialistic ambitions had not led her into the first world war and the one we were now bringing to her own soil. I hated the Nazis with every throb of my heart and all the more perhaps because as a student of German I had developed a liking for their language and an appreciation for many of their contributions to civilization. At the same time, however, my mind was filled with images of their atrocities and of our dead comrades. I wiggled my toes in Big Rodgers' socks.

Our platoon's first combat action in Germany was to seize a hillock. We dug in for the night on the bank of a ravine only thirty yards from a machine gun nest. A Krauthead rifleman kept the Arab and Wild Bill pinned down half of the next day and even tried to throw a grenade into their hole. At nightfall Berkely joined them. The enemy joker who had been after them all day finally killed himself with his own grenade.

Around midnight a stiff counterattack was unloosed on us. The Nazis advanced up the ravine in considerable strength, determined, it seemed, to get us. Berkely rushed up and down the line firing his tommy gun to simulate greater numerical forces than we had. Pierson threw seventeen grenades. When Duquesne's rifle jammed after three rounds, he threw it at a group of three Krautheads and gained enough time during their confusion to scatter them with a grenade. Just when our ammunition was about gone, an attack by another platoon hit the enemy's right flank at Em Phal and forced them to withdraw.

Hitler pitted some of his paratroopers against us at Em Phal who had already repulsed the efforts of two platoons to take the town. They were fierce, stubborn, crafty, ingenious warriors. For example, four of them yelled "Kameraden" to one of our patrols and then walked forward to surrender. But when our men arose to make them prisoners, they dropped to the ground and an MG 42 behind them wounded six out of ten boys.

A G 2 report informed us that 16,000 Germans were planning to attack our positions at one the next morning. In order to increase our chances for successful resistance, it was decided to take Em Phal at all costs. My platoon drew the assignment.

The platoon was to attack at eight P. M., all three squads participating. Once the town was taken, one squad would stay, with orders to fight until killed. The other two would remain in reserve. We tossed coins to determine which squad did what. Squad leader Winters drew the task of spearheading the attack, Berkely of remaining in reserve and I of garrisoning the town.

The captain called me in for briefing. He looked at me with the kind of sorrowful sympathy shown to deathbed patients and said: "Carter, you are in a position that few men ever get into in a war. You will be on a suicide mission in Em Phal tonight. You and your men will stay there no matter what happens. Good luck!"

I gulped and said, "Thanks."

Berkely requested permission to go with us, but it wasn't granted.

I gathered my squad composed of Butler, Finkelstein, Guitry, Nixon and Sokal and told them how it was. They listened in silence and said nothing. We spent the afternoon getting ready, determined if we were to leave the war in Em Phal, to leave the town full of dead enemies.

As the hour for the attack approached, our mortars began to shell the town and heavy artillery the positions beyond it. At eight o'clock, Winters, his lantern jaw set for a repetition of the kind of action for which he was famous, led the platoon through the rain-soaked darkness and sighing winds into the objective. We found no sign of enemy paratroopers, but the Arab, accompanied by Duquesne, made sure by tossing grenades among the ruins. Duquesne hurled a gammon grenade against an iron-barred window and got wounded, but not seriously, in several places. He had to go to the rear for treatment.

The two other squads helped us dig in. I had my men collect all the ammunition which our buddies could spare. Each ended up with twenty grenades and six hundred rounds of ammunition. Berkely and the other boys shook hands with us and wished us luck. Then they left.

Three of my men, with Sokal in charge (his arm wound had not been too serious) were on one side of the town and Finkelstein, Nixon and I on the other, each group deployed in triangular formation. We all sat in the black night, gripping our weapons—Nixon his automatic rifle, Finkelstein his Garand, I my tommy gun—awaiting the 16,000 enemies who were scheduled to attack us at one o'clock. There was an element of comedy in our situation: six men against 16,-000!

I was counting my grenades and tommy gun magazines by touch when a white rabbit darted by within hand's reach. Before I identified it, I made a move to empty my gun at it. I thought of *Alice in Wonderland*.

"Carter," whispered Finkelstein, "rats are jumping into my hole! What am I gonna do?"

Little Finkelstein, who feared no man on earth, feared rats as Berkely did snakes.

"Bat 'em in the teeth with your rifle and toss 'em out!"

"I wish the damned Nazis would come! The noise I plan to make with this Garand would skeedaddle 'em so fast they'd catch their front legs in their bunghole."

"I wish the bastards would hurry," said Nixon. "I'm ready to fill their butts full of hot lead. I don't like it this way, but since this is the way it's got to be, I want to get it over."

Butler, Guitry and Sokal were too far away to talk to in a whisper, but I knew they thought as we did. The jig was up and the curtain was about to fall. We would ring it down, goddammit, with a Wagnerian finale, or at least try to.

So we crouched in our holes and waited impatiently. Memories, faces and landscapes flooded before my mind's eye. Squatted in the darkness in my small hole, I saw the valley between Duffield and Pattonsville, Virginia, my mother's house, the campus at Lincoln Memorial University, my room above the old dairy barn and thousands of other back-home objects which flowed before my mental vision in intimate detail. My mind would switch suddenly from associations of home to those of war: The original platoon in Africa, Sicily, Salerno, Volturno, Anzio; Carlton, Hastings, Oldring, Olson, T.L., the Master Termite. Then with inexplicable suddenness

I was reliving high school and college, resurrecting memories of Betty Duff, Katherine T. and Jeanne B., a sweet girl in Tennessee. In adolescent reverie I wondered whether the latter would be impressed when she learned that I croaked on a suicide mission. At this very moment my mother could be writing a letter which would read, "Look after yourself and don't take any chances. Things are looking up now and I hope to have you back with me soon." Then I thought of Carlton lying on the trail and recalled his last words, "Tell the boys I wish them luck."

A machine gun firing into the ruins snapped me back to reality. I grinned sardonically and self-chided: "Carter, what the hell! Soon you'll be softening yourself with self-pity and you know damned well that ain't good." As I walked over to Nixon, I pondered how different it was to be facing death well armed on the ground compared to getting it in a plane or in a jump.

"Nixon, give 'em a magazine to let 'em know we're around."

I went back to my hole and watched him trigger long belches of red flame toward the machine gun. When he finished, I yammered out thirty tommy gun slugs. The machine gun stopped shooting.

One o'clock. No attack. Two. Three. Four. Five. Six. Seven. Daylight. No attack. Emotionally and mentally geared to die in heroic roles, we were almost disappointed. Still it was damned good to be alive! My corned beef and crackers never munched better than they did in that early dawn.

The intolerable agony of lying cramped for hours in his tiny trench sent Nixon scurrying to a nearby barn. An enemy artillery man spotted him. In a moment the wind was shell-burnt all around us. He ran for his hole and as he dived a shell burst three feet from him, but not soon enough to get him. As I lay flat on my back I saw a building twenty feet in front of me come tumbling down. I barely had time to bury my face in my hole to escape an avalanche of dust and brick flecks. A second shell felled a tree across my hole. I called several times to see if the boys were okay, but got no answer. I was on the point of leaving my hole even at the risk of drawing more shells and go to them when I discovered that I was calling only in a whisper. I had been paralyzed by fear without realizing it. Finally I pumped man-sized sounds of enough volume from my voice box to be heard. They all answered and reported. Finkelstein was half buried by a near miss. Butler was slightly nicked by sharapnel, Nixon had his hole shaded by a cut-off hedge, Guitry had got hit by a brick, but was unhurt. Sokal answered, "I don't dare feel the seat of my pants!"

We were relieved at eight after twenty-four hours in Em Phal. Gruening, who was a member of the relief squad, told us before we left about the adventures he'd had during the day. Slinking along a hedge he came face to face with a storm trooper. They stared at each other, their guns leveled, and then backed away without firing. A few yards from the point of this encounter, he caught another storm trooper urinating and took him prisoner. And finally to round out his day, he'd shot a sniper in the belly six hundred yards away.

Dammit, he said as we left, "I miss Duquesne! Why did that dumb wood beetle have to hand-grenade himself? I got no one now to talk to about the NYC till he gets back." Duquesne and Gruening . . .

The Arab helped us evacuate a parachute engineer who'd been dead for two weeks. In many ways the fierce Arab had a mother's tender heart. He supervised the lifting of the young kid whose wax-colored face appeared strangely fluorescent as we carried him along in the bright moonlight. "Carry him gently, boys," said the Arab, "his mother would appreciate it."

We were already deep in our own defense zone when a bullet whined between Sokal and the Arab. The Arab leveled his tommy gun and bellowed in pleading rage: "Okay, you trigger-happy obscenity, I'm gonna kill you. Please come out and let me kill you. It ain't enough to look out for Kraut-head bullets! Oh, no! A trigger-snapping obscenity like you has to butt in! Co-operate and step out, you candy-kneed, rotten-gutted, milk-blooded caponized obscenity, so I can kill you!"

"Arab," laughed Finkelstein, "you're blowing your barrel. No man'll step out to be killed!"

"Captain," the Arab reported, "I'd have killed a trigger-happy joe tonight if I could have seen him. I'm warning that the next one of our jokers who shoots at me without reason is a dead man!"

"Arab," smiled the captain," go ahead. Some of them need killing."

38. The Arab Makes a Dedication

The captain called for the Arab one dark, rainy night and said, "Sergeant, you are going on patrol."

He paused. The Arab said nothing.

"You're gonna go out front and see what the score is."

"What do you want, captain, a prisoner?"

The officer leaned back in his chair, studied the Arab a moment, and replied, "Don't make any particular effort. Just find out the score."

The Arab collected Guitry and Nixon and stomped off to the platoon front.

At one o'clock three dark figures slid over a bank, crept to a hedge beneath, and lay still for some minutes. The Arab with his tommy gun was in the lead, followed by Nixon with another tommy, and then Guitry with an automatic rifle. They listened. From behind the hedge came a weird, gurgling, sucking, chewing sound. The Arab crawled over to investigate and came back vomiting. It was a hog eating a cadaver. He led the patrol on up the hedge, his moral anatomy pinging because of what he had seen.

Since it was anybody's soil and anything could start happening anywhere, the Arab lay down and snaked along the hedge, his two men close behind. Visibility was about three feet. Fortunately there was enough wind to cover up slight noises. A hundred and twenty-five yards on, they heard the sharp, metallic click of a rifle being pushed off safety not five feet away through the hedge. "And thrice he heard a breech-bolt snick, though never a man was seen," recollected the Arab as he covered the hedge with his gun. They crawled on. As they advanced a white blur at the corner of the hedge began to take the shape of what could be a low stone or concrete pillbox. The Arab covered it with his tommy. To open fire would be disastrous. He tightened up the nerves in his belly and crawled closer. It was a dead cow.

The three men continued their creeping advance. A barbed-wire fence intertwined with the hedge advised caution. It might be a bobby trap. He left it strictly alone, hoping as they bellied on that the clever enemy had not strung wires vertically across their path of advance. Finally he came to a hole in the hedge and peered through it in furtive expectancy of getting a blast of lead from a standing type foxhole he could indistinctly discern in the cavernous night.

He drew his P-38, laid his tommy gun on the bank and slithered up to the hole. It was empty. He whispered to Nixon and Guitry to crawl through and to cover him as he led the way up the enemy-held side.

The Arab elbowed and kneed his way up a mound of dirt and slid into another empty hole. Newly opened tin cans still smelling of fresh food indicated that the occupant had moved out but recently. As he progressed up the hedge the number of holes increased until their pattern of frequency averaged one every ten feet. The empty holes prompted the habitually cautious Arab to conclude that the enemy had left and that it was safe to stand up. Nixon and Guitry arose to their feet also. He peppered his pace to a gait which soon doubled the distance between him and Nixon, whom he could now barely see. He swung around to the right, intending to halt a moment so that they could overtake him, and there not three feet from him a Nazi paratrooper stood with his back to him manning a machine gun. The enemy made a quarter turn, saw the Arab and grabbed a P-38. The Arab pulled the trigger of his tommy back and held it. The tommy gun spiraled its pattern of 45 slugs in a long stitch extending from the right side above the belt to a point just under the left shoulder.

"Nixon," shouted the Arab, "come help me search him. We might find some useful information." They found nothing, but carried along the machine gun and a Karbiner 98. Fire from three machine guns escorted them through the hedge and over the bank to the safety of platoon lines.

That night as the Arab sat drinking coffee, he pulled off his boots and held up his long feet, covered by socks once white but now nearly black and almost rotten.

"Big Rodgers," he said, "it is my honor and privilege to dedicate another enemy to your spirit."

"As long as my socks last, I feel like I'll have luck," said Gruening. "Duquesne lost one of his. I ain't superstitious, but maybe Grandpa wouldn't have got hurt if he'd had both of T. L.'s socks. When I'm braking for the New York Central, I always carry a certain kind of bandana. Twice I didn't have it and each time I nearly got it. Course the bandana didn't have nothing to do with it . . . I ain't superstitious!"

"Gruening," said Berkely, "I'll bet you believe in ghosts!"

"He carried an extra load of grenades all night one time in Italy," said the Arab, "just to have plenty of ghost protection. He figured, I guess, that the slivers from a grenade would splinter up a spiritual shadow whereas a slug would make just one dent!"

"Arab, some day I'll push you on the track of the New York Central and run a fast train over you!"

"Big Rodgers saved my life," the Arab reminisced. "Once he shot a Krauthead who had dead aim on me. Another split second and I'd have gone west."

"I was pinned down by machine-gun cross fire on Hill 687," I said. "Big Rodgers saw a Nazi slipping toward me. He could have been killed but he left his own foxhole to dogtag my ambitious son of a bitch."

"Arab," said Casey, "they say you got the Silver Star!"

"It was a mistake," growled the Arab, half pleased, half griped. "It should have gone to Gruening for capturing a prisoner while urinating!"

"Arab, I'll run every train on the New York Central over you. I hope the scurvy soul you ain't got corrodes in hell till it won't burn!"

"What did the Arab do to get the Silver Star?" asked Butler.

"He saved a woman!"

"What do you mean, Finkelstein?"

"He reserved two women in a Naples hotel and saved one for the next night!"

"Arab, how did you get the Silver Star?" asked Nixon.

"Ask Berkely. He got one too."

"How did Berkely get the Silver Star?" asked Butler.

"He saved Rateye," said Larkin.

"What from?"

"A hungry sow which mistook him for a corpse."

"Why did he save him?"

"So he could keep doing his job and keep him on the payroll, eh, Berkely?"

"Obscenity, obscenity, obscenity," obscenitied Berkely. The finger had been put on the ulcer in our outfit. Officer Rateye didn't rate. For five minutes everybody obscenitied with Berkely.

After the boys had relieved their need to obscenity goof-off officer Rateye, silence and cigarette smoke reigned. Suddenly Casey electrified us with one of the few reflective comments I ever heard him make.

"Big Rodgers was a man. If he'd a talked his religion to me, I'd have listened. But he didn't. I took off my socks the other night to wash my feet in a canal. A sniper got after me and I had to leave barefooted. When I went back, they were gone. I wish I had 'em."

For a long time we sat silent, all who knew him evoking in reverie the huge, lonely figure of Rodgers, the religious Alabamian who volunteered for hazardous duty in Normandy on D-Day and who killed forty Germans before a sniper shot him through the head.

Square-jawed Winters spiraled a puff of cigarette smoke and clipped off the remark:

"Jokers, we've been lucky! Why we aren't all dead, bedamned if I know!"

39.   Willie Mullins Receives a Letter

Life on the front continued its baseball rhythm of long monotonous pauses interspersed with comic and tragic incidents and moments or hours of intense anxiety and action.

The company had moved into a particularly vulnerable position on the right flank in the open fields the day Willie Mullins got a letter from his wife which did more to erode our morale than could any conceivable amount of shells, rain or hard luck. Willie loved his wife and respected her dignity enough, in spite of the biological urges which belabored him, to stay away from the temptresses who talked love in strange tongues. He was first in line for his mail, read and reread his wife's letters and carried them with him till rain, sweat and mud made them illegible. He sent every penny he could save to her to put in the bank for the little house they planned to buy when the war was over. It had never occurred to him that the sweet young girl who sat on his knees, ran her fingers through his hair, caressed his closed eyes, and kissed him tenderly in the corners of his mouth could be a two-timer. He was fighting for her and the kind of free life he vaguely associated in his unlettered naïve thinking with the purposes of the war.

Willie had just returned from an overnight sojourn in some old houses a few yards from no man's land. It had been a strenuous night, filled with the usual tensions and noises, plus the nerve-scraping detonations of diabolically contrived new rockets we called "screaming meemies." This new gun rocketed six projectiles at a time, each containing thirty-five pounds of high explosives which in their trajectory shrieked with increasing sirenlike intensity, giving one the feeling of being personally pursued by a banshee from hell. They exploded in bursts of flame and sparks, sending glowing fragments for hundreds of yards in every direction. This weapon while not very accurate was hellishly terrifying. Many times during the night Willie's vision of the little house faded. His Adam's apple pistoned his dry throat and his chest tightened at the thought of dying before he held his wife on his knee again and felt the soft plush of her plump breasts pressing against him.

Berkely handed him his letter. He read it twice, his eyes bulging. First he threw it on the ground and stomped it. Next he shot at it. Then waving it he charged straight towards no man's land, cursing and storming every bound, described a wide arc and came back to our line panting and foaming.

"Having female trouble, Willie?"

"Arab, read this letter to the boys."

The Arab read: "Dear darling Willie, I have bad news in one way, but in another way it's good news. I am pregnant. Life was so hard without you, sweetheart. You have no idea what all I've been through. If you'd really loved me, you'd have found a way to come back from over there. I know you will understand. It will be kinda nice now, won't it, to have a little one already here when you get back. Do write, Willie boy, and tell me everything is all right. Loads of love from your loving bunny!"

The Arab finished reading the letter and handed it back to Willie with a comment that pretty well summarized our feelings.

"Willie don't answer her! Never see her again! And in future dealings with women, Willie, don't build your life around one. Our mothers are good women so there are good women. Maybe the girl back home is okay, maybe not. As for me, a woman is a thing of beauty and a source of joy, but fragile and fleeting like a rose. 'Gather in the day,' *carpe diem*. That's Latin, jokers. Now, Willie, we'll get you drunk and find you a dainty damsel the next time we go on leave."

"I can't forget her, Arab! I love her!"

"Love?" The Arab lifted his eyebrows in ironically comical disbelief. "Love, Willie, may be a state of idiocy. You don't want to be an idiot, do you?"

"I love her, I love her, I love her!" Suddenly Willie grabbed the letter and began again to run in wide circles, screaming, "I love the bitch, I love her, I love the bitch, I love her!"

Late in the night Willie Mullins went crazy and left the front in a strait jacket.

The scene filled us with bitterness. Most of us, during long, hard months of blood, death and hardship, had set some girl on a symbolic pedestal of purity and devotion. We needed something more personal and close and idealistic than the dependable affections of our families. The comradeship developed by men in battle and military association, although a powerful tie and cementing bond difficult for civilians to understand, nevertheless does not suffice. Even the toughest soldier feels the need for a speck of emotional romanticism and of spiritual purity. When the Master Termite got sentimental about Angel, Duquesne about Jelly, Casey about the beat-up Leicester widow, and even the Ancient-Greek-thinking Arab about a waitress in Middleboro, they unconsciously distilled the perfidious impurities, real or potential, of their Dulcineas into perfumed loyalties and flattering devotions. After years of absence and months of nightmares, exceeding even the most gruesome conceptions of literary naturalism, the pug-nosed, freckle-ugly anybody's girl back home who occasionally wrote you a note which she signed "with loads of love," began to build up in the imagination as a symbol of ideal feminine values. The idealized fixations of men in love with wives or sweethearts were, of course, all the more hungrily longing and obsessingly poignant.

I saw more than one Willie leave in a strait jacket. As long as the boys fought in the belief that their sacrifices and hardships meant at least enough to the woman they loved to hold her loyalty, they could usually endure the hell of mechanized battle. When cruel letters jackknifed their faith, their moral fibers crumpled and some of them fell apart.

Within a few days, the fast pace of events had filled our lives with enough comic and tragic incidents to sickle over somewhat our vicarious bitterness. Gruening and his squad had spent the night guarding a British artillery outpost from sudden attack. At daylight as he went from hole to hole to arouse his men, he stopped on the bank of a dugout to get a better look of a man's head he could see dimly about six feet below. As he struggled to climb out, a composed voice said:

"But really, old man, you're standing on my head! Do you mind?"

Gruening billy-goated out and stared down at the unruffled Britisher.

"Thanks awfully, old man! A bit disagreeable, what?"

Later in the day, the apostle of the New York Central observed the marks of his boots on the face of a British captain.

Berkely, who was observing for an 81 mortar one day, directed fire so accurately that our mortarman blew a German's trousers thirty feet into the air. The next day the giant, unarmed, carrying several five-pound cans of coffee, unexpectedly rammed into a storm trooper behind a hedge. He hurled a can at the Nazi, who dropped his gun, caught the coffee with the flash of a Yankee outfielder and took off grinning triumphantly.

Two of our boys, Corcoran and Cox, disappeared from the same hole without a trace. One day when Nixon was snoozing in it, he awoke just in time to scare away a big boar which was on the point of jumping on him. Casey affirmed that a big boar he'd seen roaming around could have carried them off. But no one else believed it. The men simply vanished without any trace of struggle.

"It's a bloody, blooming lie, ain't it so, blokes," said a Limey one day to Berkely, Wild Bill, the Arab and me, "that you American blokes have been shining up to our wives back in England?"

I remembered Willie Mullins.

"Your wives wouldn't look at us, Limey!" I said.

"They're regular Penelopes, Limey!" said the Arab.

"That good or bad, Yank?"

"Good."

"I been saying, I have, it was a bloody, blooming lie and you tell me I'm right, eh, Yanks?" he said turning to Berkely and Wild Bill.

"Every damned word of it," they chorused.

"Let's shake hands!"

We shook hands with the reassured Limey and went our way, coddling our consciences in silent uneasiness.

40. Nixon Wakes Up in Panties

There was a particularly "wearing" outpost in a little group of houses called Wassen Waal smack on the Holland-German border. To reach it a plain perhaps a mile and a half in width had to be traversed in full view of the enemy. The dozens of wrecked and charred gliders gave it the appearance of a beach strewn with skeletons of monstrous fishes. The disintegrating bodies of hundreds of Germans, half buried in the mud, lay scattered among the small bushes, abandoned patches of potatoes, sugar beets, shell holes, and ruined houses. The heavy rains had bleached the clothing and faces of the dead men to a ghastly pallid-purplish tinge. The air was permeated with the peculiar sickeningly sweetish odor of death in winter. In the hot months death has a different smell.

Across a road on the east side of the Wassen Waal were the enemy outposts; ours were on the west side. It was a tough spot. My platoon registered little enthusiasm when its turn came to wade through the dead men to carry out the order, "Go to Wassen Waal tonight, and remain there until dawn."

As darkness fell, the platoon moved down a wagon road toward the little spot. Rateye was leading the mission with only ten troopers between him and the enemy.

Things went unusually well during the first half of the march. We stopped twice to chase hogs off cadavers. Casey even slaughtered a vicious boar with his dagger. Casey couldn't stand to see a hog eat a cadaver. "I'll never eat a dirty pig again," he confided to me. "I hate the filthy cannibals. They're worse than buzzards."

We had attained a point about halfway to our objective when we saw thirty-six balls of white glowing fire ascend into the air several thousand yards to the east. The flock of missiles neared us with a great hissing noise and plunged into the earth slightly on our left flank. The explosion resembled the kind of sound I can imagine Atlas would make if he were beating great rugs in the canyon. The center was a glaring red disc which dissolved into flaming steel and streams of sparks which were hurled high into the sky. We relaxed a bit when the vast clouds of smoke drifted high overhead and merged into the night.

After a brief interval our attention was focused on a point which must have been at least twenty-five miles distant. We saw a thin pencil of yellow light rise from the ground and climb perpendicularly to a height of at least 25,000 feet. At that altitude the yellow turned to red and the object vanished. We conjectured that it was a V-2 headed for Antwerp or some other spot in the Lowlands.

War, I reflected, was getting somewhat beyond the reasonable bounds of courage when an inanimate mass of steel and explosive could be guided to a target 150 miles away. It made us feel ineffectual and futile. As long as we manipulated our

own weapons individually and faced weapons manipulated individually by the enemy, we could feel the confidence of self-
courage and heroic determination. But the sight of the rocket
and experience in England with buzz bombs encouraged
the belief that modern science might nullify and even mecha-
nize the human spirit.

The Arab, lying near me, patted his pocket edition of
Homer and commented:

"The Legion may be enacting the last epic of our time. If
that is the future, I want the past. Emotionally and mentally, I
am closer to the spirit of Homer than to the spirit that went
into the making of that rocket. The fact that we have to kill
other men is bad enough. To use our brains to contrive such
instruments for mass murder puts us lower than jungle brutes.
Carter, I don't believe in this kind of progress."

For the first time the Arab had expressed his thoughts without webbing them in cunning indirection and irony. I liked
him in this frame of mind and kept silent, hoping he would
go on. But instead he exploded in obscenties. "Berkely, stick
a bayonet in Rateye's obscenity so we can get to shelter before the *Nebelwerfers* mincemeat us for the hogs!"

We pushed on down the path. Two sergeants from the outpost came to guide us silently to our positions. I went with the
Arab and his men. As we cautiously advanced down a little
path, a nervous machine gunner sprinkled the area but made
no hits. The Arab set up his command post in the cellar of a
toppled-down stone house, put an automatic rifle on his right
flank, another on his left flank, a third on his rear and posted
his riflemen. Twenty yards in front was no man's land.

The cellar was about twenty feet long, ten feet wide, and six
feet high. The ceiling itself, at least four feet thick, was covered by several feet of rubble. Hundreds of cans of food, plus
stacks of old clothes, had been stored in the cellar. Although
most of the cans had been emptied by previous outposts, we
still found large stocks of cherries, apples, pears, huckleberries,
tomato juice, and canned sauerkraut. We had struck a gastronomic bonanza.

The Arab asked me to hunt up the platoon command post
and bring back a telephone to attach to the wires already set in
position. I entered the basement of another building where I
found Rateye, Berkely, Ciconte, Moore, Larkin and a young
officer setting up headquarters. Berkely went out to check on
the outposts.

Ciconte opened his 300 radio whose groans brought a
spatter of bullets into the rubble. Rateye observed with good
sense that we would be safer with the radio turned off. We sat

and smoked. A mortar a few hundred yards away landed a shell in the ruins above us. Part of the basement roof fell on our heads. Rateye trembled. Larkin noticed it and began to snicker to himself. I checked the blackout and lit a candle stub. Its dim lights showed fear on the haggard face of officer Rateye. Again the Krautheads raked the rubble with bullets. Lacking the strong arm of Berkely to lean upon, Rateye was beside himself with terror. Larkin openly laughed at him. When Berkely finally came in, Rateye asked him in a nasty tone. "Where you been, sergeant? Digging holes for your men?"

The giant exploded in wrath. He characteristically tore his helmet from his head, hoisted it high and threw it onto the rubble-packed floor where it clanged and crashed and set echoes to going. Before they died away, the mortar shelled more rubble down on us, bullets began to plow up the roof. Larkin guffawed. Berkely roared, oblivious of danger: "I had to put the men into position when you wouldn't stir." He picked up his helmet and hurled it down again. "Maybe you ought to get somebody else to earn my pay." Rateye began to apologize. The scene made me morally sick. I went back to the Arab's position.

We hooked up the telephone. The Arab called little Finkelstein in and handed him a can of pears. Then he called Ciconte on the phone: "Ciconte, listen closely to the sound that will come over the phone." He handed Finkelstein a spoon. The little guy chomped and chewed lustily into the transmitter. Ciconte professed to be mystified. In a grand manner the Arab announced, "You have just now heard the sound of Finkelstein eating canned German pears. Stand by for another broadcast."

Ciconte, a chowhound by nature and by reputation, swore bitterly and to the point. The Arab grinned till his ears drooped.

Presently Berkely stumbled through the blackout curtain into the cellar. He wrenched his helmet from his head, hurled it to the floor and swore: "Arab, that yellow-bellied obscenity! The motherless bastard! I oughta pound Rateye!" The Arab handed him some pears and remained silent. Presently Berkely got into a better humor. "I scared him stiff when I threw my helmet on the floor. He almost got down on his knees to me. He is afraid a shell will drop down the cellar door. Larkin is about to bust a gut laughing at him. He is an officer in the toughest outfit in the army and yet he is afraid to step out of the cellar to see where I put the men. He asked me if the cellar was well guarded. The only way I'd ever respect him is for him to blow out his brains!"

The Arab handed the giant a can of huckleberries and a spoon and stationed him near the phone. Again he called Ciconte. "Ciconte, listen!" He nodded to Berkely. The glutton gulped down half a can of berries, making loud, smacking noises with his lips. The Arab announced: "Audience, that was Berkely breaking his fast with a can of the finest huckleberries in no man's land. You ought to try some. You ought to buy some. Listen to our next broadcast in thirty minutes."

Ciconte swore loud and long into the phone.

I accompanied Berkely to the platoon headquarters. Rateye was hunched back in a corner, more miserable than the Sad Sack. Berkely glowered at the floor; Ciconte was cursing the Arab over the phone. Winters came in to report that things were okay at his post. We sat in silence, doing the only thing the dogfaces can do in such places—smoke. I went back to the Arab quarters.

The bitter cold seeped down into the cellar and froze our marrow. The Arab had arranged for one man from each outpost to sleep while awaiting his turn. Nixon was asleep on the floor on some old German clothes. Rummaging in a box, I found a clean pair of rayon panties which were thirty inches broad without stretching. My body would have fitted perfectly in one of the pant legs. We sat and tried to imagine a woman big enough to fill out such gigantic panties. I put them over Nixon's head to keep him warm. The Arab scrutinized them carefully and allowed that after looking for his ideal woman for years, he had at last been lucky enough to find her drawers. His ideal, he said, was a woman two and one half ax handles in width by standard measurement across the stern. He'd found one two ax handles wide in Sicily, he averred, but she was sixty-two years of age and had eight kids and five grandkids. "Jokers, take any woman prisoner who can wear them panties. Orders!"

Nixon awoke, clawed the garment from his head and inspected it. His eyes bulged progressively like a balloon being inflated. He drawled: "Makes me feel at home to know that a shapely female has been in these parts. The German who owned that woman could have sold his ox team and his mattress!"

Inasmuch as it was too dangerous for the entire platoon to be bunched in the open at one time, it was decided that the squads would leave their positions a few minutes apart just before dawn and then regroup as a unit in a wood on the edge of the plain. The last squad to leave would be that of the platoon officer and his assistants. Rateye broke all precedents, however, by leading the first squad. Going forward he manifested no zeal to be first, but on withdrawls he set such a fast pace that his men couldn't keep up.

Berkely, Gruening, Casey, Winters and I brought up the rear. When we rejoined the boys in the wood, we found Rateye turning in circles with no idea of the direction of our positions. We finally reached them, but Rateye was still too confused to find his hole. Gruening, standing beside his own burrow, called out to him:

"Sir, I'm lost. I don't know the way home."

"Where are you, Gruening? I'm lost too."

As he slid into his hole, Gruening replied: "I'm in my dugout, Sir. Where are you?"

"Not where he ought to be!" echoed a chorus of buried voices.

41. The Arab Goldbricks on Psychiatry

The next afternoon we were relieved by Canadian troops after six weeks of uninterrupted front line combat. We hiked eighteen miles before setting up bivouacs in some rain-soaked pine thickets. But we didn't mind the moisture or the cold. The thought that we had fought desperate battles and survived warmed the cockles of our hearts. Of the old boys, only Duquesne and Pierson, who had accidentally shot himself in the leg with a pistol, were not along, but neither being seriously hurt, we expected to have them back with us soon. Although tired we sat around until late at night rehashing the campaign. Buddies from other companies came over to our bivouacs to renew friendships and to relate their adventures. The different accounts of the same battle clarified many happenings which for the individual soldier in his foxhole had but a fragmentary meaning.

The following morning we were carried by trucks into Belgium. The national hero, as Wild Bill put it, seemed to be "an eight-year-old kid who had kidney trouble." The number of statues of a king's or *bürgermeister's* son (history doesn't make it clear whether he was a bourgeois or aristocrat) who got lost and when found was urinating in a corner, almost equaled the population. I am sure that if to the number of statues were added the realistic miniature souvenir models of *mannequin-pisse*, which every fifth citizen tried to sell us, they'd exceed the number of citizens by far. Most of us crossed into France with an endless variety of the emblem of universal unity.

We set up headquarters in France not far from Reims. The brass didn't show proper appreciation, we thought, for our military achievements. The way we got it, we were to stay in France for two months just taking it easy: Plenty to eat, no hard training, lots of passes to Reims, Paris, the Riviera, England, and a good big old-fashioned Christmas. Our packages would catch up with us, we'd have big Christmas trees, roast turkey and plenty to drink. Wonderful—*seulement*, as the French say, things got off to a bad start. Passes came in driblets, drink was scarce, and the chow no better if no worse than before. We had inspections, close order drill, extended order drill, weapons training and every other annoyance that could be invented to add to the fatigue of tired front line combatants.

When eventually we did get passes to Reims, the troopers took the town by storm. We left a shameful record for which I apologize to all Frenchmen, but I think part of the blame should be farmed out to the top brass. After all, old fighting men should not be treated like eighteen-year-old recruits. But maybe it would have happened anyway. I'm afraid that the people of Reims will henceforth judge the American way of life by our conduct. They would be wrong, of course; but after all, most people form opinions on what they see and what they hear, and the citizens of Reims saw plenty. It is fortunate that most of them didn't understand what they heard.

We were in France through November and early December. Attention World War I veterans: It was still raining! The Arab got disgusted with training in the rain and betook himself to the regimental aid station, intending only to get some pills to relieve his head cold. A fine young officer M.D., new from the States and medical school, stared at the bloodshot eyes, heavy mustache, lean cheeks, tousled hair, and generally wild, restless appearance of the scurvy Arab. Being ambitious to make a name for himself, he saw in the Arab an opportunity to make a remarkable diagnosis which would add to his prestige. He asked: "Do you have nightmares, do you dream of battle, do you fancy you hear the voices of women screaming, do you hear bells ringing in your ears, were you ever knocked out by a shell?" and so on.

The Arab, highly entertained by these slurs at his sanity, replied, "Hell yes, lieutenant, I have nightmares, I hear bells ringing, I hear the voices of whores screaming bloody murder on dark nights! I was knocked out by a shell and my nerves are shot. I am about to blow my stack, but that is all right, as I am always about to blow my stack, but never do. I never have time!" He leered menacingly at the doc, then leaned forward and whispered confidentially: "Lieutenant, I ain't crazy, not yet. I got as much sense as I ever had."

The cagey doc, noting what he fancied to be maniacal gleams in the eyes of the Arab, made a memorandum of his symptoms, told him to report to a field hospital nearby, and then dismissed him.

The wily Arab, reflecting that he was onto a good racket to get out of training, loped up to the hospital, entered the waiting room, pulled out a recently acquired volume of the *Araucana* and began to read. Presently a tall captain came around and took the slip the Arab handed to him. A surprised look immediately came over his face. He drew down his lower lip with a thoughtful air and batted his eyes. The Arab drew down *his* lower lip with a thoughtful air and batted *his* eyes. The captain backed off a few feet, surveyed his patient with concern and decided to pass the buck. "Sergeant," he said, "you sit right there. I'm sending you down to Reims for consultation."

Presently the captain returned and ordered the Arab to get into an ambulance and go to Reims. He arose, stuck his *Araucana* in his pocket and went around the corner to a dental clinic where he remained for fifteen minutes; then he returned to the waiting room and reabsorbed himself in the deeds of Caupolican. The doc strode in, grasped him by the shoulder and howled, "I told you to climb into that damned ambulance. What in hell do you think you've been doing?" The Arab clucked his tongue reprovingly, gazed at him with pity and said in a mild voice, "Why, captain, you distinctly ordered me to walk over to the dental clinic. I went over there and waited awhile, but I decided that you must have made a mistake. I can't understand why you'd give such an order to a man waiting for an ambulance. Do you feel all right, captain?"

The harassed brass hat, badly in need of a sedative, ordered him to get on the next ambulance. None being available, the doc ordered him to return next day. The Arab informed the boys in his company that he at last had blown his stack and was on greased skids to the nut ward. Knowing of course that his insanity was a clever maneuver to achieve some objective not apparent at the moment, they capitalized on the situation to have some fun.

When the curious character went to chow, jogging along

in his loose-jointed custom, mess kit dangling from his hand, he was assailed from all sides with jibes, catcalls and interrogating remarks: "Arab, I hear ye've blown your lid. Think nuthin' uv it . . . it has bin coming fer years. You never had much sense and now you've proved it. How do you do it? . . . I'd like to miss some training meself. I ain't been crazy lately; it might be an interestin' pastime?" The Arab parried all questions with calm composure and affirmed that it took an intelligent man to blow his stack: "Now, you half-witted jokers could never go crazy. Any fool could plainly see that you were only goldbricking."

Next day the Arab went to a hospital in Reims, handed his papers to a little major and inquired where he could find the psychiatrist. The major, who happened to be the high priest of the booby hatch, looked suspiciously at the Arab and growled: "Who sent you here? Are you pulling my leg?"

"No, sir, I ain't pulling your leg. It ain't my idea that I'm crazy. I blame it on a doc back in Sissonne. If you don't want to see me, I'll go back to camp. To hell with being nuts anyway! It ain't no fun!"

The major led him into his office, gave him a physical examination and questioned him at length. The Arab raved for thirty minutes: "Major, I'm as sane as you are, but at *times* I *do* feel strange. I'm always sleepy. I could lie down on the floor here and sleep the clock around. I can't hear well. I can't remember orders. I hear voices speaking to me in the dark. I wake up trembling with fear . . . I have horrible dreams of killing people ever since I shot a Kraut's head clean off his shoulders. If I don't like a man, I want to rub him out. I specially want to shoot up the officers. I may shoot Rateye any day now. It would benefit the nation to kill that sonuvabitch."

The major, astonished and intrigued by the frank confession of blood lust, albeit a trifle doubtful of the veracity of the Arab's story, patted him on the back, gave him a bottle of medicine, and opined that it must be his blood pressure, which seemed a little high. "Come back a week from today and in the meantime stay on quarters and do no work. Here's an order."

The Arab got drunk on the way to camp, staggered into his room, hit the sack and for a week got out of bed only for nature's needs. His fellow jokers, fed up with weapons training in the rain, watched his maneuver turn into the purest of goldbricks, but in spite of being envious, their admiration for the wily warrior moved up ten notches.

A week later the Arab, refreshed and fit, rolled reluctantly from his bunk, and measured the doses of medicine in the bottle. His Ulyssean cunning wanted to forestall the possibility of being trapped into the confession that he hadn't taken a drop of it. He even tasted it so that he could describe its flavor to the major if the latter pulled any psychiatric tricks out of his nest of nut snares. Then he heaved the bottle out the window and set off for the hospital.

The company clerk stopped him on the way out. "Arab, you're ranking man for a forty-eight hour leave in Paris, but but since you're crazy and taking treatment at the hospital, I don't reckon you'll be able to go."

"Crazy, hell," snarled the Arab, who had longed for Paris for months. "Hold that pass for me and damn your ornery soul. When I come back here tonight, I'll be the sanest man in France."

The Arab briskly trotted into the major's office. "How do you feel, sergeant?" Major, I feel like a fresh-burped baby. My head is as clear as a bell. I sleep like a dead man. I don't want to shoot anyone except the Nazis. I even like officer Rat-eye! Sir, it must have been that medicine and that week on quarters."

The major reluctantly gave him a clean bill of health. "Your case was *so* unusual," he said plaintively. "I had hoped to further psychiatric research by studying it in detail. I don't know how to explain your remarkable recovery."

The Arab muttered beneath his breath as he left the office: "Pass to Paris!"

42. "Mac, I've been a Bad, Bad Boy!"

Most of the old boys except Duquesne, who had lucked a trip to England to see Jelly, were among the forty-eight who got passes. We entered Paris as a unit, our pockets filled with French Republic banknotes and our wills with the determination to dispose of them. We split into two groups, one headed by Winters consisting of Wild Bill McMurtry, Sheraton, Casey, Knowlton and Nixon, and the other led by Berkely composed of the Arab, Gruening, Finkelstein and me. Winters and his crowd disappeared in the direction of Montmartre. I persuaded Berkely to head for the Latin Quarter. An older brother who had studied in France had recommended the Hôtel de

Versailles as a place to stay and the Café du Dôme as an interesting spot to hang around.

We managed to find a taxi and had the driver take us down the Champs-Elysées, through the Place de la Concorde, around the Jardin du Luxembourg, by Notre-Dame, the Louvre and other points we'd heard about, and finally drop us at the hotel. The manager said his hotel was so full it bulged, but when we showed him our roll of bills, he emptied it fast enough, without budging from his desk or telephoning, to give us two rooms. Berkely, the Arab and I took one with two beds, Finkelstein and Gruening the one with a single double bed. Then we headed down the Boul Mich, drinking from bar to bar, till we finally came to the Café du Dôme. The champagne, cherry brandy, calvados, cognac, beer and wine set little elves to gamboling about in the calves of our legs, diffused a pink alcoholic glow over the old city, and brought a soulful gaze filled with cultural longing into the Arab's blue eyes.

"Jokers," he announced, "I am going to make a cultural tour of Paris. I feel the need to take a close look at some of the things we saw as we rode in the taxi. For years I've heard of this most highly cultured city. Now I'm gonna really look it over. I'm going to see the Louvre, Notre-Dame, look at some of the old books in the little stalls on the banks of the Seine, see the Tour Eiffel, the Hôtel des Invalides, and all the other great historical points I can come across. But first I need to alcoholize the itch in my throat. I want to put so much drink in my bladder that when we get back to the Rhineland I can urinate like Rabelais' giant (remind me to tell you about that giant, jokers, he ended a war by simply relieving his urge of nature on the enemy) and wash the Nazis into the North Sea."

We had another round of drinks at the Dôme and moved on to another café.

"Berkely," said Finkelstein, "I'll buy you one drink for each minute you speak in praise of Rateye."

"I'd rather become a eunuch and join the WCTU."

"Well spoken, giant," said the Arab. "I'll buy the next salvo. Let's toast Big Rodgers and the boys we left in Italy. T. L. wouldn't drink himself, but I know he'd appreciate a toast."

We lifted our glasses in deference and in reverence to the members of the platoon now forever *in absentia* and went to look for a restaurant.

An aggressive caterer erupted from a small eating place, pointed with his right hand to a menu in his left and entreated. "Come in, Messieurs! Good food!" He rolled his eyes and batted his winkers in furtive intimacy. "I beleve *vous autres américains* might call eet zee black market."

Berkely figured it was just a dump, but I had heard that French eating places could not always be judged by their outward appearance. We decided to try it. Soup, fish, steak, vegetables, pastries, cheese, fruits, black coffee, pousse-cafés, we had the works, with appropriate wines for each course. It was a marvelous feed, at an exorbitant cost of course, but for men living with death, money means little.

The spot had a certain *gemütlichkeit* about it, so we ordered a quart of Hennessy.

The Arab looked at his watch. "Jokers, it is two P.M. As soon as our digestive juices have worked through the stuff in our bellies and as soon as we can see the art work that undoubtedly went into the making of the bottom of that bottle of cognac, I shall embark upon a cultural tour of Paris, known to Roman antiquity as Lutetia. You ignoramuses are cordially invited to go along."

"Arab," said Gruening, "our pass just lasts forty-eight hours. We've used up nearly half of it already and I ain't goosed a chick yet."

"Gruening, you must remember the spiritual things. Pleasures of the senses leave craving memories, those of the spirit peace and tranquility. Besides, we'll find a chicken roost tonight."

Grinning Finkelstein burn-cured his burps with an ounce of cognac. "Arab, you've talked me into it."

"I knew I could depend on you, Finkelstein. What about you, Berkely?"

Berkely squirmed and looked at me. "I'm willing if you are."

"I'm willing," I said. The whimsical Arab was always interesting and enigmatical. Perhaps he would lift the veil again as he had at Wassen Waal on the real self or other selves which ticked with the camouflage of his irony and contradictions.

"Carter, I feel toward you like a brother. Sometimes I think that we must have been weaned from the same teat. Gruening, I promise we'll find a railroad museum if you'll go. You might even see an NYC switch engine."

"I feel I'm wasting my time, dammit, but I'll go."

"Perfectly ripping, old boy," said the Arab in a fair English accent. "Let's belly the rest of that bottle and be off!"

The mixed drinks had our knees wobbly and the big dinner our heads groggy.

"The Louvre will be our first stop, jokers. Keep an eye sighting for a taxi."

A hatch of chicks clucked and wiggle-jiggled up to us.

"Be firm, Gruening," said the Arab. "It's mind over matter this afternoon and matter over mind tonight."

Gruening shook off a tart-spiced number: "Listen, baby, I'm after culture."

"*Je ne comprends pas!* You like me, no?"

"Yuh! Arab, to hell with culture!" He looked around. "Arab! Arab!"

We spied the scurvy fellow, a chick under each wing, a malicious grin on his sly face, burning the pavement around a corner.

"That eel-oiled, flap-lipped bastard, that—!" exploded Gruening. Duquesne's pal hoisted the chick over his brawny shoulder and disappeared with her, kicking and giggling, into her place of business.

Believe it or not, Berkely, Finkelstein and I actually did go to the Louvre.

At daylight the wrecked Arab dragged into the room, Berkely eyed him caustically and inquired:

"How did you like Mona Lisa?"

A blush spread over his pale face and he hung his head.

"Mac," he said in a wee voice, "I've been a bad, bad boy! Maybe the government will have a pension for old paratroopers and I can see her smile in my old age."

43. There Would Be No Christmas!

As Christmas approached, our emotions alternated between sad recollections of the bleak days on the rugged Italian peaks of a year ago where Olson, Oldring, Hastings, Carlton, and the Master Termite left us forever and the joyful anticipation of a real holiday season abounding in roast turkeys, stuffed with oyster dressing, candies and packages from home. In contrast of the fifth of whisky for our entire company on Christmas Day, 1943, we would have at our disposal seventeen truckloads, it was rumored, fast moving northward from southern France.

December 17, 1944. A bunch of us old boys, meaning

those of us who had left the States with the original platoon, and a few we considered old men because of their long action with us since our campaigns had started, were sitting around planning a big Christmas party. Suddenly, the new company commander dropped into our midst like a shell.

"Men, we're hot! An urgent mission is coming up. There's been a break-through. We've got to be ready to leave by eight o'clock in the morning with complete combat equipment. I want to see all the noncoms."

There would be no Christmas!

"Okay, men," said Berkely as soon as we returned from our briefing. "Get hot! Draw your K rations and D bars. You may need them before we're done. Arab, you, Winters and Gruening check on your squads." Duquesne was back with us, busted to a private for going on a big drunk and resisting the MP's. It griped and at the same time tickled him to take orders from Gruening.

We inspected our equipment and prepared to leave in an atmosphere of indescribable tension and disconsolate melancholy. We knew nothing except that some group in the Allied Armies was getting hell stomped out of it and we were being sent up as trouble shooters. We were trouble shooters all right. We could and would get the job done whatever it was. *But, but but . . .*

By now the sands of our destinies were surely trickled through. Men like Duquesne, Gruening, Berkely, Finkelstein, Larkin, Casey, Nixon, the Arab, Winters, Carey, Fox and me had outlived 200 percent replacements in the company. We were refugees from the law of averages. In live battles men must die, even old soldiers. We looked at each other gloomily, each secretly reflecting. "Who will get it this time? Some of us will be dead in a few days." I didn't want it to be me and neither, it goes without saying, did I want it to be any one of my comrades.

No one seemed sadder than the Arab over the turn of events. For a while that night after we had finished packing he sat around like a shriveled sack of blue gloom. Finally he said:

"Jokers, I know you bastards don't like poetry, but I'm goin' to recite some to you and if you don't like it you can go blow it! It tells how I feel when I think about that liquor we won't drink and the turkey bones we won't gnaw. Now listen all you wise guys, who thought we had it made, to the way a poor soldier sonuvabitch just like us told it in a poem about the Spaniards fighting the Araucanian Indians down in Chile:

> "No man can lucky feel himself to be
> Until he's witnessed life's uncertain end
> Nor fully freed by the tempestuous sea
> Until he's anchored safe within the port.
> Unsurely follows good on good for men,
> On bad luck following bad he can depend;
> Prosperity's feeble reign but briefly lures
> But misery's hold implacably endures."

"That joker had a crud all right," Duquesne said, shaking his head sadly, "but my pal Gruening has left better verses than them on every privy wall along the New York Central."

"Arab, I thought you was goin' to tell us how he cussed out the ole man or roto-reamed the purple out of a bunch of brass for getting him in such a dam' mess!" said Finkelstein.

"Arab, that ain't so good!" said Larkin.

The Arab pulled a large rag from a pocket and covered his face, giving the impression that he was crying. Suddenly the rag fell and there he was sucking the last drops out of a half pint of brandy. He tossed the empty flask to Duquesne and said, "Duke, I was saving you a drink, but you ain't deservin' of it. I'm going to write my girl in Tennessee a letter so I can get away from you maggot brains."

We all wrote short letters home telling everybody we were well and looking forward to a big Christmas. We wished the usual season's greetings and expressed the usual optimisms about the war's early end and anticipations of getting home maybe sooner than we expected. Then we hit our bunks to toss and pitch and dream.

We had coffee at the Red Cross at four in the morning. Many of the boys talked loud and laughed often to stifle their tensions and saliva the dryness on their throats. As we sipped the warm coffee we hoped it would scald or drown the butterflies in our stomachs and warm the icy imaginings of losing a leg or an eye, or being gelded by shrapnel, into resigned acceptance of whatever fate had stored for us.

Old friends from different platoons and from sister companies visited and smoked and sipped and chided. "Well, you beat-up old stallion, here we go again. Keep your tail down, you old son of a bitch. It ain't that you're worth a damn and deserve to live, but you owe me money. And I just wouldn't have the heart to tell your mother why I lent it to you." "Hard luck! I knew you were going home on rotation, but I didn't know it was to be tomorrow. Justice on Anzio was to go too. Well, he lived to make it in spite of sixty-three days of hell. Good luck!" "Mac, don't argue with an MG 42. Just keep your tail down. And don't try to outrun an 88!" "Listen, joker, the shell ain't made with my initials on it. I'm going to live to be a grandpa."

Young faces turned into lean hard lines, relaxed lips into thin slits and smiling eyes into uncommunicative colored half-marbles. We examined and re-examined our weapons, made long thrusts with bayonets, worked the safety on automatic rifles, half loaded A-6 machine guns, checked the reticle on field glasses, set the sights on Garand rifles, oiled carbine magazines and 45 automatics. Preludes to battle and good-bys to Christmas. . . .

We pieced together enough scraps of information to learn that von Rundstedt had launched a powerful counter-attack in the Ardennes in Belgium which had overrun several divisions and was threatening Liége and other strategic positions. The 101st and 82nd Airborne Divisions were being thrown in to halt the drive until reinforcements could be brought up.

Miserable pawns on the checkerboard of battle, we rode in rain-soaked trucks all day and all night, piled off in the cold of a rain-fog morning on December 19 and slogged along for miles through squashy piles of watery snow. We spent the day in a drippy pine forest and then at nightfall resumed our march, which lasted until our muscles became numb and the bones in our feet dissolved into formless, motileless paste. At dawn (December 20) we finally halted on a roof that circled the top of a high hill and began to dig into the hard clay. Below in the valley was a small river. Elements of the 30th Division were defending its west bank and they were having trouble. It was in this area that the Legion would come to grips with the enemy, but with little or no knowledge of their numerical strength or resources.

We spent the morning on the hill, peering down into the impenetrable fogs and wondering what was happening beneath their sheltering cover. By early afternoon, the atmosphere having cleared enough to give us fair vision, we reassembled our equipment, backtracked a few hundred yards and then headed down into the valley. As we marched,

American artillery shells went over to land far ahead of us.

Duquesne had forebodings. "Gruening," he lamented, "Old Duquesne is going into his last battle. I know it, god-dammit, I know it. I've lived out my days. Remember me, Gruening, when you tighten brakes on the New York Central. And send a present to Jelly when you get back to the States."

Gruening obviously uneasy because Duquesne was serious, said, "You drunken old wood beetle, quit jammering. You'll get my job on the New York Central. You're too damned worthless to die."

"Old Duquesne is going into his last battle, Arab. I done lived out my days."

The Arab looked sadly at Duquesne. "Last night I dreamed I went fishing in the north fork of the Powell in southwest Virginia. The channel was dry and in it half-buried in the sand was my volume of Homer."

Finkelstein laughed at them. He laughed at everything, especially death. "You jokers say that before every scrap. You'd be dead and rotted if you'd popped off every time you said your number was up. By rights I should have been dead long ago. Why the hell should I start to sweat now?"

Our Company, C, followed Company B down a winding road overarched by interlacing branches of evergreens. Ahead we heard sporadic firing. Soon Aydelot, who had been leading battalion reconnaissance, came marching past us with a tall SS prisoner. Firing became so heavy that B Company got pinned down. We hid among some trees to avoid the sweep of machine gun bullets, interspersed occasionally with 20 mm cannon shells which snapped the branches over our heads, and waited for night to come.

The Arab observed with the interest of a laboratory psychologist the reactions of the brand-new platoon lieutenant as he got his baptism of fire. He turned to Casey and me and commented:

"Inexperienced, but probably okay."

Larkin, Sheraton and Casey bellied over to join us. The Arab looked at Larkin and said:

"If you ain't given Casey satisfaction yet for casting reflections about his English widow, I think you ought to do it. It would be awful to die owing Casey a black eye."

Larkin looked at Casey, who shook his head in disinterested negation. The iron-fibered silent giant spoke dolefully. "There's something about this business that puts me in mind of a funeral. I can't put my finger on it. I had a feeling like I got now once when an Oregon stallion almost tromped my guts out at the Pendleton Round Up. If Larkin gets it, I want him to get it without a black eye. And I don't want to get it with one. Larkin, good luck!" A glow of comradely warmth came into Casey's usually icy eyes. It was a bad sign. Never in our battles had I sensed such despondency or such mellow resignation. I was uneasy. The braggadocio irony of former preludes to battle inspired a form of cock-sure optimism. Casey was right. We were going into battle with the sadness of mourners. I didn't say so, but I too felt the ominous pull of uneasy premonition.

In early twilight the company moved to the left and stopped in a dense forest to await orders. They came. Orders always came. Lieutenant Freisinger called his noncoms together:

"Men, there is a strong Krauthead roadblock a few hundred yards away on the edge of an open field opposite this woods. Just behind the roadblock is a town called Cheneux. At seven thirty we are going to shove off with our platoon in a skirmish line in the lead for C Company. B Company will push off at the same time on the other side of the road. Headquarters' 1st Battalion is going to back us up with 81's and machine guns. Be sure to keep the line dressed. Make as little noise as possible. The enemy will be shelled for fifteen minutes before we take off. We're going to break through that roadblock, take that town and hold it. That is all, men." Just that and nothing more. . . .

44. De Profundis . . . .

A chilly quietness filled the dark wood where we lay immobile in the leaves and smoked, hiding the glow of cigarettes beneath blankets.

"Carter," said the Arab. "Big Rodger's socks rotted off my feet. I don't feel lucky. And I keep thinking of the dream in which I saw my volume of Homer lying in the dry channel of the north fork of the Powell nearly covered with sand."

"Arab, I'm wearing one of T. L.'s socks. Berkely has the other. But nothing will make a damn this time. Our luck's run out."

"Carter," said Finkelstein, "I thought better of you. You're acting like the others. You'll live to be a history professor with your students wishing the Krautheads had killed you!"

"Finkelstein," said the Arab, "we are makers of an epic. In a few minutes we will write maybe the concluding canto."

The promised artillery barrage whistled overhead into the enemy lines. There was still no sign of the two tank destroyers, armed with 90 mm guns, whose mission it was to proceed down to the road as we attacked and knock out any Krauthead armor which stopped us.

After looking at our watches scores of times, the appointed minute to move forward finally ticked to its end. We climbed to our feet and slowly formed in a skirmish line. Lt. Freisinger, accompanied by Berkely, both bulging fantastically large in the darkness, paced up and down in front of us. The order came down the line to move forward.

The thirty-three men in our platoon, spearheading for the two platoons following us, ground into motion and began to advance in a dressed skirmish line, noisily and clumsily breaking sticks as they went. At any second we expected *it* to come like a wind-driven gust of burning hail. The silence continued save for the steady sound of a string of men picking their way through a dry forest. A few cords of stacked wood lying between us and the field made it necessary to form in a single file. We formed again in a skirmish line on the edge of the field, crisscrossed at forty or fifty yard intervals by barbed-wire fences. An enemy dressed in skirmish formation advancing across such a terrain was a machine gunner's dream. I felt my senses plummet into a pit of leaden numbness. I heard Duquesne whisper to Gruening:

"This is it!"

Now we were in the open field. And still death's bullet scythes which we knew would mow that level ground were not unleashed. We made unavoidable noises crossing the two- and three-wire-strand fences. The comfort of the pile-driving explosions of our artillery ahead did not atone for the absence of the two tank destroyers.

Our men, strung out unevenly now because of difficulty in getting across, under and through the wires, had nearly reached mid-field and were beginning to climb another fence when it happened. Suddenly thousands of tracer bullets, uncannily beautiful despite their lethal purpose, arched and crisscrossed above us. Their flickering flames turned the night into day and men into targets. The air was filled with the yellow glow of hissing 20 mm cannon shells, the sputter of machine guns and the roar of exploding mortar shells dumped on our comrades just below us.

I was halfway over a fence when little Finkelstein, already across and a few feet in front of it, was struck by a 20 mm shell which exploded his hand grenades and set him afire. He ran back a few feet and collapsed in the barbedwires.

Stunned by the first burst of enemy fire, our line faltered. Dimly, I heard the bull voice of Berkely: "Go forward, men! Kill the bastards who killed Finkelstein!" I continued forward in a daze. About five feet to my left a steady stream of tracers felt for me. Twenty mm cannon balls, systematically currying the field, exploded in vicious little firecracker puffs of flame. A field piece methodically shelled the center of our advance. Mortar shells kept chewing up the second and third platoons behind us. Machine guns warped and woofed their straight stitches across and through the zone ahead. It was worse than a Dantesque nightmare; it was man-made mechanized hell.

For years, it seemed, since leaving little Finkelstein on the fence, I had been walking down the field toward the guns. Gradually the noise of battle disappeared, as had the past and the future, and all my thoughts but one: *I know I'll die because my life is forfeit, but I hope I'll last long enough not to go empty-handed.* I walked forward firing my rifle, but could not hear its detonation.

"I've got it good." It was the feeble voice of the Arab, who lay in a pool of blood almost in my path of attack. I fell to my knees beside the old warrior and started to give him first aid. "It ain't no use." The wily look in his friendly eyes had dissolved into the same kind of sweetness I saw in Carlton's. "Tell the boys, if any of them are left, that I wanted to give a better account of myself." He tried to say something else, but was too weak. As I started to go, I stepped on his volume of Homer, which was blood-spattered and shot nearly in half. I put it on his chest and felt his heart. It was still. I folded the hero's arms across his beloved book and rushed on.

For a few minutes, except for a meeting with Kong, I was alone in my little private strip of hell. As I lay under a fence clearing my jammed rifle he wriggled past me like a snake, his white teeth shining in his dark face, his tommy gun thrust forward.

"Kong," I asked, "where in the hell are you going?"

He replied out of the corner of his mouth as he continued to crawl.

"Gotta go get those bastards! Gotta go get those bastards!"
He vanished to the left.

I continued on down the field, firing until my rifle burned in my hands, cursing insanely, getting closer and closer to the starting points of the bullets which had killed Finkelstein, the Arab, and so far as I knew at the moment, most of my other buddies. I realized that my bayonet stub was loose and wondered if it would wobble too much. Ahead three forms skulked in the darkness by a machine gun. I reloaded and charged. A burst of slugs smoked past me. When I was within a few feet of them, they started to run. I put one knee on the ground and leveled off eight slugs. Then I hit the ground and rolled to escape a machine pistol blast.

The sector in front of me now being quiet, I walked to the left about thirty feet. I found Casey, riddled by MG 42's. lying a few yards in front of a machine gun nest. In it were four dead SS troopers. I roared in rage and hate and started toward the right where B Company seemed to be having rough going. At the moment Berkely surged out of the night, his little finger bleeding from a machine gun slug, his hand paralyzed. He had shot two machine gunners, thrown his empty rifle at a third and was leaping forward to strangle him when automatic rifleman Avant saved him the trouble. Unable to handle a gun, he was on his way to help the medics.

"Casey is over there," I said. "The Arab is gone too."

"Duquesne got it in the head and Gruening in the belly. Both bad!"

We slapped each other's shoulder and separated into the night.

About a hundred yards away I found Technical Sergeant William Walsh, B Company, of Waunakee, Wisconsin, trying to recognize his platoon in the face of deadly fire from the flak wagons forming the roadblock. He was yelling:

"Let's go men! We got to take that town. We can't stop now!"

He didn't realize at the time that most of his men were dead or wounded. He thought apparently that they were backing down on him.

"I'll go with you, Knobby."

We rushed toward a monstrous shape spurting flame into the darkness, off whose metallic sides the bullets sparked and whined in feeble ineffectualness. Diving into a ditch on the right, I spotted six similar iron-age monsters sitting in a circle steadily spewing machine gun bullets and small cannon shells and glowing intermittently from gun flashes and tracers like half-fired coke ovens on rainy nights. From a nearby ditch I could hear Walsh above the pain-filled cries of troopers already wounded by armored fire exhort his few remaining men and give them instructions.

Ten feet away, on the other side of the road, was an armored vehicle whose 20 mm, I observed, was no longer firing. I reflected that it must have jammed. A pair of hands pushed out of the turret hatch and emptied a machine pistol into the road. I readied a grenade, thinking to myself, "I'll stop your clock when you stick that gun out again!", crawled over to its side and crouched. I *felt* without hearing a sound that the hatch grate was being opened and arose halfway to toss in my grenade. Before I made a move, however, an egg grenade thumped me between the shoulder blades and bounced off in an arch traced by sparkling blue burning powder. I dived back across the road and sprawled into a barbed-wire fence. Unable to extricate myself from the tangled mess in which I had lacerated my face and hands, I waited humbly and numbly for the missile to explode. When it did, something hit and numbed my shoulder and back. The thought that I was wounded did not deter me from wriggling free of the wire and diving into a water-filled ditch squarely on the wounded rump of a trooper who squalled in pain. I quickly moved off him, too concerned about the armored car whose motor was starting to roar, to have time to inquire whether he needed aid, much less to apologize. I felt panic-stricken as the thing backed up at an angle and stopped, facing me. Now, I thought he will lower the boom on this ditch, because he must have seen me or else he wouldn't have tossed out the grenade.

Just when I thought the jig was up, the motor stopped, the hatch cove opened and three men hurtled out. I leveled my gun and fired until they fell either because they were hit or in order to take cover.

Walsh and his men apparently now gone, I decided to cut back to the left to see how the battle was going for my own company. On hands and knees I crawled past the abandoned armor and on down the road a few yards until I saw another tank which also seemed silenced. I bellied near it, carefully inspected it and the nearby terrain, and then stood up to take a better look.

Behind me erupted the horrible thudding growl of a machine cannon. As I bounded I felt a red-hot rip tear through my right arm. Simultaneously, a heavy shock loosened my right hand's grip on my rifle, whose weight now fully on my left hand swung me away from the cannon toward a large enemy truck.

As I staggered along, Walsh passed me, also wounded, heading for Cheneux where he won the DSC. A stream of blood as big as my thumb cascaded down my arm. I began to call frantically for first aid. I had tottered less than a hundred yards when I began to feel deliciously weak. Violet and red flashes began to flicker before my eyes. I sank to the ground.

When I regained consciousness, Ciconte was kneeling beside me. He took off my jacket and coat, slipped loose my belt and put it on my arm as a tourniquet. Suddenly he picked up his gun and threw a fast shot. "That Krauthead won't try to slip up on anybody else!" Then he knelt gently by me again, gave me a shot of morphine and rechecked my tourniquet.

I think I must have fainted about every fifty yards on the way to the station. Once when I collapsed across the wire fence, unable to move and not really caring whether I did or not, Winters' hard-boiled voice croaked sardonically in my ear: "Broch, I don't want to disturb your rest, but do you intend to spend the night on that barbed-wire fence?"

So Winters was still alive! A wave of moral comfort flooded me and I grinned to myself at his question. "Why, no, Winters, I don't want to sleep here," I answered, "but I can't seem to get off the damned thing."

He helped me across and asked Esman to look after me.

Nixon, a shell in his back, passed me on the *via dolorosa,* as did Sokal, who had a fairly serious head wound.

I asked Nixon about Larkin and Sheraton.

"Dead. And so is O'Connell."

Of the old boys only Berkely and Winters and I remained and I might bleed to death. Finkelstein afire on the fence, the Arab with his hands folded across his Homer, Casey lying in front of his four victims, Duquesne and Gruening deathly wounded, and now the bad news about old warriors Larkin and Sheraton!

My mind backflashed to the original platoon; a gentle weariness overcame me. The will to live which had put motion into my wobbly legs seemed to dissolve into nostalgic longings. I sank to the ground. Why should I still live when men as good or better lay dead? What was there to live for? For three years my buddies had been most of my life. The more than three hundred days of front line combat had welded our comradeship into a reality which faded civilian memories to dreamy nothingness. Without these brave men alive in the world, I could not conceive of much to look forward to. The thought of new faces in the platoon revolted and embittered me. A feeling of bottomless loneliness brought tears to my eyes.

As I lay without energy or will to move on, I felt a ring banging in my ears which was followed by an hallucination of extraordinary vividness. I was lying by the side of a trail the Legion had once marched along somewhere in Italy.

From around a bend in the distance I saw a column of soldiers appear who marched steadily toward me at a fast pace. As they came closer I could see that they were neatly dressed as if for inspection or leave, but curiously enough their shoes made no noise on the gravel path. I strained my eyes to see if I could identify any of them as soon as they came within recognition distance, but their faces seemed hid in a hood of fog. Then just as the lead man passed directly in front of me the vapor dissolved and I saw it was Hastings. He smiled at me without slowing his step. As soon as he moved by me, the fog again settled over his head. The second man was Oldring, the third Olson, the fourth Carlton, the fifth the Master Termite, and so on. One by one, their marching rank determined by the time of their death, the old boys filed by, each smiling and all giving the impression of being in a great hurry to reach some destination.

The Arab, marching fifth from the rear, smiled and said: "Ross, if you hurry, you can overtake us."

None of the others had spoken.

The tail man was Duquesne. He said nothing, but beckoned to me to follow.

When I regained consciousness, I was struggling to get to my feet. I wondered if in my delirium I had got up to try to follow our column of phantoms.

A few steps farther on I collapsed again. As I blacked out, I realized dimly that it was beginning to snow.

Epiloque

In the late afternoon of a sunshiny day in August, 1947, the Berkely of this story and I walked slowly up a hill about midway between Duffield and Pattonsville, Virginia, to a small family cemetery. Berkely, wearing a paratrooper's uniform, stopped before a fresh grave, saluted and for several minutes stood at attention with tears rolling down his tanned cheeks and his lips and chin quivering. On the tombstone was written:

Ross S. Carter
January 9, 1919—April 18, 1947
Paratrooper in The 82nd Airborne Division

Berkely and I sat down under a small tree in the cemetery. For a long time neither of us spoke. Life in its promiscuous vicissitudes stages many ironical performances, but certainly few which could equal the one responsible for our visit to this grave. Ross Carter survived the Battle of the Bulge and the other experiences related in this book only to die of cancer. Just two years and four months after the hallucination described in the last chapter, the author joined the Arab, Duquesne and the rest of his buddies in his Legion platoon of phantoms.

It was not until several days after the Battle of the Bulge that the author, recovering in the 62nd General Hospital in Paris from his arm wound, learned more about what had happened on the disastrous night of December 20. He told me he first got the information from Lt. Colonel Harrison, who survived the battle without a scratch, but got his jaw broken the day following when a truck crashed into his jeep.

The boys took the town of Cheneux, killed the majority of five reinforced companies of elite SS troops, and captured ninety-five armored vehicles, twenty-four machine guns and much other equipment. But they paid the price. Out of two and one half companies of paratroopers, 211 were killed or wounded in the thirty-five minutes that the battle lasted.

Of the thirty-three men in my brother's platoon, only nine were able to walk the next morning and four of them had slight wounds. Of the old boys, only Berkely, Carey, Winters and he still lived.

In good shape except for a weak arm and low blood count, Ross rejoined his outfit on February 26. "It was when I walked into the room occupied by the third platoon," he wrote me, "that I became conscious of extreme age—and loneliness. The beardless, smooth new faces, unlined by privation and long-continued life with and thoughts of death, swiveled to look at me. Berkely, Winters and I, alone remaining of the forty men of one proud platoon which sailed the Atlantic in the spring of 1943, belonged to a past, inaccessible, even incomprehensible to those beardless youths. They looked at us as museum visitors at rare and strange fossils of prehistoric reptiles, disbelief in their eyes."

Compared to their other campaigns, the final one, which took them to the Elbe River where the paratroopers met up with the Russians, was a picnic. Berkely, picked to go home on rotation, left before it began. The author went through it without mishap and was discharged from the service in early June 1945.

It is not strange that the calm of civilian life impressed Ross and Berkely, who was immediately adopted into the Carter family, as abnormal and incredible. As the twilight draped the little valley in purple shadows and sound-proofed it to silence, except for the call of a whippoorwill or the baying of a foxhound, Ross would listen intently for a while and then say: "It doesn't seem real. I have to pinch myself to realize that I'm here. This silence makes me nervous. It seems unreal to be alive. I should have died a long time ago."

For days he and Berkely, each wearing several tiers of decorations including the silver and bronze stars, celebrated and slept. Each maintained that the other was the bravest man and the best soldier in the army. The comradeship which had developed as a result of dangers faced, overcome and endured together, was a bond as strong and probably stronger than that which bound him to his brother or sisters. Coupled with this feeling of comradeship toward Berkely was a nostalgic identity with, and an extraordinary emotional loyalty to, their dead comrades, the bravest, most daring, most loyal men in the world, in the best division in the army! No man, I am certain, ever took greater pride in his outfit or comrades or manifested greater loyalty toward them.

Ross talked almost constantly about the heroic deeds of the dead men who had participated with him in the epic adventures of his regiment. Like Arab, he was a great reader of Homer and of epic literature in general. For him, Duquesne, Casey, Berkely, the Arab, Carlton, Gruening, Sheraton, Finkelstein, T. L. Rodgers, and the others, in battle and in pleasure, combined individual action and zestful living to a degree which rivaled the heroic proportions of Homer's Greeks.

Ross's powers of observation, sensitiveness to dramatic and human values, sense of humor and ability to communicate what he had felt and experienced both orally and in writing, prompted me to ask him one day whether he had considered writing a book about the adventures of the boys in his platoon. He said he had. Several of us encouraged him to get to work on it before the wash of civilian life began to erode the poignancy and freshness of his memories. He began to write last summer, 1945, and by midautumn had completed a manuscript of considerable length. While he wrote, Berkely slept. From time to time, my mother reports, he would wake him up to check a detail or date. Often he would tell the story to members of the family before he wrote it.

In the course of the summer he had renewed acquaintance with his professors at Lincoln Memorial University, Harrogate, Tennessee, where he had majored in history, and with many former classmates and fellow students. For a while he considered the possibility of enrolling in some graduate school to study history.

In November, 1945, less than six months after they were discharged, Ross and Berkely re-enlisted in the paratroops. Ninety days later they were back at Fort Bragg, N. C.

A few months later after his re-enlistment, Ross volunteered for training with the 505th Parachute Regiment in Alaska. En route, a black mole, which had become sensitive and inflamed, was removed from his back while he was in Seattle. He went on to Alaska, but had to return for additional surgery, following which he was given a ninety-day leave.

It was not until February, 1947, when my brother went to the Walter Reed Hospital, that I had a chance to see his manuscript. He had not had time to edit it, harmonize the style or incorporate into his story certain revisions and changes which he now felt should be made. He asked me to read the manuscript carefully before coming to visit him so that we could discuss it in detail. During the week I was with him, he spent many hours briefing me on the editorial work he entrusted to me.

Berkely and I discussed the author and his manuscript until the sun began to saw into the mountains. Then he arose and said:

"I'll go now to say good-by to Ross."

He again stood at attention for some time before his grave. When he rejoined me, he said: "I have known a lot of brave men, but here on this hill lies the bravest."

> Boyd G. Carter
> Lincoln, Nebraska
> August 1950

Have You Read These Current Bestsellers from SIGNET?

☐ **THE FRENCH LIEUTENANT'S WOMAN by John Fowles.**
By the author of The Collector and The Magus, a haunting love story of the Victorian era. Over one year on the N.Y. Times Bestseller List and an international bestseller."Filled with enchanting mysteries, charged with erotic possibilities . . ."—Christopher Lehmann-Haupt, N.Y. Times. (#W4479—$1.50)

☐ **LOVE STORY by Erich Segal.** The story of love fought for, love won, and love lost. It is America's Romeo and Juliet. And it is one of the most touching, poignant stories ever written. A major motion picture starring Ali MacGraw and Ryan O'Neal. (#Q4414—95¢)

☐ **JENNIE, The Life of Lady Randolph Churchill by Ralph G. Martin.** In JENNIE, Ralph G. Martin creates a vivid picture of an exciting woman, Lady Randolph Churchill who was the mother of perhaps the greatest statesman of this century, Winston Churchill, and in her own right, one of the most colorful and fascinating women of the Victorian era. (#W4213—$1.50)

☐ **THE AFFAIR by Morton Hunt.** Explores one of the most engrossing and profoundly troubling of contemporary concerns. Morton Hunt allows the reader to enter this secret underground world through the actual words and experiences of eight unfaithful men and women.
(#Y4548—$1.25)

THE NEW AMERICAN LIBRARY, INC.,
P.O. Box 999, Bergenfield, New Jersey 07621

Please send me the SIGNET BOOKS I have checked above. I am enclosing $_____(check or money order—no currency or C.O.D.'s). Please include the list price plus 15¢ a copy to cover mailing costs.

Name_____

Address_____

City_____State_____Zip Code_____
Allow at least 3 weeks for delivery